CONTENTS.

I.

PAGE

PHŒNICIA—THE COUNTRY—ITS POSITION AND
PRODUCTS 1–19

Phœnicia the "Palm Land," 1—Length and breadth, 2—
Frequent importance of small countries, 3—Four regions in
Phœnicia—description of them, 3, 4—Character of the coast-
line, 4, 5—Productivity of the Mediterranean, 5, 6—Advantages of the geographical position, 6–9—Southern Phœnicia—
Carmel, 10—The Litany—the plain of Tyre, 11—The plains
of Sarepta and Sidon, 11, 12—The plain of Berytus, 12—The
Nahr-el-Kelb, 14—Rugged tract between the Nahr-el-Kelb
and Tripolis—plain of Tripolis, 14, 15—Northern Phœnicia—
chief towns, Orthosia, Marathus, Aradus, Antaradus, and
Laodicea, 15—Boundaries of Phœnicia, Casius, 15–16—Bargylus, 16—Lebanon, 16–19.

II.

THE PEOPLE—THEIR ORIGIN AND ETHNIC CHA-
RACTER 20–39

Flow of Semitism westward, 20, 21—Movement of the Phœni-
cians from the Persian Gulf to the Mediterranean, 21, 22—
Occupation of the coast tract, about B.C. 1400-1300, 22, 23—
Nations of the Semitic group, 23—Phœnician language closely

PAGE

allied to the Hebrew, 24—Physical characteristics of the
Semites, 24, 25—Moral characteristics—Pliability, 25-27—
Depth and force, 27—Yearning after dreamy ease, 27—Love
of abstract thought, 28—Religiousness, 28, 29—General character of the religion, 29-32—Baal and Ashtoreth, 32—Melkarth, 33, 34—Adonis, 35—Eshmun, 35, 36—Introduction of
foreign gods, 36, 37—Degradation of the religion, 37—Scepti-
cism as to a future life, 38—Practical ability of the Phœnicians,
38, 39.

III.

THE CITIES—THEIR POSITION, PRINCIPAL FEA-
TURES, AND MUTUAL RELATIONS   .   .   40-55

General pre-eminence of Tyre, 40—Tyre a double city, 41—
The continental Tyre, 41—The Island Tyre, 41-45—Magnificence of the architecture, 45, 46—Position and plan of Sidon,
46-48—Berytus and Byblus, 48-50—Tripolis, Marathus, and
Simyra, 50, 51—Aradus, 51, 52—Ramantha or Laodicea, 52,
53—Akko, now Acre, 53, 54—Relations of the cities one to
another, 54, 55.

IV.

THE COLONIES   56-71

Settlement at Memphis, 50—Colonies in Cilicia, 57, 58—In
Cyprus, 58, 59—In Rhodes, 59—In the Ægean Sea, 59, 60—
Navigation of the Black Sea, 60, 61—Islands off the coast of
Greece, Cythera, Salamis, Eubœa, 61, 62—African colonies,
Utica, Carthage, Leptis Magna, 63, 64—Colonies in Sicily,
Eryx, Egesta, Palermo, 65—Gaulos, Malta, 66—Colonies in
Spain, Tartessus, Gades, Malaca, Carteïa, 66-69—Colonies in
Sardinia, Tharros, and others, 69—Settlement in the Scilly
Islands, 70—Possible settlements on the Red Sea, 70, 71—
Summary, 71.

V.

EARLY PHŒNICIAN ENTERPRISE — SIDONIAN
ROVERS IN PRE-HOMERIC TIMES   .   .   72-88

Earliest Phœnician vessels, "long ships," or ships of war,
"round ships," or merchantmen, 72-74—Phœnician biremes;

PAGE

74, 75—Perils of the Mediterranean storms, 75–77—Rock-bound coasts, 77, 78—Pirates, 78—Story of the rape of Io, 79–81—Fact of Phœnician kidnapping, 81, 82—Story of Eumæus, 82–84—General commercial honesty of the Phœnicians, 84, 85—Excellency of their wares, 85–87—Limits of the early Phœnician enterprise, 87, 88.

VI.

RISE OF TYRE TO THE FIRST RANK AMONG THE CITIES — HIRAM'S DEALINGS WITH DAVID AND SOLOMON 89–106

Transfer of Phœnician ascendency from Sidon to Tyre, and its causes, 89, 90—Tyrian, colonization of Gades, 90, 91—Power and magnificence of Hiram about B.C. 1050, 91, 92—Relations established by Hiram with David, 92–94—Friendly intercourse between Hiram and Solomon, 94, 95—The timber trade, 96—The Tyrian metallurgy, 96–98—The Temple substructions probably Tyrian, 98, 99—The ornamental metal-castings certainly made by the Tyrians, 99, 100—Other works of about the same date, 100, 101—The Jews and Tyrians engage in joint commercial enterprise, 101–103—Cession of territory made by Solomon to Hiram, 103—Contest of wits between the two, 103, 104—Death of Hiram, 104—His supposed tomb, 104–106.

VII.

ITHOBAL AND AHAB—DARKER ASPECT OF THE PHŒNICIAN RELIGION. 107–117

Obscure period of Phœnician history, 107, 108—Accession of Eth-baal or Ithobal, and marriage of his daughter, Jezebel, to Ahab, 108, 109—Phœnician worship introduced into Samaria, 109, 110—Spread of the corrupt religion into Judæa, 110—Nature of the Phœnician Baal and Astarte worship, 110–112—Sacrifice of children, 113, 114—Horrors of the Astarte worship, 115–117.

VIII.

Story of the Founding of Carthage . . 118–128

The story, as commonly told, 118–120—Its untrustworthy
character, 120, 121—Attempt of Movers to separate the false
from the true, 121—Supposed historical features, 122–125—
Supposed mythical details, 125, 126—Supposed intermixture
of history with the myths, 127, 128—Doubtful character of
Movers' method and conclusions.

IX.

Phœnicia's Contest with Assyria, and her
Position as Assyria's Tributary . . 129–148

First contact between the Phœnicians and Assyrians, about
B.C. 880, 129, 130—Relative power of the two nations, 131–
133—Submission of Phœnicia to Asshur-nazir-pal, 133, 134—
Continuance of peaceful relations for a century and a half, and
consequent prosperity, 134, 135—Assyrian encroachments lead
to hostilities, 135, 136—War of Shalmaneser IV. with Elulæus,
136–138—War of Sargon with the same, 139, 140—War of
Esarhaddon with Abdi-milkut, 140, 141—Baal, made king by
Esarhaddon, revolts—War between Esarhaddon and Baal,
142—Baal conquered by Asshurbanipal, 143, 144—Revolt
and reduction of Arvad or Aradus, 144, 145—Reasons for the
general discontent—the tribute, 145, 146—The enforcement of
homage, 146, 147—The passage of Assyrian armies, 147—
The severe treatment of revolted towns, 148.

X.

Phœnicia's Recovery of Independence—Her
Commerce at this Period . . . 149–164

Decline of Assyria, 149—Phœnicia recovers her independence,
about B.C. 630, 150—Phœnician commerce at this time, as described by Ezekiel, 151–153—Ascendency of Tyre, re-established, 153, 154—Extent of the commerce, 154, 155—Phœnician
caravan traffic, 155–157—Picture of a Tyrian caravan at Babylon, 157–160—Picture of one at Van or Urumiyeh, 160–162—
Commodities derived by Tyre from her sea commerce,
162–164.

XI.

PHŒNICIA'S CONTEST WITH BABYLON . . 165–174

Phœnician independence threatened by Egypt, 165—Battle of Carchemish—Phœnicia submits to Nebuchadnezzar, 166, 167—Revolt of Tyre and Sidon, 168—Reduction of Sidon, 169—Long siege of Tyre by Nebuchadnezzar, 169–172—Tyre forced to surrender, 173—Her resistance heroic, 174.

XII.

THE CIRCUMNAVIGATION OF AFRICA, AN EPISODE
    IN PHŒNICIAN HISTORY 175–180

Phœnicians willing to befriend Pharaoh-Neco, 175 — Circumnavigation of Africa undertaken by them at his instance, according to Herodotus, 176—Credibility of the narrative, 177, 178—Confirmation of the story from the report brought to Neco with respect to the position of the sun, 178, 179—Credit due to the Phœnicians for their success, 179, 180.

XIII.

PHŒNICIA UNDER THE BABYLONIANS . . . 181–185

Change of government at Tyre—Kings superseded by judges, 181, 182—Tyre and Sidon attacked by Apries and conquered, 182, 183—War of Nebuchadnezzar against Apries, 183—He recovers Phœnicia, 184—Kingly government re-established at Tyre, 184, 185—Fidelity of Phœnicia to Babylon.

XIV.

PHŒNICIA UNDER THE PERSIANS . 186–211

Sovereignty over Phœnicia claimed by Cyrus, 186, 187—Disputed by Amasis, who annexes Cyprus, 187—War between Cambyses and Psamatik III., 188—Cambyses' need of a navy,

PAGE

and Phœnicia's submission to him, 188, 189—Cyprus follows
Phœnicia's example, 189, 190—Refusal of the Phœnicians to
attack Carthage, 191, 192—Arrangements of Darius favourable to Phœnician commerce, 193, 194—Phœnicia's contribution to the Persian revenue and navy, 194, 195—Excellence of
the Phœnician ships, 195-197—Sidonian vessels sent with
Democedes to survey Greece, 197—Phœnicia's part in the
Ionian revolt, 197-201—Phœnicia's part in the attack made
by Xerxes upon Greece, 201-203—Further aid given by
Phœnicia to the Persians against the Greeks, 204, 205—
Phœnicia turns against Persia in the war with Evagoras,
205, 206—Alliance of Sidon with Nectanebo II., King of
Egypt, 207, 208—Sidon destroyed by Ochus, 209—Friendly
relations with Persia re-established by Esmunazar, 209, 210—
Period of tranquility, 210, 211.

XV.

ALEXANDER AND THE PHŒNICIANS—SIEGE AND
DESTRUCTION OF TYRE   .   :   .   . 212-236

Mentor's advice to use the Phœnician fleet against Alexander,
unheeded, 212, 213—Battle of Issus opens Phœnicia to him,
214—Alexander occupies Marathus and Byblus, 215—Aradus
submits to him, 215—Sidon receives him within her walls,
215, 216—Tyre promises submission, but declines to receive
him into the Island City, 216, 217—Alexander's rage at this,
217, 218—The determination of the Tyrians to resist Alexander, not blamable, 218-221—Preparations of the Tyrians,
222—Alexander commences his mole, 222, 223—Difficulty of
the work, 223, 224—The Tyrians succeed in destroying it,
224, 225—Alexander begins the work afresh, but makes little
progress, 225, 226—He succeeds in collecting a powerful fleet,
and establishes a blockade, 226-228—Alexander completes
the mole, and begins the assault, 229, 230—Attempt of the
Tyrians to raise the blockade fails, 230, 231—Desperate defence of the walls, 231, 232—Last general assault successful,
232-234—Further resistance within the walls, 234, 235—Cruel
treatment of the Tyrians, 235, 236.

PAGE

XVI.

PHŒNICIA UNDER THE GREEKS AND ROMANS . 237–249

Phœnicia contended for among Alexander's "Successors," 237—Falls finally to the Seleucidæ, and is treated with favour, 238—Tyre disapproves the conduct of Epiphanes towards the Jews, 239—Phœnicia generally abets his scheme for selling the Jews as slaves, 239–241—Spread of Hellenism over Phœnicia, 241—Short subjection of Phœnicia to Tigranes, 242—Phœnicia made a Roman province, but certain privileges granted to Tyre, Sidon, and Tripolis, 242, 243—Roman Tyre receives the Gospel, 243, 244—Gradual spread of Christianity over Phœnicia, 244, 245—Development of Phœnician literary activity, 245–247—Origen at Tyre, 247—Porphyry and Methodius, 247, 248—Latest Phœnician authors, 248, 249.

XVII.

PHŒNICIAN ARCHITECTURE . . . 250–274

Scantiness of the remains, especially in Phœnicia Proper, 250, 251—*Maabed* of Marathus, 252, 253—Other shrines in the neighbourhood, 253—Temples of Tyre have left no trace, 253—Phœnician stone masonry, 253, 254—Plans of temples—Temple on coin of Byblus, 255, 256—Temple of Paphos, 257—Walls of towns—remains of Aradus, 257–260—Sepulchral monuments—the Mêghâgils, near Marathus, 260–264—Two other tombs, 264–267—Tombs excavated in the rock, 267–270— Subterranean sepulchral chambers, 270, 271 — General character of Phœnician architecture, according to Renan, 272–274.

XVIII.

PHŒNICIAN MANUFACTURES AND WORKS OF ART 275–326

Manufacture of the purple dye, 275—Shell-fish producing it, 276–280—Methods employed, 280, 281—Story of the original discovery, 281, 282—Manufacture of glass—supposed accidental discovery, 282, 283—Objects in glass—Aggry beads,

PAGE

283—Other objects, as vases, bottles, drinking-cups, cylinders, &c., 284—Manufacture of textile fabrics, 284, 285—Metallurgy —Works of Hiram for the Temple of Jerusalem, 285— Sidonian metal-work celebrated by Homer, 286—Bronze dishes found at Nimrud, and elsewhere, 286-289—Coins, 289, 290—Phœnician sculpture, 290—Bas-reliefs on tomb at Amathus, 291-295—Reliefs on walls of sepulchral chambers, and sarcophagi, found at Sidon, 296-308—Phœnician art of navigation, 308-310—Phœnician mining, 310-312—Phœnician carving in ivory, 312, 313—Phœnician gem-engraving, 313-315—Phœnician ornamental metallurgy—Objects found at Curium in Cyprus, 315-324—Merits of the metal-work, 324, 325—Possible greater merit of the lost works, 325, 326.

XIX.

PHŒNICIAN LANGUAGE, WRITING, AND LITERA-
TURE 327-350

Semitic character of the language, generally admitted, 327— Account of the alphabet, 327, 328—Alphabetic signs rather improved than invented by the Phœnicians, 328-330—Their alphabetic signs not derived from Egypt, but still a picture writing, 330—Extreme simplicity of their characters, 330, 331—Adoption of their alphabet by the nations of the West, 331, 332—Phœnicians wrote from right to left, 332—Extant Phœnician literature—Inscription of Esmunazar, 332-336— Shorter inscription of Tabnit, 336, 337—Curt legends on native offerings, 337—Later literary efforts—Fragments of Philo Bybl us. 337-347—Estimate of their value, 347, 348— General estimate of the Phœnician nation, 349-350.

INDEX 351

LIST OF ILLUSTRATIONS.

	PAGE
THE TOMB OF ESMUNAZAR . . . . *Frontispiece*	
PASS AT THE MOUTH OF THE NAHR-EL-KELB . .	8
SOURCE OF THE RIVER ADONIS	13
PASS IN THE LEBANON	18
BAAL AS A SUN-GOD	30
ASTARTE, FROM A STATUETTE FOUND IN CYPRUS .	31
MELKARTH, FROM A STATUETTE	33
COIN OF GADES	34
PLAN OF THE ISLAND TYRE	43
PLAN OF SIDON	47
REMAINS OF THE WALLS OF SIDON	49
CHART OF ARADUS	51
COIN OF LAODICEA, WITH BILINGUAL INSCRIPTION .	53
COIN OF TARSUS, WITH PHŒNICIAN INSCRIPTION .	57
PHŒNICIAN GALLEY, REPRESENTED ON A COIN .	72
PHŒNICIAN GALLEY, FROM A PAINTING . . .	73
PHŒNICIAN BIREME, FROM AN ASSYRIAN BAS-RELIEF	73

PAGE

MONUMENT NEAR TYRE, KNOWN AS "HIRAM'S TOMB"   105

PLAN OF TYRE IN ALEXANDER'S TIME .   .   .   220

SHRINE AT AMRIT OR MARATHUS   251

GROUND-PLAN OF THE SAME   252

WALL OF GEBEIL, SHOWING BEVELLING .   .   .   254

WALL OF TORTOSA, SHOWING BEVELLING .   .   255

PHŒNICIAN TEMPLE, ON COIN OF BYBLUS (ENLARGED)   256

GROUND-PLAN OF TEMPLE AT PAPHOS .   .   .   257

REMAINS OF THE CITY WALL AT ARADUS .   .   258

PHŒNICIAN SEPULCHRAL MONUMENTS, KNOWN AS

"THE MÉGHÂZILS"   261

PLAN AND SECTION OF A TOMB AND MONUMENT

AT AMRIT OR MARATHUS   262

THE MONUMENT, RESTORED   263

SEPULCHRAL MONUMENT AND ENTRANCE TO TOMB

AT AMRIT, RESTORED   265

TOMB AT AMRIT, KNOWN AS THE BURDJ-EL-BEZZAK,

RESTORED   266

SECTION OF THE SAME, IN ITS PRESENT CONDITION   267

SEPULCHRAL CHAMBERS AT AMATHUS .   .   .   271

SHELL OF THE MUREX TRUNCULUS .   .   .   276

EMBOSSED PATERA FROM CURIUM   287

COIN OF GADES   289

BAS-RELIEF ON THE SIDE OF A SARCOPHAGUS FOUND

AT AMATHUS   .   .   .   .   .   -   292

PAGE

CONTINUATION OF THE BAS-RELIEF ON THE OPPOSITE

    SIDE OF THE SAME   293

SCULPTURES AT THE TWO ENDS OF THE SAME   .   295

ENGRAVING ON A PHŒNICIAN GEM — WARRIORS

    FIGHTING   315

PHŒNICIAN BRACELETS FROM CYPRUS   .   .   316

PHŒNICIAN BRACELET AND NECKLACE FROM THE

    SAME   317

NECKLACE FOUND AT CURIUM IN CYPRUS   .   318

ANOTHER NECKLACE FROM THE SAME   .   .   319

VASE IN ROCK CRYSTAL, WITH FUNNEL AND GOLD

    COVER, FROM THE SAME .   .   .   321

RINGS, EARRING, AND FASTENING FOR THE HAIR,

    FROM THE SAME.   323

THE PHŒNICIAN ALPHABET   333

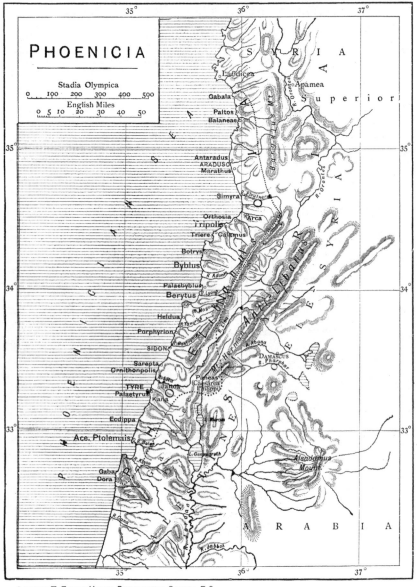

PHOENICIA

Stadia Olympica

| 0 | 100 | 200 | 300 | 400 | 500 |

English Miles

| 0 | 5 | 10 | 20 | 30 | 40 | 50 |

S   Y   R   I   A

Laodicea

Apamea

Gabala   S u p e r i o r

Paltos

Balaneae

Antaradus
ARADUS
Marathus

Simyra

R. Eleutherus

Orthosia   Arca
Tripolis
Triere Calamus

Botrys

Byblus

R. Adonis

Palaebyblus
Berytus

Heldua

Porphyrion

SIDON

Sarapta
Ornithonpolis

TYRE
Palaetyrus
Kana

Ecdippa

Ace. Ptolemais

Gaba
Dora

DAMASCUS
R. Pharpar

Paneas
Caesarea
Philippi

L. Merom

L. Genesareth

Alsadamus
Mount

A   R   A   B   I   A

R. Jordan

R. Crocus

R. Jabbok

LONDON: T. FISHER UNWIN, PATERNOSTER SQUARE, E.C.

THE STORY OF PHŒNICIA.

I.

THE COUNTRY—ITS POSITION AND ITS PRODUCTS.

AT the eastern end of the Mediterranean, facing towards the west, and looking out on the Levantine Sea, or " Sea of the Rising Sun," was the scanty, but fortunately situated, tract which the Greeks and Romans knew as PHŒNICIA, or, " the Region of Palms." On the sandy belt which borders the Mediterranean from Gaza in the south to Casius in the north, this graceful and striking tree—so different from any growth indigenous to the West—flourished in great abundance, and drawing the eye of the early Greek trader, previously unacquainted with it, caused him to designate the newly discovered region, whereto his enterprise had brought him, by the name of " Phœnicé " — " the Palm land," or " the country where the palms grew." At first the term was used, with a good deal of vagueness, of the Syrian coast generally between Asia Minor and Egypt; but ultimately, when it broke upon the Greek intelligence that the tract in question was inhabited by three nations, politically and ethnographically distinct, the geographical nomenclature was conformed to the ethnologic facts, and the name "Phœnicia" became confined to the more central portion of the coast region only, that towards the north taking the name of Syria, or the country of the Syrians, and that towards the south the name of Palestine, or the country of the Philistines. Shorn thus of its two extremities, Phœnicia was reduced to a tract about two hundred miles in length, extending along the Eastern Mediterranean from a little below the thirty-third to a little below the thirty-sixth parallel.

The width of the country was very disproportionate to its length. Even if we include in it the whole of the mountain range which shuts in the Cœle-Syrian valley upon the west, and was certainly its extreme eastern boundary, we shall find that nowhere along the entire length of two hundred miles did the width exceed a maximum of thirty-five miles, and that generally it did not amount to much more than half that distance. Phœnicia is like Chili, a long narrow tract, squeezed in between the mountains and the sea, widest in the north, between the thirty-sixth and thirty-fifth parallels, and gradually narrowing, until towards the south, about latitude 33°, it can scarcely be said to have had a breadth of more than one or two miles. It is a liberal estimate for the area to reckon it at 4,000 square miles, which is less than that of at least one English county.

Size, however, is a very insignificant element in that aggregate which determines the importance or unimportance of a country. In antiquity, Sparta,

Athens, Carthage, had but small domains. In the Middle Ages Genoa, Venice, Pisa, Florence, were equally circumscribed ; but each of them had a world-wide influence. Later, Portugal, Holland, England, through the momentum of their strong individualities, did their great deeds, and set their mark on the world's history, from a comparatively small *pied à terre.*

But, if the size of Phœnicia was insignificant, its position, soil, products, geographical and political relations to the countries around it and about it, were such as naturally to bring it to the forefront of history at an early period. Phœnicia consisted of four regions. The sandy belt along the coast was admirably suited for the date-palm ; and the thick groves of palm-trees which are even now seen about Beyrout and Jaffa may be taken as indicative of the general appearance of the coast-line in early times, before the necessity of finding timber for house-building had thinned the naturally luxuriant growth of the palm bosquets along the Levantine shore. Inside the sandy belt is a rich and fertile plain, a region of orchards, gardens, and cornfields, varying from one mile to twelve miles in width, and even under unskilful cultivation abundantly productive. "The cultivated tract presents for the most part an unbroken mass of corn, out of which rise here and there slight eminences in the midst of gardens and orchards—the sites of cities," or villages. The gardens are gay with the scarlet blossoms of the pomegranate, the orchards famous for the enormous oranges which diversify the green foliage of their shady groves. Eastward the plain is bounded, for the most part, by low swelling hills, suited for the growth of the vine, the olive, and the mulberry, which anciently were largely cultivated throughout the entire region. As the hills rise higher and higher, cultivation ceases, except in favoured spots, and the vineyard region is succeeded by a tract of wild mountain-land, in part bare, in part clothed with hanging woods or with noble forest-trees—oaks, chestnuts, sycomores, terebinths, and, above all, that glory of Syria, the cedar, with which no other forest-tree can compare. The mountain region varied in its elevation from about 5,000 feet in the north, where it was known as Casius and Bargylus, to above 9,000 feet in the south, where Lebanon culminates in the snowy peak of Makmel.

The coast-line of the region, though not deeply indented, was sufficiently irregular to furnish a number of tolerable harbours; and when art was called in to assist nature, it was found fairly easy to construct ports, which, according to ancient ideas, left little to be desired. Jutting promontories furnished protection from prevalent winds on either side of them, and in some cases bays, like that of Acre, were almost land-locked; elsewhere, as at Tyre, Sidon, and Aradus, small littoral islands, or rather islets, gave the necessary shelter; and everywhere it was possible to excavate in the low ground near the shore artificial basins of a sufficient size to receive twenty or thirty of the small galleys of ancient times. The blue Mediterranean, tideless, and mostly calm during the summer time, incited to navigation. Cyprus, distinctly visible on the western horizon from Casius and many parts of Bargylus, offered a new world to the adventurous ; and Cyprus conducted to Cilicia, Caria, Rhodes, Cnidus, the Sporades, and the Cyclades. Inexhaustible supplies of timber, fit for ship-building and for oars, were laid up in the three mountain regions which shut in Phœnicia to the north and east —in Casius, Bargylus, and Lebanon, to all of which the Phœnicians had free access at all times ; and thus nature pointed out, as it were, to the Phœnician people their vocation, and made them the connecting link between the East and the West.

The smiling sea, which lay in their front, and invited them to trust themselves to its calm and placid surface, contained also in its depths a treasure, which ultimately, as much as anything, brought the Phœnicians to their high position among the nations. The Mediterranean waters off the Phœnician coast, and especially off the tract between Mount Carmel and Tyre (lat 32° 50' to 33° 20'), abound with two species of shell-fish capable of furnishing an exquisite dye. These are the *Buccinum lapillus* and the *Murex trunculus*. The *buccinum* derives its name from the form of the shell, which has a wide mouth, like that of a trumpet, and a spiral form, terminating in a small rounded head. The *murex* has the same general form as the *buccinum*, but the shell is more rough and spinous. The mollusks which inhabit these shells have a receptacle or *sac* behind the head, in which a very minute portion of a colourless, creamy fluid is contained, having a strong smell of garlic. If it be carefully extracted by a hook, or a pointed pencil, and applied to wool, linen, or cotton, and the material be then exposed to a strong light, it becomes

successively green, blue, red, deep purple-red, and, by
washing in soap and water, a bright crimson, which
last tint is permanent. Although the shell-fish
capable of producing this dye are not confined to
any single locality, and the secret of extracting it
was known to many ancient nations, yet nature seems
to have so far favoured Phœnicia, that through all
antiquity she maintained a pre-eminence over all
other purple-producers. Something may have been
due to art : her chemical knowledge may have exceeded that of other nations, and have found employment in the purple industry ; but it is only reasonable
to suppose that her admitted superiority in the trade
rested primarily on her having an inexhaustible
supply of the best fish, furnishing the brightest dye,
and perhaps a little on the brilliancy of her sunlight,
which brought out the tints more vividly than the more
subdued radiance of a cloudier and duller heaven.

But, besides her possession of valuable products,
Phœnicia had also a position, geographically and
politically, which favoured her rise to importance.
In the first place, she was greatly protected by the
mountains which shut her in on the north and east,
and by the peculiar conformation of her coast. To
the armies which traversed the Cœle-Syrian vale on
their way from Mesopotamia to Egypt, or from Egypt
to Mesopotamia, the mountain range upon the west
was, for the most part, a barrier which they did not
seek to surmount, and which they would have had
difficulty in surmounting. Their hosts ransacked the
mountain region to a certain elevation, for purposes
of plunder, and especially to cut and carry off the

precious cedars, which were accounted of as highly
at Nineveh and Egyptian Thebes as at Jerusalem
(1 Kings v. 6 ; Ezra iii. 7 ; Isa. xiv. 8). But they
rarely, if ever, passed the crest of the mountains, or
entered the territory, which was most properly
Phœnicia, to the west of the ridge. They might
sometimes look down from the crest upon the "Sea
of the Setting Sun"; but they were seldom tempted
to approach it, much less to make Phœnicia their line
of march from north to south. The coast route was,
in fact, by nature impracticable for an army. At
intervals along the shore spurs from Lebanon extended right across the Phœnician plain, and formed
promontories which descended precipitously into the
sea, leaving no room for a road, and requiring to be
surmounted by "steps" or zigzags, such as were
known to the Greeks and Romans under the name of
Climaces (κλίμακες). One such promontory shuts in
the plain of Acre on the north, and is known as the
Ras-en-Nakura, or "Headland of the Entrance";
another, some miles to the north, bears the name of Ras-
el-Abiad, or "White Headland," being formed of snow-
white chalk interspersed with black flints, and this
was called anciently "the staircase of the Tyrians";
a third shuts in the course of the Lycus to the south,
and, until surmounted by engineering skill, must have
been impassable to an army ; a fourth, a little south
of Tripolis (Tarabolus), is called the Ras-esh-Shekah,
and blocks the way between Tripolis and Byblus.
Though Assyrian and Egyptian monarchs contrived,
in course of time, to overcome these natural obstacles,
they continued to be obstacles nevertheless ; and it

VIEW OF THE PASS SOUTH OF THE NAHR-EL-KELB.

was probably to mark their sense of physical obstructions with difficulty overcome, that the conquering kings who from time to time forced their way through the southern Phœnician territory, erected those trophies of their success on the rocks south of the Lycus, which are still to be seen at the present day.

Further, Phœnicia lay in the natural course of trade between the East and West, and offered the readiest route for the interchange of the commodities of Asia and Europe—of the wealthy kingdoms, which, from a remote antiquity, had grown up in the great Mesopotamian lowland, and of the wilder yet still favoured regions to which the Mediterranean Sea gave access, the isles and coasts of Hellas, and the remoter shores of Italy and Spain. A much frequented caravan route led from Tiphsach (Thapsacus) on the Euphrates, by way of Damascus, to Tyre ; and another passed from Asia Minor, by way of Hamath, to Tripolis and Aradus. Tyre, situated " at the entry of the sea," was "a merchant of the people for many isles " (Ezek. xxvii. 3), and her sister cities were almost as favourably circumstanced. From a date which cannot be placed later than the twelfth century B.C. the carrying trade of the world belonged mainly to Phœnicia, which communicated by land with the Persian Gulf, the Euphrates, Armenia, Cappadocia, and Anatolia, by sea with Egypt, Greece, Italy, North Africa, Gaul, and Spain.

But it is time to pass from this vague and general sketch of the country, whose "Story" we are about to tell, and to enter on a more particular description of its topography.

On the south, the natural boundary between Phœnicia and Philistia, or the country of the Philistines, was the strong promontory of Carmel, which projects further into the sea than any other on this line of coast, and has an elevation of 1700 feet above the sea level. Carmel, as its name implies, is a fruitful and park-like region, containing rocky dells of much beauty, deep jungles of copse, shaggy groves of olive trees, and many patches of dwarf oak, which give it altogether a wooded and green appearance. It is a long ridge, extending eighteen miles in a south-easterly direction, and separating between the plain of Sharon, which naturally belonged to Philistia, and that of Jezreel or Esdraelon, which was Canaanite. Inside Carmel, on the coast, began "the plain of Acre," a fertile tract, stretching along the shore a distance of about twenty miles, and extending inland to the hills of Galilee a distance of three or four miles, watered by two principal streams, the Kishon and the Belus, with "a rich soil, perhaps the best cultivated and producing the most luxuriant crops, both of corn and weeds, of any" in this part of Asia (Stanley). On the north this plain is shut in, as above mentioned, by the headland known as the Ras-en-Nakura, which leaves no beach between itself and the sea, and has to be surmounted by a set of zig-zags. The Ras-en-Nakura is followed within a short distance by the Ras-el-Abiad, another very similar promontory, after which the traveller enters upon "the plain of Tyre," the widest of the whole coast, which reaches from the Ras-el-Abiad to the mouth of the Litany (Leontes), a distance of fifteen miles, and expands near Tyre to a width of five miles. The hills which border the plain are low, and cultivated to their summits. The plain undulates gently, and is fertile, bearing good crops under a very rude system of cultivation.

The Litany, which is the principal river of Phœnicia, rises near Balbek in the Cœle-Syrian valley, at an elevation of 10,000 feet above the sea, and forces its way through Lebanon by a deep and narrow gorge, in which it frets and chafes many hundred feet below the eye of the spectator, descending precipitously, and at last debouching upon the plain by a ravine, about five miles north-east of Tyre. It has been compared to "a monster serpent chained in the yawning gulf, where she writhes and struggles evermore to escape from her dark and narrow prison, but always in vain, save only near the sea-shore, where her windings reach a close." [1]

The course of the Litany through the plain is not more than about five miles. It is ordinarily a stream of considerable width and depth, but in dry seasons dwindles to a rivulet, which may be easily crossed by the traveller.

The "plain of Tyre" is followed by that of Sarepta, which is a continuation of it, and which merges into that of Sidon, the three plains having nearly the same character, but with a gradual contraction as we proceed towards the north. The distance from Tyre to Sidon is about twenty miles, and the entire length of the plain from the Ras-el-Abiad to the elevated piece of coast between the Bostrenus and the Tamy-

[1] Van de Velde, "Travels," vol. i. p. 113.

ras (lat. 33° 40′) about thirty miles ; but the average width does not much exceed two miles. The river of next importance to the Leontes (Litany) is the Bostrenus, which flows from the western flank of Lebanon, and enters the sea about two miles north of Sidon. The Sidonian plain is of the highest fertility, and produces the finest fruits of Syria.

North of the Bostrenus, the hills again closely press on the shore, and a rugged tract supervenes between the Bostrenus and the Tamyras, which is, comparatively speaking, unproductive. Crossing the Tamyras (Damour), we enter on " the plain of Berytus," which is watered by the river Magoras, and has all the richness of the most favoured portions of the region. The projection of the coast, which here juts out into a headland, comparable to that of Carmel, gives the lowland an unusual width, and enables the traveller to obtain a view of Lebanon, which is most striking. The plain itself is covered with gentle undulations. Berytus (Beyrout) is embosomed in gardens and orchards more extensive and luxuriant than those of any other town along the entire coast. The orange tree and the mulberry grow in profuse abundance ; the palm flourishes, though it does not produce fruit ; and the vines bear grapes of excellent quality. The climate is delicious, intermediate between the colder one of Northern Syria and the somewhat oppressive heat of the southern Palestinian coast. In the "plain of Berytus" the beauty and fertility of Phœnicia culminate ; and it is not surprising that of all the Phœnician cities Berytus should alone have maintained its prosperity.

SOURCE OF THE RIVER ADONIS

Once more, between the Magoras and the Lycus—
now the Nahr-el-Kelb—a steep cliff projects into the
sea, forming the southern side of the valley through
which the Lycus discharges its waters, and the
northern boundary of the Beyrout plain. Egyptian
engineering skill first surmounted this obstacle by
means of a road scooped out of· the chalk, and
carried at a high elevation round the headland.
Later on the Romans made a second road at a lower
level—a road which is broader and of more gradual
ascent, and which continues in use at the present
day.

The chalk formation still hugs the shore to the
north of the Lycus, which issues into the sea by a
deep and narrow chasm, the nearly perpendicular
walls of which are two hundred feet in height.
Another steep cliff projects into the sea seven or eight
miles further north, a little below the thirty-fourth
parallel ; this cliff was called Climax anciently, and
is now known as the Ras-Watta-Sillan. Like the
other " Climaces," it had to be surmounted by steps
or " ladders," and formed a barrier which an army
could scarcely cross. The coast continues elevated
from this point to Byblus, or Gebal, which occupied a
hill directly overlooking the sea, a few miles north
of the famous river Adonis, fabled to run with blood
on one day in the year. Between Byblus and the
promontory of Theouprosopon, now Ras-esh-Shekah,
the chalk hills recede a little from the shore, and
on a narrow strip of land stood Botrys, the modern
Batroun, a port with an artificial harbour. A rugged
tract follows, incapable of cultivation, spur after spur

from Lebanon descending nearly to the sea ; but from Tripolis (Tarabolus) the plain begins to expand, and, after crossing the Eleutherus or Nahr-el-Kebir, where Lebanon terminates and Northern Phœnicia begins, we enter upon a tolerably open country, watered by numerous streams from Mount Bargylus, and cultivable for a distance of about fifteen miles from the coast in corn or vineyards. The principal towns of this region were Gabala, now Jebilee, Balanea, Antaradus, and Marathus ; off the shore, at a short distance, was Aradus, on its rocky islet ; and in later times flourished the Greek cities of Heraclea, Laodicea, and Orthosia.

The boundaries of Phœnicia, as already stated, were Carmel upon the south ; Casius upon the north ; upon the east Bargylus and Lebanon. Carmel has been already described. With a few words upon the other Phœnician mountain regions, we may terminate this account of the Phœnician country.

Casius is an outlying and detached fragment of the mountain-group known as Taurus, Anti-Taurus, and Amanus, transported by a freak of nature to a distance. The rocks whereof it is composed are of igneous origin, and give to its outline that sharp and pyramidal form in which the Syrian ranges are deficient. The sides of the mountain are clothed with forest trees, such as belong to the growth of Asia Minor and of Southern Europe rather than of Syria and Palestine. The chalk, so prevalent in Syria, just touches its southern edge. Above this all is supercretaceous limestone, or else granite, trap, or schist, peak mounting over peak, and the whole culminating

in a lofty cone, 5,699 feet above the level of the sea.
on which in ancient times stood a temple consecrated
to the worship of the Casian Jupiter.

Bargylus is a mountain tract of no very great eie-
vation, intervening between the Orontes valley to the
east, and the low plain of Northern Phœnicia to the
west.   It is mainly of chalk formation, but contains
some trap and serpentine in places.   Its general outline is tame and commonplace ; but it encloses many
beautiful valleys and ravines, gradually worn in its
sides by the numerous streams which flow eastward
and westward, to the Orontes or to the Mediterranean.
The upland regions are for the most part bare, or
covered with dwarf myrtle or occasionally with fern.
But some portions, more especially towards the north,
are well-wooded, being covered with forests of oak
and pine.   Elsewhere there is abundance of thick
brushwood; and the frequent villages are embosomed,
almost without exception, in orchards and gardens ;
figs, vines, and olive-trees alternating with pomegranates, mulberries, and walnuts.   Apricots, peaches,
and nectarines also abound, and many tracts are
suited for the growth of wheat, maize, melons, cucum-
bers, and other vegetables.   Fountains and rills of
water gush out on every side, cheering the eye with
their freshness, always pleasantly cool, and sometimes
" chilly cold."

Lebanon, the glory of Syria, stands separate from
Bargylus, divided from it, first, by a broad plain,
known as El-Bukeia, and then by the gorge of the
Nahr-el-Kebir.   The axis of the Lebanon range is
slightly deflected from that of Bargylus, running from

N.E. by N. to S.E. by S., whereas that of Bargylus is nearly due north and south. The range extends in one long unbroken dorsal ridge from Jebel Riban in the south to Jebel Akkar in the north, a distance of above a hundred miles. Geologically it is, in the main, of secondary formation, consisting of limestone of the early cretaceous period ; but "the valleys and gorges are filled with formations of every possible variety—sedimentary, metamorphic, and igneous. Down many of them run long streams of trap and basalt, occasionally there are dykes of porphyry and greenstone, and then patches of sandstone before the limestone and flint recur." The elevation rises gradually as we proceed northward, until the range culminates in the peaks about the cedars, which are estimated to attain a height of from nine thousand to ten thousand feet. The scenery is throughout most beautiful. Garden cultivation carpets the base of the mountain ; above this is, for the most part, a broad fringe of olive groves ; higher up, the hill sides are carefully terraced, not an inch of ground being wasted ; and among sharp cliffs and pointed rocks of a grey-white hue are strips of cornfields, long rows of dwarf mulberries, figs, apricots, apples, walnuts, and other fruit trees. Gorges, ravines, charming glens, deep valleys, diversify the mountain sides ; here and there are tremendous chasms, with precipices that go sheer down for a thousand feet ; tiny rivulets bound and leap from rock to rock and from terrace to terrace, forming chains of cascades, refreshing and fertilizing all around. In the deep gorges flow copious streams, shaded by overhanging woods of

DESCENT FROM THE PASS OF LEGUIA, IN THE LEBANON.

pines or cedars ; and towards the summit are in
several places magnificent cedar groves, remnants of
the primeval forest which once clothed the greater
part of the mountain.   Above all towers the bare
limestone of the dorsal ridge, always white enough to
justify the name of Lebanon ("White Mountain"),
and for eight months of the year clothed with a
mantle of snow.

II.

THE PEOPLE—THEIR ORIGIN AND ETHNIC
CHARACTER.

THE earliest inhabitants of the Syrian seaboard, which in course of time came to be known as Phœnicia, were apparently the Canaanites. This people, a Hamitic race closely connected with the Egyptians, Ethiopians, and primitive Babylonians, spread itself at a remote date over the entire coast tract from the borders of Egypt to Casius, and formed the dominant population as far inland as the Cœle-Syrian valley, the lake of Gennesaret, and the deep cleft of the Jordan. But, from about B.C. 2000, Semitic immigrants from the East began to find their way into the territory ; and by degrees permanent lodgments were effected, which transferred the rule and government of almost the entire country from the Hamites to the Semites— from the Canaanites and Philistines to the Hebrews, the Phœnicians, and the Syrians. In the emigration of Terah, his family, and his dependants from " Ur of the Chaldees " to Harran, Sichem, and Hebron, we have a specimen of the movements which were in progress at this early period, whereby the thickly-

peopled countries on the shores of the Persian Gulf
discharged their superfluous population into the more
sparsely populated regions of the West. Chedor-
laomer's expeditions (Gen. xiv. 1–12) indicate a pressure of the same kind; and there are traces in the
early Babylonian monuments of other Babylonian
monarchs having pursued the same policy. Semitism
flowed westward from the lower valley of the Euphrates to the shores of the Mediterranean; and the
best positions in the important region intervening
between Taurus and the frontiers of Egypt passed
into the possession of Semitic races.

According to the " Father of History," who, despite
his detractors, is still recognized as an authority
second to no other, by the best critics, the Phœnicians at a date anterior by some generations to the
siege of Troy swelled the migratory movement
whereof we have given instances, and passed of their
own free will from settlements on the Persian Gulf to
the shores of the Mediterranean. This statement,
which he calls "their own account of themselves," is
confirmed by the respectable authority of Justin, who
not only regards the fact of the migration as certain,
but traces to some extent the line of march. "The
Tyrian nation," he says, "was founded by the Phœnicians, who, being disturbed by an earthquake, were
induced to leave their native land, and to settle, first
of all, on the Assyrian lake, and afterwards on the
shore of the Mediterranean, founding a city there
which they called Sidon from the abundance of the
fish; for in the Phœnician tongue a fish is called
Sidon." Another quite independent testimony

ascribes the foundation of Ashdod to "fugitives from the Erythræan sea." Renan sums up the evidence when he says : "The greater number of modern critics admit it as demonstrated, that the primitive abode of the Phœnicians must be placed on the Lower Euphrates, in the centre of the great commercial and maritime establishments of the Persian Gulf, conformably to the unanimous witness of antiquity." [1]

The date, the causes, and the circumstances of the migration are involved in equal obscurity. The motive for it assigned by Justin is absurd, since no nation ever undertook a long and difficult migration on account of an earthquake. If we may resort to conjecture we should be inclined to suggest that the spirit of adventure gave the first impulse ; and that afterwards the unexampled facilities for trade, which the Mediterranean coast was found to possess, attracted a continuous flow of immigrants from the sea of the Rising to that of the Setting Sun. The entire movement may have covered the space of a century, or even more. It was probably complete before the Israelites quitted Egypt, since the Sidonians of the Book of Judges, who "dwelt careless, quiet, and secure," are apparently Phœnician Sidonians, luxurious, peace-loving, and indisposed to exertion.

But whenever and however the Phœnicians came into possession of the tract of land known to the ancients as Phœnicia, which is a matter that must always be open to discussion and doubt, it is at any rate certain that for a thousand years—from the four-

[1] Renan, "Histoire des Langues Sémitiques," II. 2, p. 183.

teenth century to the fourth century B.C.—a great and remarkable nation, separate from all others, with striking and peculiar characteristics, occupied the region in question, drew upon itself the eyes of the whole civilized world, and played a most important part in history. Egypt, Judæa, Assyria, Babylon, Persia, Greece, Rome, came successively into contact with the country and its settled inhabitants, while almost the whole known world made acquaintance with its hardy mariners, who explored almost all seas, visited almost all shores, and linked together the peoples from Spain, Britain, and the Fortunate Islands in the West, to India, Taprobane, and the Golden Chersonese in the East, in the silken bonds of of a mutually advantageous commerce. It is with this people and their characteristics, that we have in the present section to deal, the people who of all antiquity had most in common with England and the English—the people who first discovered the British Islands and made them known to mankind at large, the people who circumnavigated Africa, and caused the gold of Ophir to flow into the coffers of Solomon.

What, then, were the characteristics of this people? In the first place it was, as has been already stated, Semitic. It belonged to that group of nationalities which occupied the middle place in the ancient world between the Aryan nations which filled the north, and the Hamitic ones which lay towards the south. It was more or less intimately connected with the Assyrians, Babylonians, Syrians, Hebrews, Moabites, Edomites, and Arabs. This is seen, in the first place by its language. The character of the Phœnician language is now sufficiently known to us by inscriptions upon tombs and altars, cippi, votive tablets, vases, candelabra, gems, and coins, amounting in all to several hundreds, and for the most part very fairly legible. These show it to have been almost as closely allied to the Hebrew as German to Dutch, or Portuguese to Spanish. "The words most commonly in use, the particles, the pronouns, the forms of the verb, the principal inflexions (and, we may add, the numerals), in Phœnician are identical, or nearly identical, with the pure Hebrew." [1] *El*, is "God"; *Bal* or *baal*, "lord"; *melek*, "king"; *adôn*, "lord"; *ab*, "father"; *am* or *em*, "mother"; *ben*, "son"; *bath*, "daughter"; *akh*, "brother"; *ish*, "man"; *ishah*, "woman" or "wife"; *beth*, "house"; *eben*, "stone"; *abed*, "servant"; *deber*, "word"; *shemesh*, "the sun," &c. Yet still Phœnician is not mere Hebrew; it has its own genius, its idioms, its characteristics. The definite article, so frequent in Hebrew, is in Phœnician extremely rare. The quiescent letters, which in Hebrew accompany the long vowels, are for the most part omitted. The employment of the participle for the definite tenses of the verb is much more common than in Hebrew. Aramaisms are more frequent. The feminine termination of nouns is never *h*. Peculiar forms occur, as *ash* for *asher*, *alonim* for *elohim*, *'amath* for *'am*, "populus," and the like.

Semitism carries with it certain physical and certain moral characteristics. The Semites were of a

---

[1] Renan, "Histoire des Languages Sémitiques," pp. 189, 190.

complexion intermediate between the pale races of
the north and the swart inhabitants of the south.
They had abundant hair, sometimes straight, sometimes curly, but never woolly, like that of the negro.
They were of medium height, but rather tall than
short, and had features not very unlike the Aryans of
Caucasians, but somewhat less refined and regular.
The brow was heavy, the nose broadish and inclined
to be hooked, the lips a little too full, the chin a little
too developed. In the frames there was a good deal
of variety. While the Assyrians, Babylonians, Phœnicians, and Hebrews, inclined to stoutness and
massiveness ; the Syrians and Arabs were, in general,
lean, spare, and agile. On the whole, the Phœnicians,
probably, both in form and feature, very much resembled the Jews, who were their near neighbours,
and who occasionally intermarried with them (1 Kings
xi. 1, xvi. 31 ; 2 Chron. ii. 14).

The moral characteristics of the Semites, or at any
rate of the more western ones, have been said to be,
first, pliability combined with iron fixedness of purpose ; secondly, depth and force ; thirdly, a yearning
for dreamy ease together with a capacity for the
hardest work ; fourthly, a love of abstract thought ;
and fifthly, religiousness, together with an intensely
spiritual conception of the Deity.[1] These qualities
are said to have especially distinguished the Phœnicians, the Arabs, and the Jews.

Phœnician "pliability" is strongly evidenced, not
only by the success of their colonization, which could
only have been attained by a wonderful power of

[1] E. Deutsch. "Literary Remains," pp. 160, 161.

adapting themselves to the most diversified conditions of human life, and to the ideas and feelings of almost all the varieties of uncivilized man, but also by the relations which they are found to have established with the great civilized nations of their time, the Egyptians, the Hebrews, the Assryians, the Babylonians, the Greeks, and the Persians. Jealous as the Egyptians were of foreigners, and disposed as they were to exclude them altogether from their country, they were so won upon by the Phœnicians as not merely to carry on with them an extensive trade, but even to allow them a settlement in their capital, and a temple in which they could worship their own gods. Phœnician deities actually found their way into the Egyptian Pantheon, where Baal was recognized as "Bar," and Ashtoreth as "Astaret," and Anaïtis as "Anta," and Chiun as "Ken," and Reseph as "Reshpu." With the Hebrews they were always on the most familiar and friendly terms, manning their ships (I Kings ix. 27), intermarrying with them (*ibid.* xi. I ; xvi. 31), lending them artificers (*ibid.* v. I ; 2 Chron. ii. 13), trading with them (I Kings v. 9; Ezra iii. 7), supplying them with cedar-wood, and almug-trees, and works in bronze, and dyed cloths, and receiving in return "wheat of Minnith and Pannag, and honey, and wine, and oil" (Ezek. xxvii. 17). Assyria and Babylon encouraged their trade, protected their caravans, and gave their merchants free passage through Western Asia from the shores of the Mediterranean to those of the Persian Gulf. The Greeks accepted from them letters and weights, welcomed them to their ports, and, though to a considerable extent their rivals in trade, were never weary of singing their praises. Persia, which depended on them for her marine, treated them with exceptional favour, so long as they were her subjects, permitted them to retain their own kings, taxed them lightly, and allowed them to reach a high pitch of prosperity.

" Depth and force " are qualities of a people which do not readily admit of demonstration. We rather feel them as involved in the *tout ensemble* of a nation's history, than deduce them from any particular facts or circumstances. The thousand years of Phœnician greatness, the dangers which they confronted, and the vicissitudes through which they passed unharmed, may, however, be adduced as indications, at any rate, of a tough fibre and a vital energy, not the heritage of many races, and may incline us to acquiesce in the view, that " depth and force " were among their characteristics.

The "yearning after dreamy ease " is apparent in the intensity of the Phœnician luxury described by the Prophet Ezekiel (chap. xxvi. 16 ; xxvii. 3–25 ; xxviii. 13), and its combination with a " capacity for the hardest work " is shown by the unwearied activity of the nation throughout its whole career in ship-building, in manufactures, in mining, in colonization, and in commerce. No people of antiquity passed habitually more laborious days than did the great bulk of the Phœnician nation ; perhaps none more enjoyed the delight of rest from toil and indulgence in comfortable ease when the active business of life was accomplished.

The general Semitic "love of abstract thought," so noticeable among the Hebrews and the Arabs, can scarcely be said to have been a leading characteristic of the Phœnicians. There are, it is true, but few remains of the Phœnician literature ; but, neither the fragments which exist, nor the accounts of the literature which have come down to us from the Greeks and Romans, give reason to believe that much of it was concerned with philosophy or abstract speculation. A certain Mochus—a Sidonian—is indeed said to have written a treatise on the doctrine of atoms, and speculations concerning creation and the early condition of man are the main subject of Philo Byblius's introduction to his Phœnician History. But the bulk of the Phœnician writings seem to have been of a practical character, consisting mainly of histories, geographical treatises, and books of travels. The Phœnicians were, on the whole, too busy, too much occupied with the affairs of practical life, to give much attention to speculation or abstract reasoning.

On the other hand, the Phœnicians possessed, in a strong degree, the general Semitic quality of religiousness. The temple was the centre of attraction in each city, and the piety of the inhabitants adorned each temple with abundant and costly offerings. The kings were zealous in maintaining the honour of the gods, repaired and beautified the sacred buildings, and not unfrequently discharged the office of High Priest. Both they, and their subjects, bore, for the most part, religious names—names which were regarded as placing them under the protection of some deity. Their ships bore images of gods as their figure-heads. Wherever they went, they carried with them their religion and worship, and were careful to erect in each colony a temple, or temples, similar to those which adorned the cities of the mother country.

It must be confessed, however, that the religion of the Phœnicians was not, in the historic period, of a very elevating or improving character. Originally, indeed, the Phœnicians would seem to have been monotheists, and to have possessed a lofty idea of the great Power which had created, and which ruled, the world. They called Him El, "great"; Ram or Rimmon, "high"; Baal, "Lord"; Melek or Molech, "King"; Eliun, "Supreme"; Adonai, "my Lord"; Bel-samin, "Lord of Heaven," and the like. They regarded Him as wholly distinct from matter, and believed Him to have brought into existence all other beings, and all material things. But this belief was early overlaid and corrupted. The different names of God passed by degrees into different gods; new deities were invented or imported, as Ishtar from Babylon, and Thoth and Ammon from Egypt. Monotheism passed into Polytheism. Instead of worshipping a single supreme God—El, the "great" or Eliun, the "Supreme" One—the Phœnicians, like so many other peoples, broke up their primitive conception into a number of fragments, and made of each fragment a distinct and separate personality. Baal or Baal-shemin, "the Lord of Heaven," became a deity distinct from El, and the first object of Phœnician worship. He was represented as the son of El, or sometimes of Uranus, and as the practical

BAAL AS A SUN-GOD.

ASTARTE.

ruler of the world during the current cycle. At the
same time he had a solar aspect, and seems to have
been, by some, actually identified with the physical
sun, as Ra was by many in Egypt. Whether there
was any real connection between Baal and Bel is
doubtful, since there is a root letter in the one (בעל)
which is wanting in the other (בל). At any rate, Bel
had no solar character in Babylon, and was far from
being at the head of the Pantheon in the early times.
With Baal was associated, as a sort of counterpart,
or complement, the great goddess, Ashtoreth (עשתרת)
or Astarte, who was especially worshipped at Sidon,
but received also a widespread, indeed a general,
acknowledgment. Her ordinary character was that
of a nature-goddess, the queen of increase and
fecundity ; but, as Baal had a solar, so she had a
lunar character, and was often represented with horns,
or with the crescent moon upon her head. The
character of her rites will be spoken of in a later
chapter. Baal and Ashtoreth maintained from a very
early date to the latest period of Phœnician nationality
a supremacy, or at any rate a pre-eminency over all
the other personages of the Phœnician Pantheon.
Among secondary deities were the following :—El,
Melkarth, Dagon, Hadad, Adonis, Sadyk, Eshmun,
the Kabeiri, Atergatis or Derketo, Onca, and perhaps
Beltis. A few words must be said concerning each.
El or Il, originally the name of the supreme God,
became in the later Phœnician mythology a subordinate deity, whom the Greeks compared to their
Kronos, and the Romans to their Saturn. He was
especially worshipped at Carthage, and is perhaps to

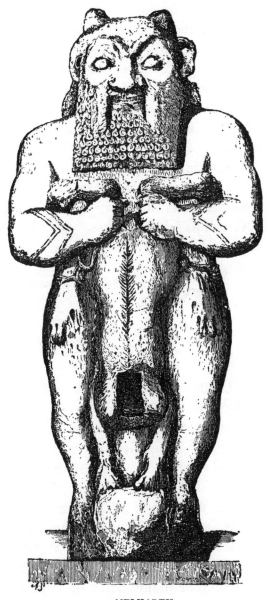

MELKARTH.

4

be identified with the Ammonite Moloch. Human
sacrifices were offered to him, and a tale was told of
him, that he had been himself the first to sacrifice his
own son, Jeoud, in a time of distress and calamity.
Melkarth was perhaps originally a mere aspect of
Baal—Baal considered as the god of cities, or of a
particular city. He is called in one inscription " Baal
Tsur," " the Lord of Tyre," or " the Baal of Tyre ";
and he was certainly looked upon as in a peculiar
way the guardian and protector of that town. His
name is explained as meaning " City King," and
appears in Greek as " Melikarthos " or " Melikertes."

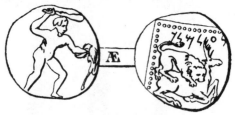

COIN OF GADES.

The Greeks identified him with their Hercules, but
for what reason is not very apparent ; however, the
Phœnicians caught at the idea, and in their later coins,
Hercules, modelled upon Grecian types, makes his
appearance frequently as representative of the
Phœnician deity. Dagon, the god of Ashdod in
Philistia (1 Sam. v. 2 ; Mac. x. 84), was probably one
of the deities adopted by the Phœnicians from
without. It is generally supposed that he had the
form of a fish, and images of fish-gods have certainly been found in many parts of Western Asia ;
but there is no ground for regarding Dagon as
one of them beyond a very doubtful etymology.

"Dag" (דג) in Hebrew means "a fish," but Philo
Byblius suggests for Dagon quite a different deriva-
tions making him a "Corn-god" (Σίτων), the discoverer of wheat, and the inventor of the plough.   In
Philistia he held a high place, but in Phœnicia he was
quite subordinate, and it is simply on the authority of
Philo that he is admitted into the Phœnician
Pantheon. Hadad, Adad, or Adod, was primarily a
Syrian god, and seems to have represented the sun in
the later Phœnician system.   One of his titles was
"King of the Gods," but he was certainly not regarded by the Phœnicians as a deity of very exalted
pretentions.   Adonis held a much more important
position.   The word is properly Adonai (אֲדֹנָי), "my
Lord," and was probably in the olden times an epithet
of Baal, but later it became a designation for the Sun-
god, or rather for the sun in certain of its relations.
The sun in winter, withdrawing himself from the
northern hemisphere, was considered to suffer a
temporary death ; and this was typified by the death
of Adonis through a wound inflicted on him by
the tusk of a boar, as he hunted in the heights of
Lebanon.   The river Adonis, really swollen and dis-
coloured by the autumn rains, was considered to be
reddened with his blood ; and the Phœnician maidens
flocked yearly to the banks of the stream, to weep
and beat their breasts for his loss. Sadyk, "the Just
One," appears to have been an embodiment of the
Divine attribute of Justice.   He was the son of
Agruêrus, and the father of Eshmun and the Kabeiri,
who discovered the art of working in metal, and were
the first to build ships. Eshmun was by the Greeks

identified with Asclepias or Asculapius ; but here again it is difficult to discover any grounds for the identification. Eshmun was Sadyk's eighth son, whence his name, which is to be connected with the Hebrew שְׁמִינִי "eighth." He was, according to the myth, a beautiful and chaste youth, much given to hunting, with whom Astarte fell in love, and whom she would have forced to be her paramour, had he not emasculated himself to escape her. The Kabeiri (probably כְּבִּירִים *i.e.*, "great gods") were gods of navigation, and also gods presiding over the working in metal ; they were represented as dwarfs and misshapen, like the Egyptian Phtha-Sokari, and the Greek Hephæstus. Atergatis or Derketo, was more properly Philistinian than Phœnician. The principal seat of her worship was Ascalon ; and we may perhaps best regard her as a nature-goddess, akin to Ashtoreth. Onca was a divinity of a higher type : the Greeks compared her with their Athene, who was the goddess of wisdom, and to a certain extent adopted her into their Pantheon. Beltis, if a Phœnician deity at all, which is uncertain, can only be the Babylonian goddess of the name transported to the shores of the Mediterranean.

It is certain that the Phœnicians, or at any rate those of the later times, having once embarked in polytheism, were not averse from adopting into their system new and extraneous gods. From the inscriptions it appears that the Ammon and Osiris of Egypt, and the Tanata, or Anaïtis of Syria, were among the deities of most account in the later ages. Ammon, indeed, who is called "Hammon" (חמו), is identified with Baal, and never addressed as a distinct and separate deity ; but Anaïtis and Osiris are clear additions to the later Pantheon, as also is Thoth, if we may accept the statements of Philo Byblius. It is, of course, palpable that, when once the line of monotheism is overstepped, no limit of number can be established on any intelligible and defensible principle.

With polytheism there came naturally a degradation of the idea of god, an identification of Baal with the sun, and of Ishtar or Ashtoreth with the moon, an inclination towards licentious orgies, and a belief that the anger of the supernal powers was best averted by the offering of human sacrifices. Aphaca in Lebanon, near the sources of the river Adonis was one of the places where religious prostitution prevailed in its grossest and most revolting forms, and throughout Phœnicia and its colonies there was an established practice of offering up human victims in time of public calamity. Familiarity with such bloody rites naturally tended to brutalize a people whom the influences of trade and commerce would otherwise have softened and refined, and this may account for the " violence " with which they are taxed by Ezekiel (ch. xxviii. 16), for their cruel treatment of prisoners on some occasions, and for their habitual indulgence in piracy, kidnapping, and the other horrors attendant on the traffic in slaves. The Phœnician religion rather excited the passions than restrained them, rather blunted the moral sentiments than gave them force or vigour. Fear of divine vengeance may have exercised a certain deterrent influence, and held men back from some forms of sin ; but the aggregate results of the religion upon the moral character of the people was probably injurious rather than beneficial.

The Phœnicians seem to have had but small expectation of a future life. A usual expression for death was "the time of non-existence." Those who died "went down into silence," and "became mute." Their spirit "vanished," "disappeared "— ceased to be, "like a day that is past." The only continuance that they, for the most part, expected or desired, was to be still borne in remembrance among those who remained upon the earth. On one gravestone alone do we find a hope of future existence indicated, rather than declared, in the curt phrase with which the inscription ends—"after rain the sun shines forth."

Altogether, the Phœnicians must be said to have fallen very far behind most of the other Semitic peoples in the domain of thought, of speculation, and of ideas. It was their glory to be practical. "By industry, by perseverance, by acuteness of practical intellect, by unscrupulousness, and, if they thought the occasion called for it, by want of faith, by adaptability and pliability when necessary, and dogged defiance at other times, by total disregard of the rights of the weaker, they obtained the foremost place in the history of their times, and the highest reputation, not only for the things that they did, but also for many things that they did not. They were the first systematic traders, the first miners and metallurgists, the greatest inventors, the boldest mariners, the greatest colonizers—while elsewhere despotism overshadowed as with a pall the whole Eastern world, they could boast of a form of government approaching to constitutionalism ; of all the nations of their time they

stood the highest in practical arts and science " [1]—
they were masons, carpenters, shipbuilders, weavers,
dyers, glass-blowers, workers in metal, navigators,
discoverers, beyond all others ; if they were not
actually the first inventors of letters, at any rate they
so improved upon the mode of writing which they
found in use, that their system has been adopted, and
suffices, with a few additions, for the whole civilized
world ; they were the first to affront the dangers of
the open ocean in their strong-built ships, the first to
steer by the Polar star, the first to make known to
civilized nations the remoter regions of Asia, Africa,
and Europe ; they surpassed the Greeks in enterprise,
in perseverance, and in industry ; at a time when
brute force was worshipped as the main source of
power and only basis of national repute, they succeeded in showing that as much fame might be won,
as much glory obtained, as real a power constructed by
arts as by arms, by the peaceful means of manufacture,
trade, and commerce, as by the violent and bloody
ones of war, massacre, and conquest. They set an
example which has been followed in the past by
Miletus, Corinth, Genoa, Venice, Portugal, Holland,
and to some extent by England—an example which,
it is to be hoped, will be far more largely followed in
the future, when the rage for military establishments
is past, and the rivalry of nations is diverted from the
warlike channels in which it at present flows to the
peaceful ones, which alone have the sanction of
civilization and Christianity.

[1] Adapted from E. Deutsch, " Literary Remains," pp. 162, 163.

III.

THE CITIES—THEIR POSITION, PRINCIPAL FEATURES, AND MUTUAL RELATIONS.

AMONG the Phœnician cities the one which first challenges attention, and which requires to be described at the greatest length, is the city of Tyre. In a certain qualified sense Tyre may be regarded as the capital of Phœnicia. If not the most ancient, it was, at any rate during the historical period, by far the most important of the towns. Known to the Hebrews from the time of Joshua as "the strong city" (Josh. xix. 29), often mentioned as Tsor on the early Egyptian monuments, attracting so much the regards of the Greeks as to extend its name in their geographical nomenclature to the entire tract of sea-coast on which it stood (for "Syria" is most properly explained as a softened form of "Tsyria"), from the age of David to that of Alexander politically first and foremost among the states, Tyre is to Phœnicia what Miletus was to Ionia, almost what Rome was to Italy —the natural leader and head, the directress and monitress, the national impersonation and embodiment.

It is among the most remarkable peculiarities of

Tyre, that it was a double city—a city made up of two wholly distinct parts—one, a littoral island about three-quarters of a mile in length, separated from the mainland by a strait about half a mile wide, and the other a town upon the opposite shore. The town upon the shore was known to the Greeks and Romans as Palætyrus, or "Old Tyre"—its twin sister was "the island Tyre," or "New Tyre," or "Tyre" emphatically. Nature's own arrangement seems to have been to place a group, or string, of some seven or eight islands off the Syrian shore in lat. 33° 30′, the general axis of the group being parallel to the shore, and two of the islands towards its centre being much larger than the remainder. This natural breakwater afforded sufficient protection against the prevalent winds to make the strait between the row of islands and the coast a convenient roadstead. Here, then, on the continent, about half way between the mouth of the Litany and the Ras-el-Ain, the original city grew up in the maritime plain, which is about five miles in width at this point. It was strongly fortified by massive walls and towers, and by degrees extended itself over the plain, until it attained a circumference of about fifteen miles. No more particular description can be given of it, since it was ruined in the Assyrian and Babylonian wars, and all traces of it have disappeared, if we except a few broken arches, running northwards from the Ras-el-Ain towards the sandy isthmus, which now joins "the island Tyre" to the shore.

Of the "Island Tyre" a more detailed description may be given. It appears that from a very early date the two principal islands of the group, or string, above described, were occupied by settlements, the smaller one, which lay to the north, or north-west, of the other, being made the site of a great temple to Melkarth, while the larger one was wholly covered with houses which were many storeys in height, and closely crowded together in the narrow space. This state of things continued till the time of Hiram, the friend of David and Solomon. Hiram filled up the channel between the two main islands, thus uniting them into one, pulled down the Melkarth temple, and erected a new temple to Baal and Ashtoreth on a different site, and utilized the whole space of the Melkarth temple and its *temenos* for houses and other buildings. He also greatly enlarged the main island towards the east, filling up the sea with stone and rubbish to a considerable distance on that side, and obtaining thereby a broad space, which he laid out in streets and squares. One of these latter was known as " the Eurychôrus ;" it was probably a large open place, surrounded by grand buildings like the Piazza of St. Mark at Venice, and served as a meeting-place for the assemblies of the people, as well as for other purposes. By these means the " Island Tyre " attained a circumference of twenty-two stadia, or about two and a half miles.

It remained to provide the " Island City " with harbours. Nature had done no more than to furnish a breakwater, behind which was a tolerable roadstead, but one only partially sheltered towards the south by the trend of the shore, and without any shelter at all towards the north, where the strait lay open to the full force of the north wind. A safe anchorage-

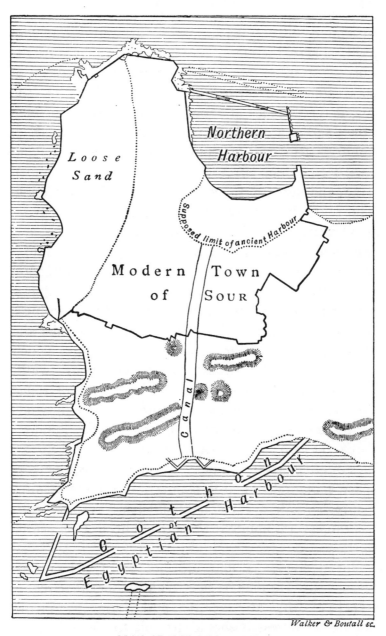

PLAN OF THE ISLAND TYRE.

ground could only be secured by art and engineering skill. These, therefore, were called into play. At the north-eastern extremity of the island two piers of solid stone were carried out from the shore into the sea, at the distance of about a hundred feet from each other, and to a distance from the shore of about seven hundred feet, which, running nearly due west and east, formed an effectual barrier against the north wind, and secured to vessels the needful protection. The outer line of wall may be regarded as a mere breakwater. The inner one was an actual pier, and was deflected at its eastern extremity so as to join a low ridge of rock which formed a natural protection to the harbour on the east, and secured it against squalls from Lebanon. Another ridge ran out to meet this and completed the shelter upon this side, the mouth of the harbour between the two ridges, which were strengthened by art, having no greater width than about thirty-five yards. The extent of space thus enclosed and made absolutely safe in all winds seems anciently to have been about three hundred yards by two hundred and thirty-five yards, or an area of about seventy thousand square yards, a narrow space enough if viewed in connection with the requirements of modern ships, but sufficiently capacious to contain several hundred vessels of the size known to the ancients.

But a single harbour did not satisfy Phœnician ideas. No harbour is accessible under all circumstances of wind and weather, and Tyrian commerce required that vessels should be able to make the port of Tyre at all seasons. Accordingly a second harbour was constructed at the southern extremity of the island, which was known as "the Egyptian harbour," since it looked towards Egypt. A pier was carried out from the south-western point of the island to a distance of two hundred yards in a south-south-west direction, and a wall was carried thence in a direction a little north of east to the island's south-eastern extremity, a single opening being left in it, which might be closed by a boom. A space, eight hundred yards long and from fifty to a hundred and fifty wide, was thus walled in, and a second harbour constructed rather more capacious than the first, the area being about eighty thousand square yards. The approach to this harbour was further guarded by a breakwater thirty-five feet in breadth, which started from a small islet a little outside the southern wall of the harbour, and was carried southwards for a distance of nearly two miles.

Finally, to secure a ready communication between the two harbours at all seasons and in every kind of weather, a canal was excavated, which ran from north to south through the middle of the city, and enabled vessels to pass freely from the northern to the southern harbour, and *vice versâ*. Thus, according to an ancient writer, the fleet and arsenals of the Tyrians were placed in a condition of perfect security, " as if within a house whose doors were bolted."

Very little remains to show what was the character of the Phœnician architecture, or what pretentions the Phœnician cities had to splendour and magnificence ; but Tyre, at any rate, from the descriptions of it which have come down to us, must have been a

striking and noble city. The outer walls on the side
of the mainland were a hundred and fifty feet in
height, and were surmounted with battlements and
towers. Beyond lay the "pleasant houses" (Ezek.
xxvi. 12). These rose, in storey over storey, to a
height unusual in antiquity, and sometimes stood in
the midst of gardens and orchards shaded by vines
and olive trees. Towards the south-western extremity
of the island was the Royal Castle, or palace; beyond,
toward the centre of the city, were the great temples,
built with huge blocks of stone and roofed in with
cedar; in the eastern suburb was the grand square,
or place known as "the Eurychôrus." The natural
slope of the ground towards the west showed the
buildings in tier over tier to one who viewed the town
from the continent, and greatly increased the grand
effect of the *coup d'œil*.

Sidon, the second in importance of the Phœnician
cities, and probably the most ancient of them all, was
situated at the distance of about twenty miles north
of Tyre, on a small promontory which runs out into
the sea in lat. 33° 34'. Three reefs, or low ridges of
rock running parallel with the shore, with narrow
openings between them, offered the nucleus of a harbour, which Sidonian art converted after a while into
a small but safe haven. Two spacious open road-
steads extended themselves to the north and south of
the promontory, but these were of little use in rough
weather. Sidon could never have been, as a port, at
all equal to Tyre. Originally it was a mere fishing
station like its namesake, Beth-Saida, on the Sea of
Galilee; but the genius of its inhabitants raised it

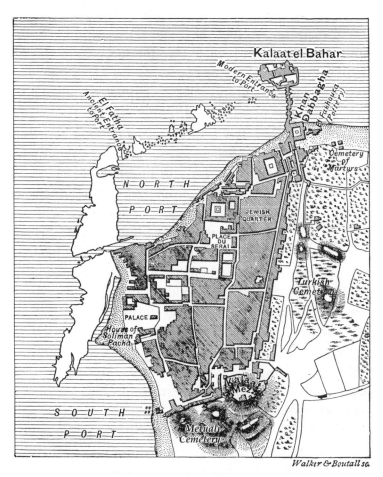

Kalaat el Bahar

Modern Entrance to Port

El Fatha
Ancient Entrance to Port

Khan
Dabbagha

Frakhoura
(Pottery?)

Cemetery
of
Martyrs

NORTH
PORT

JEWISH
QUARTER

PLACE
DU
SERAI

Turkish
Cemetery

PALACE

House of
Soliman
Pacha

SOUTH
PORT

Kala
Mez

Metual
Cemetery

Walker & Boutall sc.

PLAN OF SIDON.

into a temporary prominence ; and until about the eleventh century B.C. it seems to have been of even more importance than Tyre. The nautical skill and enterprise of the Sidonians, their textile fabrics, and their metallurgy, had become famous long before Homer's time, and their productions were widely spread over the countries bordering the Mediterranean. Sidon boasted of at least four temples, one dedicated to the gods generally, another to Ashtoreth, a third to Baal-Sidon, or the Sidonian Baal, and a fourth to Esmun, the chief of the Cabiri. Nothing remains of the ancient town except a portion of its walls.

Proceeding northwards from Sidon, the next town of any consequence is Beyrout, or Berytus, which is now by far the most flourishing city on the Syrian coast. Anciently, however, it was a place of little note, possessing no harbour of any size, and was probably subject either to Sidon or Byblus. It is scarcely mentioned in history until the time of the Maccabees.

Byblus, the Greek and Roman name for the native Gebal (Ps. lxxxiii. 7 ; Ezek. xxvii. 9), occupied a round hill close to the shore in about lat. 34° 8'. It was one of the earliest of the Phœnician settlements, celebrated as the abode of the mythic Cinyras, the father of Adonis, and at any rate well known in the time of Joshua (Josh. xiii. 5). Its people, the Giblites, were especially skilled in the hewing and squaring of those great masses of stone with which the Phœnicians were wont to build ; and we probably see their work in those recently-uncovered blocks of enormous size which formed the substructions of Solo-

WALLS OF SIDON

mon's temple (1 Kings v. 18). At a later date they were noted as "caulkers," and were employed by the Tyrians to make their vessels water-tight (Ezek. xxvii. 9). Byblus was sacred to Adonis, and was one of the chief scenes of those licentious orgies which characterized his worship. It is frequently mentioned in the Assyrian inscriptions, and appears to have been the seat of a monarchy distinct from the kingdoms of Tyre and Sidon, from B.C. 745 to B.C. 660, and again in the time of Alexander.

Thirty miles north of Byblus, in lat. 34° 26' nearly, was Tripolis, now Tarabolus. It was situated on a promontory, about a mile long and half a mile broad, which here runs out into the sea to the north-west. Beyond are a string of seven islands, affording good protection from the prevalent winds, and rendering the roadstead between them and the Syrian coast tolerably secure. Tripolis, the native name of which is unknown, was, we are told, a joint colony of the three cities, Tyre, Sidon, and Aradus, and was itself divided correspondingly into three distinct towns, each encircled by a wall of its own. It was not anciently a place of much consequence.

Nearly thirty miles from Tripolis, on the opposite side of a deepish bay, which here indents the coast of Syria, penetrating further eastward than any other, were the two small towns of Marathus and Simyra, both exceedingly ancient, the former traceable in the "Brathu" of Sanchoniathon and in the "Martu" of the early Babylonian inscriptions; the latter probably the home of the "Zemarites" mentioned in the Book of Genesis (chap. x. 18). Neither town lay upon

the shore. The rich plain seems here to have tempted
the original settlers more than the sea ; but the consequence was a lack of development. Neither Simyra
nor Marathus attained to any great prosperity. Both
probably fell early under the sway of Arvad or
Aradus, which, becoming powerful through commerce,

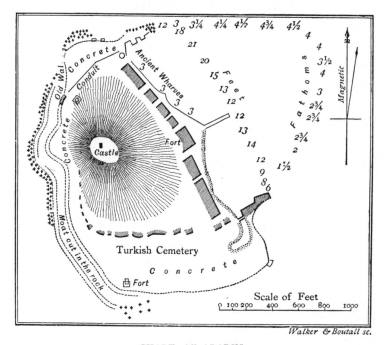

CHART OF ARADUS.

was able to extend its authority over a large tract of
the continent.

Aradus was situated on a rocky island about eight
hundred yards in length, distant nearly three miles
from the shore. It lay in lat. 34° 48′, a little further
north than Simyra. Nearly opposite, on the Syrian
coast, was Antaradus, or Carnus, its principal naval

station and port. It had also two small harbours on its eastern face. According to a tradition reported by Strabo, Aradus was a colony from Sidon ; but it may be doubted whether it was not really as old as any other Phœnician settlement. The walls were built of those massive blocks, from fifteen to eighteen feet long, which mark an early stage of architecture, when it is thought that security can only be achieved by mass, and that mass alone is admirable. As in the Island Tyre, the buildings were closely crowded together, and the houses were of many storeys, being inhabited in flats. The island was springless, and the natives had to depend for their water supply either on cisterns and reservoirs, in which the rain-water was stored, or on a submarine spring which rose in the mid-channel of the strait from a depth of fifty cubits. This curious fountain was carefully covered with a mass of lead, let down from above, which excluded the sea, while it allowed the fresh water to rise through a leathern tube attached to the lead, which conducted it to a vessel that floated on the surface. The plain about Antaradus was abundantly watered and very fertile, being traversed by copious streams from Bargylus, and boasting also of a famous fountain, the Ain-el-Haiyeh, or " Enydra " of Strabo.

Fifty miles north of Aradus, on the shore, near the mouth of a considerable river, now the Nahr-el-Kebir, lay the most northern of the Phœnician cities, known to the later Greeks as Laodicea, but originally " Ramantha." Movers conjectures that it was the earliest of all the Phœnician settlements. The ground for this suggestion is the fact that the coins of Laodicea in some instances bear the inscription, *am b'Canaan,* which is interpreted to mean " the mother city in Canaan " ; but neither the interpretation of the inscription, nor the deduction drawn from it, can be regarded as altogether satisfactory.

COIN OF LAODICEA.

Ramantha is unheard of in the early times, and not known to have flourished until the period of the Seleucidæ. It had only a small harbour, and is unnoticed by the early Greek geographers. We must reckon it among the less important of the Phœnician cities.

At the opposite end of the long line of coast, furthest towards the south as Ramantha was furthest towards the north, lay Aké or Akko, certainly one of the earliest settlements (Judges i. 31), and the one which has retained its prosperity the longest. As Ptolemaïs, Akko played a most important part in the Græco-Roman age ; as Acre, it has been famous is history from the period of the Crusades to times within our own memory. It occupied the north-western extremity of the great bay which indents the Syrian coast north of Carmel, a bay eight miles across and about four miles deep. Its own haven was small and exposed ; but on the opposite side of the bay, under Carmel, was the sheltered roadstead of Haifa ; and either at Akko or at Haifa vessels could ride securely in almost all sorts of weather. The great importance of Akko was that it commanded the entrance to the broad plain of Esdraelon, conducting to the rich valley of the Jordan, and so was, in a certain sense, as it was often called, "the key of Palestine." Its kings were reckoned next in rank to those of Tyre and Sidon during the Assyrian period ; and we find them taking part in the wars which were carried on by Shalmaneser IV. and Sennacherib.

The cities of Phœnicia lived for the most part on friendly terms one with another, but at no time formed a regular confederacy. In the normal condition of things each had its own monarch, who was quite independent of all the rest. On the approach, however, of serious danger the various towns drew together ; alliances were formed, and joint armies and fleets collected. The chief command was entrusted to a single leader, who was usually either the King of Tyre or the King of Sidon. But an inherent weakness rendered these leagues of little service. The great armies of the leading Asiatic powers could not be resisted, even by the combined forces of all Phœnicia, in the field ; such resistance as could be offered had to be made behind walls. The result was, that the towns were severally invested on the land side, and when a portion were forced to surrender, their fleets could be used by the conqueror to blockade by sea the cities which still held out. Phœnicia was forced to submit, successively, to

Assyria, Babylonia, Persia, and Macedon, her own arms being turned against herself. The several cities retained, however, a certain amount of internal independence, until the Seleucid princes made Phœnicia an integral portion of their empire.

Special ties seem to have connected, at certain times, the three principal Phœnician cities, Tyre, Sidon, and Aradus. This is implied in the tradition concerning the founding of Tripolis, which was a joint colony of the three states. It is shown still more clearly by the fact that, under the Persians, the three states had a joint Council, or Congress, which sat at Tripolis, and deliberated on matters affecting the common welfare. Indeed, as early as the time of Ezekiel, there is indication of the alliance ; since even then " the inhabitants of Zidon and Arvad " served in the fleets of Tyre (Ezek. xxvii. 8), and the " men of Arvad " helped to man the walls (verse 11).

IV.

THE COLONIES.

THE earliest maritime commerce of the Phœnicians was probably with Cyprus, Cilicia, and Egypt. Their relations with the Philistine cities were hostile, and those cities had no commodities to exchange which their own land did not furnish sufficiently. Their vessels, consequently, neglecting Ashdod, Ascalon, and Gaza, passed southwards to the ports of Egypt, and, mounting one or more of the navigable branches by which the Nile poured its waters into the Mediterranean, laid themselves alongside the wharfs which lined the banks of the great river at Pelusium, Bubastis, Zoan, Memphis, Sais, Sebennytus. At Memphis they were allowed to make a settlement. This was not, in the strict sense of the word, a colony ; but it gave them a *point d'appui* in Egypt, a fixed home, from which they could, by their mercantile ability, control most of the internal lines of traffic, and secure to themselves the choicest of the merchandise which either Egypt itself produced, or which was poured into its bosom by the rest of Africa. The early Phœnician trade was, as Herodotus

tells us (i. 1), very mainly in the " wares of Egypt "—
these they exported largely to Greece, Asia Minor,
Italy. They consisted of ivory, ebony, skins, ostrich
feathers, gums, gems, corn, papyrus, textile fabrics,
toilet articles, pottery, glass, salt fish, &c. The
Phœnicians in Memphis are said to have been
derived originally from Tyre. They had permission
to worship their own gods openly, and had a temple
dedicated to Astarte, which Herodotus believed to
have been built about the time of the Trojan War, or
circa B.C. 1250.

COIN OF TARSUS, WITH PHŒNICIAN INSCRIPTION.

A coasting voyage of about the same length as
that from Tyre to Egypt would have conducted
the Phœnicians of Tripolis and Aradus to Cilicia.
The coins of Cilicia show its language to have been
Phœnician, and numerous traditions connect the two
countries in the closest way. The name itself is
derived from a Phœnician word, *khalak*, which
means " rough," or " rocky." Tarsus, the capital, was
probably, at the first, a Phœnician colony, though
subsequently it received a large number of Assyrians

into its population, and also a large number of Greeks. Its coins have the figure of a god on the obverse, with the legend, *Baal Tars*, "The Lord of Tarsus." Cicilia could furnish the Phœnicians with abundant timber for ship-building, and with many precious minerals from the spurs and flanks of Taurus.

Opposite Cilicia, within sight from its shores, and also within sight from the highlands of Northern Syria, so situated that it could not fail to attract colonists from Phœnicia at a very early date, was Cyprus. The east coast would naturally have been the first to be colonized, and here are found the Phœnician names of Salamis and Ammochosta, both situated in the great bay which indents the shore between lat. 35° and lat. 35° 30′. Thence the emigrants seem to have passed to the south, where they founded Citium, Amathus, Palæpaphos, and Paphos, together with Idalium in the interior. It is doubtful if they ever possessed much of the north coast, which at an early date was colonized by the Greeks. Cyprus offered to the Phœnicians many advantages. It had abundant mines of copper, together with some of silver and of gold. It was thickly wooded originally, and after the trees had been cleared from the plains, was richly productive of corn, wine, and oil. Its precious stones attained great celebrity. Among them were the aquamarine, the emerald, the opal, the agate, and the red jasper. Abundant traces exist of the Phœnician occupation of Cyprus, both in the coins and in the very curious remains which have been disinterred by the energy and enterprise of General Di Cesnola and others.

The shores of Pamphylia and Lycia seem to have possessed no great attraction for the Phœnicians, and at any rate cannot be shown to have been occupied by any of their colonies. Neither region was very productive ; and the Lycians, having a civilization of their own, of an Aryan type, may have been disinclined to encourage the settlement among them of a Semitic people. Anyhow, the Phœnicians coasted along these lovely regions, where the trees dip their branches into the blue limpid wave, without effecting any lodgment upon them, so far as we know, and steered their vessels for the fertile island which lay off the south-western corner of Asia Minor, the island known from the earliest times to the present as Rhodes. Rhodes had numerous excellent harbours ; its mountains were clothed with forests of pine, and towards the base with vines ; its plains produced pomegranates, olives, figs, and abundant crops of corn. The Phœnicians occupied Ialysus and Camirus under a leader called Phalas, whose name connects him with the royal families of Sidon and Tyre ; but in course of time they were forced to succumb, first to the Carians, and afterwards to the Greeks.

From Rhodes the Ægean lay open to the adventurers. Carpathos and Casos conducted them to Crete ; Telos, Cos, and Calynda to the whole circle of the Sporades and Cyclades. Their colonization of the latter is testified by Thucydides ; their occupation of the former appears from such local

names as Phœnicé (Acts xxvii. 12), Araden, Lebena,
and the like. The myth of Europa and the stories
told of Minos and the Minotaur are further indications of Phœnician influence in Crete; and some
towns, like Itanos, were expressly declared to have
been founded by Phœnician settlers. As in Rhodes,
so in Crete, Grecian colonization at an early date
put in its claim to draw the island within the sphere
of Hellenic power and activity. Phœnicia yielded,
preferring quiet retirement to an embittered contest,
and content to transfer her efforts into regions where
no rival interfered with her methods or restricted her
liberty of action.

There was not much to tempt a mercantile people
to the occupation of the islands of the Ægean until
the more northern part of it was reached, where
some of them are metalliferous. Phœnician influence
may be traced in Lemnos, Imbrus, Tenedos, and
Samothrace, seats of the worship of Melicertes (Melkarth), or of the Cabiri. But the only known
Phœnician settlement in these parts was in Thasos,
which they occupied on account of its gold mines.
These lay chiefly on the eastern coast, opposite
Samothrace, between two villages called Ænyra and
Cœnyra, and were worked successfully for a long
term of years, so that, as Herodotus says, "a whole
mountain was turned topsy-turvy in the search for
ores."

It is doubtful whether the Phœnicians proceeded
further in this direction. A few notices of late
authors assign to them some scattered settlements
on the shores of the Propontis and the Euxine; and

the tale of the " good ship Argo," which the Greeks
told of their own heroes and to their own credit, is
thought by some moderns to have had a basis of
truth in adventurous voyages conducted by Phœnician
merchants to the inner recesses of the Pontus
Euxinus. But a dark veil, impenetrable by mortal
eye, rests upon these remote times and distant
regions. It will always remain a matter for controversy whether the honour of first exploring the
Black Sea belongs properly to the Greeks of Asia
Minor, or to these still earlier navigators. To us
it seems that trustworthy evidence for Phœnician
colonization towards the north-east stops at the
mouth of the Dardanelles, and that only by allowing
imagination to guide us can we extend the area
of their migrations into the Propontis and the
Euxine.

Among the Southern Cyclades, Thera, Melos, and
Oliarus or Antiparos, appear to have been early occupied by settlers from Phœnicia, Melos being colonized
by Byblus, and itself at first called Byblus, while Antiparos was a colony of the Sidonians. From Melos,
or perhaps from Crete, the hardy navigators passed
on to Cythera, where they established the worship of
Astarte, and erected storehouses to contain the corn,
which they exported from Egypt and North Africa
for the purpose of supplying the deficiency of the
Laconian harvests.

The name of Salamis raises a suspicion that a
station off the Attic coast was found as convenient for
Phœnician commerce as a station off the Laconian ;
and the settlement of Phœnicians in Eubœa for the

purpose of working the copper mines near Chalcis is
distinctly witnessed to. Whether they also occupied
the Greek mainland, either in Chalcidicé or in the
region about Thebes, may perhaps be questioned.
An inland position like that of Thebes is scarcely
likely to have attracted them ; and perhaps the
Eastern tinge, which is found in the early history of
Thebes and Bœotia generally, may have been derived
rather from intercourse and acquaintance with the
adventurous mariners who coasted along the Hellenic
shores and readily traded with the inhabitants, than
from an infusion of actual settlers. " It may be
questioned," says Thirlwall, " whether the policy
of the Phœnicians ever led them to aim at plant-
ing independent colonies . . . on the continent of
Greece ; and whether they did not content themselves with establishing factories, which they aban-
doned when their attention was diverted to a different
quarter." Even these factories, however, would only
have been established on the sea-shore, or within a
short distance of it ; and the position of Thebes, which
was fifteen miles from the sea, seems to preclude the
possibility of its having been selected as the home of
such an establishment.

Distinct evidence of Phœnician settlements on the
western side of the Hellenic peninsula, in the Ionian
Sea, or the Adriatic, is wanting ; but if, with some
scholars of high repute, we see Phœnicians in the
" Phæacians " of Homer, we must regard them as
possessed of Corcyra in the heroic age of Greece, and
as then commanding all the commerce in this quarter.
The existence of a city, called Phœnicé, in Epirus,

and the tale which Herodotus tells of kidnapped
Egyptian priestesses sold to the Theoprotians by
Phœnician merchants, lend strength to the view that
Phœnician audacity did really brave the terrors of the
stormy Adria, and if so, we may be sure that some
"coigns of vantage" upon the coasts were seized
and held by the brave adventurers.

Here, however, the continuous line of their settlements on the northern shores of the Mediterranean,
appears to have ceased. The rock-bound coast of
Iapygia did not attract them, and they made their
way to the Western Mediterranean by a different
route. Abandoning the northern line which had led
them to the Dardanelles and the Adriatic, they coasted
southwards, and passing through the turbid waters
which the Nile pours into the eastern end of the sea,
they crept along the North African shore, without
being tempted to make a settlement, until they reached
the great projection opposite Sicily, which divides
the Mediterranean into two basins. Here a fertile soil,
a docile population, and an abundance of excellent
harbours, combined their attractions ; and in the
space of about three hundred years, from B.C. 1100
to B.C. 800, Phœnician colonists occupied all the most
eligible of the Mid-African sites from Leptis Magna,
between the Greater and the Lesser Syrtis to Hippo
Regius, six degrees (400 miles) further westward. The
earliest of these Mid-African settlements was, we are
told, Utica. Utica was situated on a spit of land, which
ran out into the Gulf of Tunis in a direction nearly
north-east, at the distance of about seventeen miles
from Carthage, which lay towards the south-west. The

river Bagradas flowed past it into the sea, a little to the east. It possessed a good harbour artificially made, which is now a lake. On the land side it was protected by steep hills ; and this fact, together with the vicinity of the sea, and the artificial defences, which were carefully kept up, rendered it a very strong place. The surrounding country was exceedingly fertile and produced abundance of corn, which was at one time largely exported to Rome. The hills behind the town contained numerous veins of various metals ; and the coast was celebrated for producing vast quantities of salt which possessed peculiar characteristics. Altogether the position was excellently chosen, and Utica retained considerable importance for several centuries after the rise of Carthage. Other Mid-African settlements founded by the Phœnicians in the early period were Hadrumetum, Hippo Regius, and Leptis Magna. Hadrumetum lay south, Hippo west of Utica. Leptis Magna was situated in the low tract now known as the Beylik of Tripoli, at a point where the table-land of the Desert falls off to the sea in a succession of mountain terraces or ridges, enclosing valleys, each of which is watered by its streamlet, and sheltered from the encroachments of sand that are so injurious on this coast.

These settlements in North Africa, together with some smaller ones, satisfied the Phœnician navigators for some three centuries, being sufficient for all the purposes of trade either with the coast tribes or with those of the interior ; and it is not probable that any further settlement would have been made in these parts, had not political discontents at Tyre caused a large number of the inhabitants to form a sudden resolve to quit the city. Such resolves were common among the mercantile cities of Greece, and may have lain at the root of Phœnician colonization more frequently than history expressly mentions. It was towards the middle of the ninth century B.C. that the discontented Tyrians left their Syrian home, and, establishing themselves in great force at a new point of the North African coast, founded a city which in a short time completely eclipsed all the other Phœnician colonies, and became one of the leading powers of the world. As the " Story of Carthage" forms the subject of a separate volume in this series, it will not be further dwelt on here. We need only note that by degrees the other Phœnician settlements in the neighbourhood accepted a position of dependence upon the new city planted in their midst, and were content to be her subject allies.

It was probably not long after their first colonies were planted on the Mid-African shore that the Phœnicians crossed over into Sicily and took possession of several of its promontories, as well as of the small islets which lie off the coast. Near the extreme western end of the island they occupied the two sites of Eryx and Egesta. Eryx on a lofty mountain, the second highest in Sicily ; and Egesta, also on a commanding eminence. Midway in the northern coast their experienced eyes marked the most commodious harbour that the island can boast, the harbour of Palermo, and their settlement of Mahanath, which became Panormus, gave them the possession of this important place. Among the littoral islands which they colonized were Motyé, and probably Ortygia, which commanded the port of Syracuse. At the same time, they laid their hands on Cossyrus, now Pantellaria, on Gaulos (Gozo), Lampas (Lampedusa), and Melita or Malta, which has the best harbour to be found in the Mediterranean.

About the same time, they pushed along the North African coast in the direction of Spain, passed the Straits of Gibraltar, and planted colonies of great importance in Bætica, the modern Andalusia. Bætica was one of the most fertile regions of the ancient world. " The wide plains through which the Guadalquiver (Bætis) flows produced the finest wheat, yielding an increase of a hundred-fold ; the oil and the wine, the growth of the hills, were equally distinguished for their excellence. The wool was not less remarkable for its fineness than in modern times, and had a native colour beautiful without dye. Like the other great rivers of Iberia, which take their course to the ocean, the Bætis washes down gold from the mountains in which it rises, and, by following it to its source, the rich mines which they contain would be soon discovered. Gold, silver, quicksilver, tin, lead, copper, and iron abound in the mountains in which the Bætis and its tributaries rise. The myth of the herds of cattle which Hercules carried off from Geryon, indicates the richness of the pastures near the mouth of the Bætis. The river was navigable for boats in ancient times as high up as Corduba, and till the seventeenth century for large vessels to Seville. The river Anas or Guadiana, which rises near the Bætis, and flows into the Atlantic through a valley almost

parallel in its direction, was also navigable to a considerable distance from the sea, and the hills which
bordered it were no less rich in metals. The ocean-
tides which enter the mouths of these rivers carried
ships far up into the land ; and the estuaries which
abound along the coast afforded similar facilities to
the inhabitants for shipping the various products of
the country. The sea was equally productive with
the land in the materials for an extensive commerce.
The warmth of the waters, and perhaps the greater
range which the ocean afforded, caused the fish and
conchylia to attain to a size not known in the
Mediterranean. The salted eels of Tartessus were a
delicacy at Athenian tables ; and the ' Tyrian tunny,'
which is mentioned along with it, came partly from
the same coast, where its favourite food abounded." [1]

In this delightful region, at a very early date,
soon after the Trojan War, according to Strabo, the
Phœnicians founded the colonies of Gadeira, or Gades,
whose name survives in the modern Cadiz, of Malaca
(now Malaga), of Abdera (now Adra), and of Carteïa
(perhaps Rocadillo). Of these by far the most important was Gadeira. This town was situated at the
north-western extremity of an island about twelve miles
long, which lies off the western coast of Spain a little
outside the straits. A narrow channel, more like a river
than an arm of the sea, and now spanned by a bridge,
separates the island from the shore, expanding, however, towards its northern end, where it forms itself
into a land-locked bay, capable of containing all the
navies of the world. Two islets lie across the mouth

[1] Adapted from Kenrick's " Phœnicia," pp. 119–121.

of the channel at this end, and effectually prevent the entrance of the long rolling waves from the Atlantic. The original city was small, and enclosed within a strong wall, whence the name " Gadir " or "Gadeira," which meant in the Phœnician language "an enclosure " or "a fortified place." It occupied almost exactly the site of the modern Cadiz, being spread over the northern end of the island, the little islet of the Trocadero, and ultimately over a portion of the opposite coast. It contained temples of El, Melkarth, and Ashtoreth or Astarté.

Malaca was situated about as far to the east of the straits as Gadeira was to the west of them. It derived its name from the Phœnician word for "salt," which was the same as the Hebrew, viz., *malakh*, its inhabitants being largely employed in the making of that commodity, and in the salting and pickling of fish. The mountains in its vicinity were abundantly productive, both of gold and of other metals, and the coins of the place indicate that the people were also engaged to some extent in metallurgy. Malaga is now known chiefly by its wines ; but we have no evidence that anciently it had any special reputation for this product.

Abdera lay still further to the east, in west longitude 3° 40'. It was situated about midway in a shallow bay, which here indents the southern coast of Spain, towards the extreme east of the rich province of Granada. The modern representative of Abdera is Almeria, or (according to some) Adra.

Carteïa was in the Bay of Algesiras, which lies immediately west of the rock of Gibraltar. The bay

is about five miles across by sea and about ten miles
round by land. It offers an excellent anchorage in
almost all winds. According to Pliny, Carteïa was
the same as Tartessus, which others place further to
the west, either at Gadeira or at the mouth of the
Bætis. But Tartessus seems to have been rather a
district than a town, as is also Tarshish in some
passages of Scripture (Gen. x. 4 ; Psa. lxxii. 10 ;
Isa. lxvi. 18, &c.). It is, therefore, not to be identified with any single Phœnician settlement, but to be
regarded as a name under which are grouped all the
Phœnician colonies of these parts, as Gadeira, Carteïa,
Belo, perhaps even Abdera and Malaca.

It may have been from Spain, or it may have been
from Sicily, that the indefatigable navigators passed
over into Sardinia, where extensive traces of their
colonization have been recently discovered. Whether
they can lay claim to have been the authors of the
famous Sardinian *nouraghés* is perhaps doubtful ; but
they have left clear marks of their presence at Tharros
and other sites in the shape of vases, pateræ, seals,
rings, and other ornaments of a thoroughly Phœnician
character ; and it will scarcely be disputed at the
present day that Sardinia was one of the places where
they had settlements.

The Phœnicians had one more colony towards the
west, which has a peculiar interest for all English-
speaking peoples. Phœnician ships from Gadeira
braved the perils of the open ocean, and coasting
along the western shores of Spain and Gaul, without
(apparently) making settlements, crossed the mouth of
the English Channel from Ushant to the Scilly Isles,

and conveyed thither a body of colonists who established an emporium. The attraction which drew them was the mineral wealth of the islands and of the neighbouring Cornish coast, which may have become known to them through the Gauls of the opposite continent.   It is reasonable to suppose that the Phœnicians both worked the mines and smelted the ores. They certainly drew from this quarter those copious supplies of tin and lead, which they imported into Greece and Asia, and from which they derived so large a profit. They called the islands and shores on which they had settled the " Cassiterides," or " Tin Islands," and related of the inhabitants that they " were clad in black cloaks and in tunics reaching to the feet, with girdles round their waists ; " that they " walked with staves, and were bearded like goats ; that they subsisted by means of their cattle, and for the most part led a wandering life."   Their tin and lead they were ready to exchange for pottery, salt, and bronze vessels.

It is uncertain whether the Phœnicians ever succeeded in establishing themselves on the shores of the Red Sea. The fact that they had a settlement at Memphis is a strong indication that the Egyptians looked upon them with favourable eyes ; and if so, it would have been natural that they should grant them a settlement on the Red Sea shore, which they must certainly have coveted.   But the only indication which we have of any such settlement is contained in the name " Baal-Zephon," which is Phœnico-Egyptian, attached to a place on the borders of the Gulf of Suez (Exod. xiv. 2, 9; Numb. xxxiii. 7) ; and this indica-

tion is too weak to be regarded as an actual proof.
They may at some periods have held possession of
Elath at the head of the Gulf of Akabah (1 Kings
ix. 26–28 ; xxii. 48), whence they seem to have made
joint voyages with the Israelites ; but Elath was
usually claimed and held by Edom.

Phœnician colonization — or colonization from
Phœnicia Proper—was thus in all probability limited
within the extremes of the Dardanelles to the north,
Memphis to the south, and Gadeira and the Cassiterides to the west. It was less widely diffused than
the Greek, and less generally spread over the coasts
accessible to it. With a few exceptions, the colonies
fall into three groups—first, those of the Eastern
Mediterranean and Ægean, beginning with Cyprus
and terminating with Cythera ; secondly, those of the
Central Mediterranean, in North Africa, Sicily, and the
adjacent islands ; and thirdly, those of the Western
Mediterranean, chiefly on the south coast of Spain,
with perhaps a few on the opposite (African) shore.
The other settlements, commonly called Phœnician
on the eastern coast of Spain, in the Balearic
Islands, in Corsica and Elba ; and again those on
the Western African coast, between the Straits of
Gibraltar and the Cape de Verde, were Punic or
Carthaginian, rather than Phœnician, and are therefore excluded from this review. They belong to the
field which h's been assigned to another writer and
to another volume of this series.

V

EARLY PHŒNICIAN ENTERPRISE—SIDONIAN ROVERS IN PRE-HOMERIC TIMES.

IF we would appreciate aright the extreme hardi-
hood, and indeed audacity, of the early leaders of
Phœnician enterprise, we must, first of all, have a
correct idea of the vessels in which they embarked to
affront the perils of the sea. Their earliest ships were
little more than open boats, being partially decked at

PHŒNICIAN COIN.

the utmost, and thus liable to be swamped by the
mere dash of the waves over their sides and prows.
They were made of fir or cedar planks, very insufficiently seasoned, and were caulked probably with
bitumen, a poor substitute for vegetable tar. The
build of some of their vessels was broad and round,

PHŒNICIAN GALLEY FROM A PAINTING.

PHŒNICIAN BIREME.

like that of Dutch merchant ships in former times ;
but the better sort of ship was always of a longer
make, and was called a " long ship," while the other
kind was called a *gaulos*, or "round " one.   The
earliest vessels of which we have any representation
were impelled both by sails and oars.   A number of
rowers, varying between thirty and fifty in the later
times, in the earlier probably fewer—perhaps no more
than ten or twelve—occupied seats on either side of
the vessel, and impelled it with oars made fast to the
vessel's side by means of a peg and a strap.   These
rowers sat all of them on a level, as in modern row-
boats ; they pulled with their faces to the stern of the
boat, the course of which was directed by the steers-
man.   If the wind served, and it was desired to sail,
a mast was raised from the bottom of the vessel, one
end placed in a socket prepared to receive it about
midship, and the mast then erected and secured in
its place by means of two ropes attached to it near
the top, and made fast to two bolts or stanchions,
one at the head and the other at the stern of the
vessel.   Across the mast, near the top, was fastened
a yard, about half the length of the mast, or a little
more ; and from this depended the sail, which was a
fairly large square sail, and could be reefed along the
yard, or loosened and let down at pleasure. There was
but one mast in these early vessels, and but one
sail.

The first considerable improvement in ship building
which can be confidently ascribed to the Phœnicians is
the construction of biremes. Phœnician biremes are
represented in the Assyrian sculptures as early as the

time of Sennacherib (B.C. 700), and had probably then been in use for some considerable period. They were at first comparatively short vessels, but seem to have been decked, the rowers working in the hold. They sat at two elevations, one above the other, and worked their oars through holes in the vessel's side.

It was in frail barks of this description, not much better than open boats in the earlier period, that the mariners of Phœnicia, and especially those of Sidon, as far back probably as the thirteenth or fourteenth century before our era, affronted the perils of the Mediterranean. Moderns are apt to make somewhat light of these perils. Accustomed to the tremendous storms of the Atlantic and the Indian Ocean, they think that in a tideless and landlocked basin, like the Mediterranean, the worst that can happen can be little more than " a tempest in a teapot." But this is rather the landman's than the seaman's view. Experienced sailors do not regard the gales of the Mediterranean as trifles, and a " Levanter " is as much dreaded by them as any wind that blows. The danger run by St. Paul on his voyage from Palestine to Rome (Acts xxvii.) was as great as any that ships are subject to on the open ocean. Even at the present day, with our improved vessels, and with all the appliances of our modern nautical science, great risks are occasionally run in the Levant, the Ægean, and the Gulf of Lyons ; nor do our underwriters exact a much lower rate of insurance from ship-owners whose vessels are engaged in the Levantine trade than from those whose ships sail to South America or Australia. A single instance from a modern book of travels may be cited in proof. " The commander came down," says Mrs. Damer in her charming *Diary in the Holy Land*, " saying the night was dark and rainy, with symptoms of a regular gale of wind. This prediction was very speedily verified. A violent shower of hail was the precursor, followed by loud peals of thunder, with vivid flashes of forked lightning, which played up and down the iron rigging with fearful rapidity. The ship was presently struck by a sea which came over the paddle-boxes, soon followed by another, which, coming over the forecastle, effected an entrance through the sky-lights, and left four feet of water in the officers' cabin. The vessel seemed disabled by this stunning blow ; the bowsprit and forepart of the ship were for some moments under water, and the officer stationed at that part of the ship described her as appearing at that time to be evidently sinking, and declared that for many seconds he saw only sea. The natural buoy-ancy of the ship at last allowed her to right herself and during the short lull (of three minutes) her head was turned, to avoid the danger of running too near the coast of Libya, which to the more experienced was the principal cause of alarm ; for had the wheels given way, which was not improbable from the strain which they had undergone, nothing could have saved us, though we had been spared all other causes for apprehension. With daylight the fearful part of the hurricane gave way ; and we were now in the direction of Candia (Crete), no longer indeed contending against the wind, but the sea still surging and tempes-tuous, and no lull taking place during twelve hours, to afford the opportunity of regaining our track, from

which we had deviated about 150 miles. The sea had
completely deluged the lower part of the ship."

Another ground on which the early voyagers,
Phœnician and other, are disparaged, is the circumstance that their vessels for the most part hugged the
shore. We see distinctly in St. Paul's voyages how
as late as the time of Nero this was the case (Acts xx.
6–17 ; xxi. 1–3 ; xxvii. 2–13) ; and there is not much
reason to suppose that the practice of the Phœnician
mariners was different anciently. But such a habit
increases rather than diminishes the peril of navigation,
since there is no nautical danger equal to that of a lee
shore. What the true sailor fears, is not the swell and
surge of waves as high as mountains, or the roar and
rush of winds under which he must scud with bare
poles, so long as he has an open and practically bound-
less space wherein to move freely. What strikes a
shiver to his heart, and makes his blood curdle, is the
sound of breakers dashing on a coast that lies to lee-
ward, for then he knows that neither skill nor daring
will serve his turn or enable him to escape. Thus the
coasting voyages of the ancients, like those of our own
fishing smacks, were more dangerous, and involved
more loss of life, than voyages in the open would have
done. The Persians lost three hundred ships in a
storm off Mount Athos, on their first attempt to invade Greece and six hundred off Magnesia and Eubœa
on their second attempt. There can be no doubt that
a considerable proportion of the ships which left the
Phœnician harbours, gallantly arrayed and well found
in all respects, failed to return to them. Some went
down in open sea swamped by the waves or capsized by

sudden gusts of wind ; some were captured by pirates ;
but the greater number perished on the rocks and
shoals which are so numerous in the Ægean, or on the
iron-bound coasts of Crete and Greece, of Asia Minor
and Italy and Spain, driven on lee-shores by furious
winds whose force was not to be resisted.

The danger from pirates was not inconsiderable.   In
ancient times, when ship met ship upon the sea, the
first inquiry made by one crew of the other was, " Are
you pirates ? "   No one thought of resenting the inter-
rogatory, which was viewed as a matter of course.
Honest answer was at once returned ; and the
piratical vessel, if the stronger of the two, boarded the
other, seized its cargo, and carried off its crew and
captain to the nearest slave-mart.   The Phœnicians
would doubtless have held their own against most
antagonists ; but sometimes they would have to yield.
Neither the Greeks nor the Tyrrhenians were enemies
altogether to be despised ; and there were several other
races which from time to time put fleets upon the
Mediterranean waters, as the Taphians and Phæacians of Homer, and the Tanauna, Sharuten, Sheklusha,
Tulshu, and Uashesh, whose combined squadrons once
attacked Egypt.   If a single galley fell in with a
piratical fleet, its fate would be certain.   No superior
skill could avail.   And the value of Phœnician merchandise would tempt the piratical tribes to waylay
their trading ships with superior numbers.

In spite, however, of these various dangers—perhaps
in some degree attracted by them, for adventurous
spirits see in danger an attraction rather than a deterrent—the Phœnician merchantmen went forth from

the Phœnician ports, and boldly traversing unexplored
seas, reached unknown shores, and, entering into communication with the inhabitants, offered their wares to
them. The earliest account of any such voyage, which
has come down to us accompanied by any detail, is
that recorded in the opening section of the History of
Herodotus. At a date considerably anterior to the
Trojan War, Herodotus says, the Phœnicians "began
to adventure on long voyages, freighting their vessels
with the wares of Egypt and Assyria."   On one occasion they " made a landing upon the coast of Argolis,
which was then the leading state of Hellas.   Here
they exposed their merchandise and traded with the
natives for five or six days ; at the end of which time,
when almost all of it was sold, there happened to come
down to the beach a numerous company of women,
and among them the daughter of the king, who was
(the Persians say, agreeing herein with the Greeks)
Io, the daughter of Inachus.   So the women began
bargaining, and were standing crowded about the
stern of the ship, intent upon their purchases, when
suddenly the Phœnicians, with a general shout, rushed
upon them.   The greater part made their escape ; but
some were seized and carried off.   Io herself was
among the captives.   The Phœnicians put the captured women aboard their vessel, and set sail for
Egypt."   The portraiture is graphic.   First, we see
the traders arrive in their light bark off the Argolic
coast, most probably at Nauplia, always the chief port
of the country, bringing with them a cargo of wares
which are chiefly Egyptian and Assyrian, either
native products or at any rate procured by the Phœni-

cians from those countries. The natives crowd down to the shore and give them a warm welcome. Soon the cargo is landed, or a part of it ; and a brisk trade springs up. The Argives have plenty of gold, and are eager to exchange it for the ivory and ebony, the skins, the ostrich feathers, the delicate fabrics, the glass and pottery, the mirrors and other toilet articles, which are exposed by the owners, who have brought them from far distant lands, and now show them off to the best advantage. Abundance of chaffering goes on ; prices are asked far in excess of the value ; but the wary Greeks are not easily imposed upon, and scarcely a purchase is made until the original price put upon the article has been diminished at least one half. So large is the cargo, so eager are the buyers, that the trade continues day after day until nearly a week has passed. During this space report of what is occurring spreads to the capital, and the attention of the first ladies in the land is attracted by the accounts given them. The king's daughter determines on pay- ing the traders a visit, and, naturally, is accompanied by a train of her attendant serving-maids, and perhaps by many ladies of the Court besides. They crowd around the place where the articles that suit them best are displayed, which is near the stern of the ship, under its shadow probably. It may be that hitherto the traders had had no dishonest intention ; but they could not resist the temptation which now offered itself. The royal maiden and her companions would be decked in all that bravery of ornament, which the researches of Dr. Schliemann on the site of Argos have recently revealed to us—golden coronals, golden necklaces, golden earrings, golden bracelets, golden brooches, golden rings, golden hair loops. They were no doubt, as Greek maidens are almost universally, beautiful. So the traders made a dash upon them after a moment's consultation with each other. Ah! then what shrieks arose, what a fluttering was there of the gentle Argive doves, what a general consternation and what a hurrying of tiny feet in rapid flight! Many—the greater part, as we are told—made their escape; but the princess and a certain number of her companions were seized and carried on board. The ship, which had its head to sea, was quickly run out into the water; the oars were manned, and the vessel was under way in a few minutes. In vain the Argive men shouted from the shore, and shot their arrows or hurled their spears against the ravishers, and ran into the water, like Cynægirus at Marathon, to detain the parting vessel with their hands, if possible—the bold rover defied them, put out to sea, and steering its course for Egypt was ere long out of sight.

Such is the story. It will be asked, what faith we are to put in it? Doubtless, as an historical narrative, very little faith indeed. Io is probably *Aah*, or the Moon; and the wanderings, to which her rape is preliminary, describe the course of the moon through the constellations, or other lunar phenomena. But as a picture of what was wont from time to time to occur on the Grecian coasts, we may accept the tale as probably a perfectly true representation. The Phœnicians, who traded regularly in the persons of men with Javan, Tubal, and Meshech (Ezek. xxvii. 13)—the Ionians of Asia Minor, the Tibareni, and the

Moschi—were inveterate slave-dealers, and not above
indulging in kidnapping, if an opportunity offered, as
appears from the relations of other writers besides
Herodotus.   Honest trade was their main purpose ;
but they could not always resist the temptation of
illegitimate gains to be obtained by piracy and man-
stealing.

The tale of Eumæus, as told by the author of the
" Odyssea," exhibits to us Phœnician traders in much
the same light as does the story of Io in Herodotus.
Eumæus, swineherd to Ulyssus in Ithaca, gives the
following account of himself to his master :—

" There is an island, Syria called by name,
    Over against Ortygia.   It may be
    That to thy ears some rumour of it came,
    When thou wast roaming over earth and sea.
    It is the land where the sun's turnings be,
    Not over-peopled, but of soil divine ;
    A good land teeming with fertility,
    Rich with green pastures feeding flocks and kine,
    A fair land fed with streams, a land of corn and wine.

    Twain are the cities, and an equal share
    Of all things is to either portioned well.
    My godlike father of both realms was heir,
    Ctesius Ormenides.   And, so it fell,
    Phœnicians with a thousand things to sell
    Came, very wolves for lucre, false of heart.
    A woman [1] in my father's house did dwell,
    Fair, tall, and skilled in every splendid art ;
    And her these schemers lured with treachery to their part.

    First by the hollow ship, when on a day
    She went to wash, one mingled with her there
    In sweet love, which so often leads astray,
    And warps to ill with its seducing snare

---

[1] In the original it is " a Phœnician woman."

The female heart of woman, howsoe'er
Toward righteousness inclined within their breast.
He parting asked her who she was, and where
Had come from. She the high-roofed house confessed
Her father's home, and thus her paramour addressed :

' I from the land of swine-famed (?) Sidon came ;
Child of rich Arebas I boast to be.
Once Taphian pirates, as I wended home,
Found me afield, and o'er the rolling sea
Led to this mansion of my lord, and he
There to the sailors a fit price consigned.'
Then said the man that loved her secretly :
' Come thou with me and thy dear father find
And mother—they yet live, with store of every kind.'

Answered the woman, and this word did say :
' Yea, such a thing might happen, would ye swear,
O sailors, not to harm me on the way.'
So did she speak ; and, when the sailors sware,
' Hush !' said the woman, ' and let each beware
That neither word to me nor sign be made,
Walking, or near the well, lest one declare
Our meeting, and my lord, of guile afraid,
Bid me plan death for you—keep quiet, and ply your trade.

When, stored and laden, ye would leave the land
Then to the palace send ye word to me.
Gold will I bring, whatever comes to hand,
Yea, and a further ship-fare, it may be ;
For in the halls I tend continually
A brave man's boy, a little sprightly thing,
Just fit for running at his nurse's knee,
My master's child—him also I might bring,
And win large wealth for you from some far-distant king.'

She, having spoken, to the fair house went.
And they, abiding with us a whole year,
Safe in the hollow bark their produce pent.
So when by traffic they much goodly gear
Had gotten, and the time to sail drew near,
They to the palace sent a man, to tell
The woman. He, with wits alive and clear,

Came with a necklace of fine gold to sell
With bright electron linked right wondrously and well.

My mother and her maidens in the hall
Handled the work and with wide eyes surveyed,
Seeming to buy : but he the voiceless call
Signed with his eyebrows, and his journey made
Back to the hollow vessel.   She then laid
Her hand on mine, leading me forth, and found
Cups in the porch and tables well arrayed,
Left by the feasters of my sire renowned,
All lately gone, to sessions of the people bound.

Three goblets in her bosom she concealed,
I wending with her in my simple thought ;
And the sun fell, and every day was veiled.
Thus we with speed the noble haven sought
Where lay the bark of the Phœnicians, fraught
With goodly cargo, very swift to sail.
Me and the woman they on shipboard brought,
Embarked, and spread the canvas to the gale,
Nor did the wind of Zeus along the waters fail.

Six nights and days we sailed the ocean well ;
But when Kronion brought the seventh day,
Artemis shot the woman, and she fell
Plump like a sea-coot in the hold, and they
Cast her to seals and fishes for a prey ;
And I was left in sorrow.   Winds and floods
Carried us in the ship to Ithaca,
And here Laërtes bought me with his goods.
Thus have mine eyes beheld these rocks and waving woods." [1]

We are not, however, to suppose that the trading
voyages of the Phœnicians, even in the earliest times,
were always fraudulent, or the gains that they made
illegitimate.   In commerce honesty is the best policy ;
and the Phœnicians would not have been so generally
welcomed as they were, alike by Egyptians, Assyrians,

[1] See Worsley's "Odyssea," Book xv.

and Greeks, unless their ordinary dealings had been according to the established rules and principles of fairness and justice. The Carthaginians, we may be sure, learnt from them that honourable conduct, which is noticed as specially observable in their "dumb commerce" with the nations of North-western Africa, whom they were accustomed to invite to traffic by a signal-fire, and to deal with in the following fashion: "When they arrive, forthwith they unlade their wares, and, having disposed them in an orderly fashion along the beach, leave them, and returning aboard their ships, raise a great smoke. The natives, when they see the smoke, come down to the shore, and laying out to view so much gold as they think the wares to be worth, withdraw to a distance. The Carthaginians upon this come ashore and look. If they consider the gold enough, they take it and go their way; but if it does not seem to them sufficient, they go aboard ship once more and wait patiently. Then the others approach and add to their gold, till the Carthaginians are content. *Neither party deals unfairly by the other;* for the Carthaginians never touch the gold till it comes up to the estimated worth of their goods, nor do the natives ever carry off the goods till the gold has been taken away." [1]

Commercial honesty is in nothing more strikingly shown than in the quality of the wares which a trading nation produces and exports. Let vamped-up goods, a specious appearance of excellence intended to deceive the unwary, and covering over bad materials

[1] Herod. iv. 196.

and workmanship with an external gloss of showy attractiveness, prevail, and commercial honesty may be pronounced dying or dead, while of commercial prosperity it may be safely prophesied that it will not survive much longer. The Phœnicians were notorious for the excellency of their manufactures, the sterling quality of their fabrics, which their customers could feel absolutely confident to be what they professed to be. The textile fabrics, the works in metallurgy, and the vases and other articles in glass which Phœnicia produced, bore the highest possible character in the early ages, and were everywhere accepted as the *ne plus ultra* of perfection, combining as they did the best materials, the best workmanship, and the highest artistic taste and elegancy. When Achilles at the funeral of Patroclus would offer as a prize for the fastest runner the most beautiful bowl to be found in all the world, he chose one which had been deftly made by highly-skilled Sidonians, and which Phœnician sailors had conveyed across the cloud-shadowed sea. When Menelaüs wished to give Telemachus what was at once the most beautiful and the most valuable of all his possessions, he selected a silver bowl with a golden rim, which in former days he had himself received as a present from Phædimus, king of Sidon. *All* the royal robes of Priam's queen, the renowned Hecuba, were the work of Sidonian women, brought from the Sidonian land by Paris, when he came to Troy with Helen ; and the choicest offering that she could find to present to Athene on behalf of her favourite son was one of these robes, the most beautifully embroidered, and the longest, which shone with the brightness of a star. *All* the marvels in metallurgy wherewith Solomon adorned his temple— the two pillars, Jachin and Boaz, the molten sea supported on twelve oxen, the lavers, the basins, the pots, and shovels, and bowls, and snuffers, and spoons, and censers—all, as needed for holy uses, requiring to be the best of their kind—were the work of Hiram, "a man of Tyre, skilled to work in gold, and in silver, in brass, in iron, in stone, and in timber, in purple, in blue, and in fine linen, and in crimson ; also to grave any manner of graving" (2 Chron. ii. 14).

The enterprise of the Phœnicians in the early ages, while Sidon was in the ascendant, did not (it is probable) take them beyond the limits of the Mediterranean ; but within those limits they would seem to have visited all coasts, to have explored all shores, to have made themselves acquainted with almost every individual island, and to have carried with them everywhere civilizing influences. Letters, if not their actual invention, received at their hands modifications and improvements, which possessed within them a principle of permanency, and are traceable in the alphabets of all civilized nations at the present day. They carried with them over the Mediterranean, wherever they went, their idea of alphabetic writing, and their peculiar alphabetical forms. In Cyprus and in Lycia they were met by conflicting systems ; but these systems gave way to theirs. Asia Minor, Greece, Italy, accepted their analysis of human speech, and the signs by which they expressed its final elements. An enormous advance must everywhere have followed the introduction of writing, and this advance was due to the Phœnicians. Trade and commerce are also, in themselves, humanizing and civilizing ; they unite men, whom otherwise their selfish interests are apt to separate ; they tend to substitute for violence and savagery a sympathy with others, a friendliness, which softens manners and leads on to kind and humane conduct. In the middle and western Mediterranean, when the Phœnicians first visited them, an extreme barbarity prevailed among most of the tribes. The Illyrians of the Adriatic tattooed their bodies, hated strangers, and were greatly given to piracy. The Læstrygonians of Sicily were actual cannibals, and feasted on any hapless wretch whom they could get into their power. Most of the North African tribes painted themselves, like our British ancestors, and went naked, or nearly so, even the women wearing only a sort of fringe-apron of leather about their persons. The influence of the Phœnician traders was considerable in gradually softening the harsher features of this widespread barbarism, and in winning over the rude savages to a condition of life less antagonistic to progress and civilization.

VI.

RISE OF TYRE TO THE FIRST RANK AMONG THE
CITIES—HIRAM'S DEALINGS WITH DAVID AND
SOLOMON.

THE decline of Sidon and the rise of Tyre have
been attributed by a large number of writers to a great
blow which Sidon is said to have received at the
hands of the Philistines, about B.C. 1250 or B.C. 1200.
About that time the King of Ascalon is reported to have
besieged the city and taken it, whereupon the population generally embarked, we are told, in their ships,
and having sailed to Tyre, settled there. The rise of
Tyre does not, however make itself apparent in
historical documents until nearly two centuries later ;
and it is, at the least, open to question, whether the
change which occurred in the relations between the
two towns was not the result of gradual internal
decline and development, rather than of any sudden
alteration in their external circumstances. Sidon's
prosperity may not improbably have led her people
on to the adoption of luxurious habits, and to an
indulgence in that licentiousness and profligacy for
which the national religion afforded only too much

excuse. Corruption of manners tends to the destruction of physical and mental vigour ; and as their
comforts and luxuries increased, and sensuous enjoyment took the place of rough and hardy habits, it may
well be that the spirit of enterprise decayed, and that
as her vigour declined, Sidon found herself surpassed
by her more active and energetic younger sister.

The first distinct evidence that we possess of the
ascendency over Phœnicia having passed from Sidon
to Tyre is contained in the very positive statements
which are made, that Gades was a Tyrian, and not a
Sidonian, colony. Sidonian colonization cannot be
traced further west than the Mid-African group of
cities, Utica, Hadrumetum, Leptis Magna, and Hippo
Regius. When, about B.C. 1100, a more adventurous
spirit showed itself, and the Straits of Gibraltar were
passed, the perils of the open ocean affronted, and a
settlement made off the coast of that Iberia, which had
long represented to the Orientals the furthest region
towards the West, it was Tyre, and not Sidon, that
made the step in advance. The step was one which
implied more than ordinary daring. Iberia beyond
the straits was regarded as the abode of monsters
like Geryon, men with three heads and six arms, so
fierce and strong that it required a Hercules to overcome them. Not far off the world ceased—the sun at
evening plunged into the ocean flood with a hissing
sound which was heard afar, and passing through the
under world returned to the place of his rising in the
East. Light and darkness, the upper and the under
world met in the neighbourhood, which was thus a
ghostly region, terrible, alarming, to be avoided by all

whose nerves were of a weak fibre, and scarcely to be visited by those who were stoutest of heart, without some considerable trepidation. The Tyrian mariners, who, notwithstanding all these dangers, real or imaginary, sailed their galleys through the Straits into the Atlantic Ocean, and the bold citizens who consented to exchange their comfortable homes in Tyre for huts or cabins on an unknown western shore, deserve that credit which must always attach to the pioneers of civilization in previously unexplored regions.

It is not long after this, that we find Tyre established in a position of great power and dignity among her sister cities in Phœnicia Proper, maintaining a hereditary monarchy in much pomp and state, greatly augmenting the size of the island capital, and increasing the number and magnificence of the temples and other public buildings. At the same time, she enters into relations with a powerful neighbouring monarchy, and concludes an arrangement which is for the mutual advantage of both communities. The king at this time is Hiram, or Huram, according to another vocalization ; he is the son of Abibaal, and has succeeded him upon the throne by hereditary right at the age of nineteen. The improvement of his capital was his first care. He enlarged the area of the city by means of considerable substructions, added to the main island a smaller one which lay off the north-west coast, made a grand square or place for the meetings of the citizens, built temples to Melkarth and Astarte or Ashtoreth, which he roofed with cedar cut in Lebanon, and probably much enlarged and improved the harbours which were so necessary for the city's safety and prosperity. Some account of these has been already given. What portion of the works which made Tyre the best and safest harbour on the coast of Phœnicia was due to Hiram is uncertain ; but it is probable that, while providing a public place for its inhabitants and a larger area for their habitations, he would not neglect the necessary means of the increase of their commerce and the protection of their navy.

Hiram's possessions upon the mainland necessarily brought him into contact with the recently formed kingdom of Israel, over which first Saul, then Ishbo-sheth, and now in his day David was king. A revolt of a continental tribe, which refused to pay its tribute, took him in person to the mainland, and it is likely that, while engaged in their reduction, he became more distinctly conscious than he might have been otherwise of the great change which had taken place in the position of the Israelites within the preceding twenty or thirty years. From a feeble and distracted people, with difficulty maintaining themselves among the unconquered remnants of the Canaanitish nations, and now falling under the sway of one of them, now of another, they had, through the warlike skill and courage of the great son of Jesse, emerged from their troubles, and become the dominant race in Syria. David had attacked the strong fortress of Jebus, which impended over his capital, and taken it, thus relieving himself from an intolerable annoyance. He had levied and organized a large military force both for defensive and offensive operations. He had com-pletely defeated the Philistines upon the south-west and had reduced them to a state of permanent subjection (2 Sam. viii. 1) ; he had smitten the Moabites, and " measured them with a line," putting two-thirds of them to death (2 Sam. viii. 2) ; he had gained a great victory over the Edomites in the valley of salt, and had " put garrisons throughout all Edom, and they of Edom had become his servants " (2 Sam. viii. 13, 14) ; he had subdued the Ammonites after a desperate struggle, and forced them to make submission (2 Sam. x. 8–14) ; he had " put garrisons in Syria of Damascus " (2 Sam. viii. 6) ; finally, he had conquered the Syrians of Zobah, Rehob, Ish-tob, and Maacah, and had pushed his northern frontier to the Euphrates (2 Sam. x. 6–19 ; 1 Kings iv. 21). Hiram saw that with such a power it was best to be on good terms. Accordingly, having understood that the king of this mighty people was about to build himself a palace in Jerusalem, Hiram took the initiative, and sent a friendly embassy to the Israelite king, with a present of cedar trees, recently felled in Lebanon, and an offer of the services of numerous carpenters and masons, to superintend the erection of the palace, and if need were, aid in its construction. The offer was readily accepted ; and the skilled artizans of Tyre came with their tools and appliances to the Jewish capital, and worked for many months in the erection of the " house," which thenceforth David made his residence. Nor was this all, if we may believe the writer of the First Book of Chronicles. According to him (ch. xxii. 4), David in his later years was busied in the collection of materials for the great temple, which he had designed to build, but the actual construction of which was reserved for his son,

and among the stores which he accumulated were
" cedar trees in abundance," furnished to him through
the good-will of Hiram, by the men of Tyre and the
Sidonians.

Later on, when Solomon had inherited the extensive empire built up for him by his father, and set
himself to carry out on a magnificent scale his father's
design to erect a temple to Jehovah, further communi-
cations of the highest interest took place between the
two kingdoms. This time the initiative was taken by
the Israelitish monarch. " Solomon sent to Huram,
the king of Tyre, saying, As thou didst deal with
David my father, and didst send him cedars to build
him an house to dwell therein, even so deal with me
Behold I build an house for the name of Jehovah, my
God, to dedicate it to him, and to burn before him
incense of sweet spices, and for the continual shewbread, and for the burnt-offerings morning and evening, on the sabbaths, and on the new moons, and on
the set feasts of Jehovah our God. This is an ordi-
nance for ever unto Israel. And the house, which I
build, is great ; for great is our God above all gods.
But who is able to build him an house, seeing the
heaven and the heaven of heavens cannot contain
him ? Now therefore send me a man cunning to
work in gold, and in silver, and in brass, and in iron,
and in purple and crimson and blue, and that can skill
to grave all manner of gravings, to be with the cunning men that are with me in Judah, and in Jerusalem, whom David my father did provide. Send me
also cedar trees, fir trees, and algum trees, out of
Lebanon ; for I know that thy servants can skill to

cut timber in Lebanon ; and, behold, my servants
shall be with thy servants, even to prepare me timber
in abundance : for the house which I am about to
build shall be wonderful great. And, behold, I will
give to thy servants, the hewers that cut timber,
twenty thousand measures of beaten wheat, and
twenty thousand measures of barley, and twenty
thousand baths of wine, and twenty thousand baths
of oil " (2 Chron. ii. 3–10). The bargain was soon
struck, for it advantaged both sides. Phœnicia had
at all times to be " nourished " in a great measure
from Palestine (Acts xii. 20). The hill-sides of
Galilee and the plains of Esdraelon and Sharon produced a superabundance of wheat and barley whereof
the natives were glad to dispose, and the highlands of
Samaria and of Judah bore oil and wine far beyond the
wants of their inhabitants. What Phœnicia lacked
in these respects, Palestine was able and eager to
supply, while to Phœnicia it was a boon to obtain a
market for her inexhaustible stores of timber, and it
relieved her labour market to furnish her neighbour
for a number of years with an army of wood-cutters,
stone-cutters, carpenters, and masons. It was as
skilled artizans that the Phœnician labourers were
welcomed by the Israelitish king, whose subjects had
small experience in those useful arts which Phœnicia
had already for ages carried to a high state of perfection ; and it must be assumed that while the rough
work was, as a general rule, executed by Solomon's
own subjects (2 Chron. ii. 17, 18), the Phœnician ope-
ratives were mainly employed in such work as needed
more delicate and careful manipulation.

The "servants of Solomon" wrought with the "servants of Hiram" in Mount Lebanon, felling the trees that were marked as fit to be cut, and dragging them down the mountain-side to the sea, or else casting them into the rivers, which in their flood season would convey the timber to their mouths, where it was collected into "floats" or rafts, which were then towed along the Syrian coast from the Phœnician river mouths to the Jewish port of Joppa (2 Chron. ii. 16). A lively image of these proceedings may be seen at the present day on the coast of Norway, where the timber intended for exportation is cut on the banks of the streams, precipitated into them, and carried down to the shore on the melting of the snows in spring ; after which it is collected and conveyed along shore to Christiana or Bergen. A like practice prevails in Switzerland along the banks of the tributaries of the Rhine ; and huge "floats," seven or eight hundred feet long by two or three hundred wide may be seen descending the great river throughout the summer time, composed of scores of smaller rafts, the materials of which have been carried down the various tributaries, and finally combined into a floa‘ ing monster at Basle or Waldshut.

The skilled workmen lent by Hiram to the Israelitish king were chiefly concentrated at Jerusalem. They consisted principally of "stone-squarers," mostly "Giblites" or inhabitants of Gebal, of ornamental wood-carvers, of metallurgists, and of persons accustomed to deal with textile fabrics. At the head of them was a wonderfully accomplished artist, who bore the same name with the king, and was by descent half-Hebrew, half-Phœnician, sprung from a Tyrian father and an Israelite mother. Hiram, the "master-workman" (2 Chron. ii. 13), son of "a man of Tyre and a woman of the daughters of Dan," was one of those universal geniuses who are common in the infancy of art, and astonish later times by their manifold and versatile powers. As Theodore of Samos was an architect, a caster of works in bronze, an engraver of signets, and a maker of minute works in the precious metals—as Michael Angelo Buonarotti was at once a painter, a sculptor, an architect, and a worker in bronze, so Hiram the Tyrian was a sculptor, a carver in wood, a man skilled in the construction of delicate textile fabrics, a caster of bronzes on the largest scale, and familiar with metallurgy in all its various branches. Whether he was also an architect, we cannot be sure. It is not said that he drew out the plan of Solomon's temple, or that for his palace, or that for "the house of the forest of Lebanon" (1 Kings vii. 2–6); but considering the total inexperience of the Israelites in architectural works of any pretension, and the fact that the Phœnicians had been long accustomed to build palaces and construct temples, it may at least be suspected that the builders employed by Solomon to adorn his capital with magnificent edifices drew their inspiration from Phœnician sources. The two pillars, Jachin and Boaz, which reared themselves in front of the temple porch to the height of between fifty-two and fifty-three feet (2 Chron. iii. 15) were modelled, apparently, on the sacred metal pillars well known to Tyre and other Phœnician cities, one of which, coated with gold, had

been recently set up by King Hiram in his capital.
The ancient forms used freely in the temple and
palace ornamentation, the lions of the royal throne
(1 Kings x. 20), the twelve oxen on which stood the
" molten sea " (1 Kings vii. 25), the " borders of the
bases " covered with lions, oxen, and cherubim, can
scarcely have been the production of Israelite hands,
which were expressly forbidden to fashion " graven
or molten images." Altogether, the Jewish Temple,
though modelled in some respects upon the " Tabernacle of the Congregation," must be regarded as
essentially a Phœnician building, at once designed
by Phœnicians and the work of Phœnician hands.

From the accounts therefore which are given of
Solomon's temple, and from the remains which exist
at the present day, we may gather, probably, a better
idea than we can obtain in any other way, of the
character which attached to Phœnician architecture
and art in Hiram's time. Hiram, we know from the
Tyrian historians, Dius and Menander, was famous
for his substructions, and the substructions of the
Jewish temple are the most remarkable which the
world contains. In Scripture we are told that "the
king (*i.e.*, Solomon) commanded, and they brought
great stones, costly stones, hewn stones, to lay the
foundation of the house" (1 Kings v. 7); and again
that the " foundation (of the palace) was of costly
stones, even great stones, *stones of ten cubits*, and
stones of eight cubits." The explorations made upon
the spot reveal an architecture of this kind, but one
even more massive and more surprising. The great
area, upon which the Temple stood, was built up on

all sides from the irregular surface of the natural rock so as to form a nearly level space. The wall now rises everywhere from fifty to sixty feet above the present surface of the ground, and in places descends eighty feet more below the present surface. Thus it had an original height of from sixty or seventy to a hundred and forty feet. In places, it is built from bottom to top of large squared stones, bevelled at the edges, and varying between three feet three inches and six feet in height. The stones, which are laid in regular courses, without cement, are of very different lengths, the longest hitherto discovered measuring thirty-eight feet nine inches. It is estimated that this stone does not weigh less than one hundred tons! Many of the other blocks are from half to two-thirds of this weight ; and altogether it must be said that the builders found no difficulty in conveying up a steep hill, and emplacing in rows, and raising up, layer upon layer, masses of a size which modern architects scarcely use for their foundation-stones. The massiveness of their work is fully on a par with that of the Egyptian pyramid-kings ; and the perfection of the cutting and fitting together of the stones is nearly equal, since it is often impossible to insert a knife into the joints.

With the power of constructing this superb masonry was combined an extraordinary skill in the execution of metal castings. The great bowl or laver, known as " the molten sea," which was forty-seven feet in circumference, and capable of containing 2,000 *baths* (1 Kings vii. 26) or 17,000 gallons, far exceeded in size any similar work of the Greeks, and would

severely tax the ingenuity of modern metallurgists
to construct in one piece.   The other lavers were
not remarkable for size, but were elegant and
highly convenient pieces of furniture.   They ran on
wheels, so that they might be readily moved from
place to place, and had an ornamentation of lions,
oxen, cherubim, and palm-trees (1 Kings vii. 27–39).
The two pillars, Jachin and Boaz, were regarded as
Hiram's *chef d'œuvres*, but were constructed, probably,
in several pieces.   The shafts, the capitals, and the
bases were certainly distinct, and it is not certain that
even the shafts were in one piece.   The wonderfulness
of the pillars was in their ornamentation rather than
in their construction.   Each was adorned with
"chain-work" and "checker-work" (1 Kings vii. 17),
with "nets" and with "pomegranates," two hundred
of these in two rows being embossed on either column
(1 Kings vii. 42).

The splendid details of the Temple and its furniture have been described in another "Story,"[1] whereto
they more properly belong.   Mention of them has to
be made in this place, because they were the direct
product of Phœnicia, and because they furnish the
surest grounds for the right estimation of early
Phœnician art, which has passed away, leaving
scarcely a trace, from the cities and country that gave
it birth, while impressing itself on a neighbouring
land, and leaving indelible marks on that land's
buildings and on its literature.   The few specimens of
Phœnician skill in metal, in glass, and in gems, which
the museums of Europe contain, are, most of them,

---

[1] "Story of the Jews," pp. 24, 25.

perhaps all of them, of later date, and, while throwing light on the Phœnician civilization of four or five centuries subsequently, are useless for the period which we are now considering. One tomb, to be described further on, and certain substructions at Tyre and Aradus, may belong to Hiram's age, but they have been very incompletely examined, and even their date is uncertain. We must form our idea of the condition of Phœnician art about B.C. 1000 from the remains which still exist of the Temple of Solomon, and from the accounts which Hebrew authors, who saw it, give of the building and of its furniture.

The Hebrew literature throws also a flood of light on the commerce and navigation of the Phœnicians in Hiram's time. The Tyrian monarch entered into a close maritime alliance with his Israelitish neighbour, and engaged with him in joint commercial enterprises of the most lucrative character. Solomon's conquest of the Edomites had given him the possession of an important port on the Red Sea, Ezion-geber, at the head of the Elanitic Gulf, not far from Elath. Whatever access the Phœnicians may have had previously to the Red Sea and the Indian Ocean through the favour of the Egyptians, it was a distinct gain to them to enjoy the free use of a new port on the southern waters, where their presence was warmly welcomed, and they were allowed to build as many ships as they pleased. In return for the opening which they thus obtained to the freest and fullest commerce with the East, the Tyrians conceded to the Israelites a participation in the traffic which they had

carried on for so long a time with the nations of the far
West.   Two trading fleets were formed, to which each
of the two nations contributed both ships and men
(1 Kings ix. 27 ; x. 22)—one, starting from Ezion-
geber, traded with Ophir on the south-east coast of
Arabia, and perhaps with the more distant East, with
India, Malabar, and Ceylon; the other, starting probably from Tyre, navigated the Mediterranean, entered
the ocean, and traded with Tartessus and Gades, perhaps with Western Africa and Cornwall.   The
Eastern navy brought from Ophir a vast quantity of
gold (1 Kings ix. 28) together with almug-trees
(ibid. ix. 11), probably sandal-wood, precious stones,
and perhaps spices (ch. x. 15).   The Western, which
made a voyage once only in three years, imported
gold, like the other, but brought in addition silver,
ivory, ebony, apes, and (and if the Hebrew word is
rightly rendered) peacocks.   The whole of this commerce was absolutely new to the Hebrews, and effected
a revolution in their habits which must have been
most remarkable.   To the Tyrians none of it was
perhaps wholly new ; but their Eastern trade was
greatly stimulated, and no doubt largely increased.
The gold of Ophir flowed into the treasury of the
state and the pockets of the merchants.   If Solomon
derived from a single voyage the amount of 420
talents (1 Kings ix. 28), or more than four millions
sterling of our money, what is Phœnicia not likely to
have obtained from a continuous trade lasting for
twenty or thirty years at any rate, probably longer ?
It may be said that they had to export commodities
to the same value as what they imported ; but in

countries where gold is largely produced, it becomes a drug in the market, and the rate of exchange is that expressed in the Homeric line—

χρύσεα χαλκείων, ἑκατόμβοι' ἐννεαβοίων—

"gold for brass, the worth of a hundred oxen for the worth of nine." The country necessarily became vastly rich, which enjoyed such a traffic.

Through his dealings with Solomon the Tyrian king obtained another advantage, which however he does not appear to have estimated very highly. Solomon, anxious to show his gratitude and good will to his august brother, made over to him a district of Galilee, bordering upon the Tyrian possessions on the mainland, and containing twenty cities (1 Kings ix. 11). The Phœnician monarch quitted his capital and made a royal progress for the express purpose of inspecting his new acquisition, but was far from favourably impressed by it. An old English adage tells us "not to look a gift horse in the mouth;" but either the Phœnicians had no such proverb, or Hiram disregarded it, for he at once gave the district a name expressive of his displeasure. The land, he said, was Cabul—"disgusting"—and though he accepted it, he made his feelings known by stamping the region with the appellation.

The "wisdom" of Solomon is said to have provoked the Tyrians to match their wits against his. Solomon had sent Hiram certain riddles to test his sagacity, and had asked for a return in kind, wagering a good round sum upon the result. The contest terminated in Solomon's favour, and Hiram had to

make a heavy payment in consequence. Hereupon,
a Tyrian named Abdemon (Abdesmun?), came to the
rescue, and vindicated the honour of his country by
correctly solving all King Solomon's· riddles, and
proposing to him others, of which the Israelitish
monarch, with all his intelligence, was quite unable to
discovered the solution. He was thus compelled to
refund all the money that Hiram had paid him, and
to forfeit a considerable amount in addition. Unfortunately, none of the verbal puzzles in question
have come down to us, and we have no means of
judging whether or no the Tyrian sphinx excelled the
Theban one.

Hiram's reign lasted thirty-four years. He was
fifty-three years old at his death, and left his crown
to his son Baal-uzur, or Baleazar. A remarkable
monument, about three miles distant from the modern
Tyre (Sur), but said to have been originally built just
outside the eastern gate of the continental town,
which thence sloped down to the sea, is known to the
present day as " the Tomb of Hiram," and may well
have been the actual sepulchre of this ancient king
It is a " grey weather-beaten " structure, bearing all
the marks of a high antiquity. Upon a pedestal
consisting of three courses of grey limestone, each
three feet thick, and the uppermost a little overhanging the other two, is emplaced a tomb or
sarcophagus formed out of a single block, which is
twelve feet long by six feet high and six feet broad.
The sarcophagus is covered over by a heavy lid in
the shape of a solid block three feet in thickness,
which appears never to have been removed. The

HIRAM'S TOMB.

tomb, however, has been rifled ; a large hole has been broken into the eastern end of the sarcophagus, and its contents, whatever they were, have been removed. Hiram has found no more secure a resting-place than Cheops or Rameses the Great; his dust is scattered to the winds ; and none can say what has become of the royal ornaments which were most likely buried with him. The monument is without inscription; it stands "lone and solitary," a fit emblem of that grand old king, who alone stands out from the rest of Phœnician antiquity in definite form and shape, a solid figure, while around him and about him all else is vague and shadowy.

VII.

ITHOBAL AND AHAB — DARKER ASPECT OF THE PHŒNICIAN RELIGION.

THE condition of Phœnicia is enveloped in obscurity from the death of Hiram to the accession of Eth-baal, whom the Greeks called Ithobalus. The names of the kings are indeed for the most part known, together with their order, and the number of years that each reigned. Hiram was succeeded by his son, Baal-uzur, or Baleazar, who ascended the throne at the age of thirty-six, and reigned seven years, dying when he was forty-three. Abd-ash-toreth, son of Baal-uzur, followed: he became king at the age of twenty, but reigned nine years only, falling a victim to a conspiracy when he was still under thirty. The crown then passed into another family, being assumed by one of the conspirators whose name is not mentioned. There seems then to have been another change of dynasty, a certain Ashtoreth becoming king at the age of forty-two, and reigning twelve years. His brother, Aserymus, succeeded at the age of forty-five, and had a reign of nine years only, dying when he was fifty-four. Aserymus was murdered by a younger brother, Phales, who held the

crown eight months only, being in his turn assassinated by Eth-baal, high-priest of Ashtoreth, who
established himself in the kingdom.   Fifty years in-
tervened between the death of Hiram and the accession of Eth-baal, during which half century nothing
is known of the history of Tyre beyond the facts
above related.

A modern writer has indeed connected with this
period a graphic narrative contained in the Universal
History of Justin, and not dated with accuracy.   But
Justin, it is certain, assigned this narrative to a far
later time, since he connected it with the wars between
Tyre and Persia, which belong to the middle portion
of the fourth century, B.C., instead of the tenth or
ninth.   We shall therefore reserve this history for
later mention, and ask the reader's attention to the
reign of King Eth-baal, and the corrupting influence
which it exercised over two neighbouring countries.

Eth-baal was, as already mentioned, not only king
of Tyre, but also high-priest of Astarte or Ashtoreth.
He seems to have been a religious enthusiast, and to
have earnestly desired the spread of the Phœnician
religion into other lands besides his own.   To effect
this purpose he married his daughter, Jezebel, whom
he had thoroughly imbued with his spirit, to Ahab,
king of Israel, the son of Omri, the founder of
Samaria.   Omri and Ahab were, both of them, bold
and warlike monarchs, of a calibre much superior to
any of the other princes who had hitherto occupied
the throne of the northern kingdom.   Eth-baal may
have hoped to gain political advantages from the
alliance, but its primary motive appears to have been

religious propagandism. The Phœnician princess took with her from Tyre the paraphernalia of her religious worship, together with a sacerdotal *entourage*, which gave her at once a court of her own creatures, a band of unscrupulous adherents, and a means of displaying the ceremonial of the new religion on a most magnificent scale. Four hundred and fifty ministering priests of Baal were attached to the worship of that god in the Israelite capital, while four hundred others, devoted to Ashtoreth, hung about the royal palace at Jezreel, and feasted daily at the table which Jezebel provided for their entertainment. Ahab was persuaded to build a great sanctuary for Baal on the hill of Samaria. " It was of a size sufficient to contain all the worshippers of Baal that the northern kingdom could furnish. . . . In the interior was a kind of fastness or adytum, in which were seated or raised on pillars the figures, carved in wood, of the Phœnician deities, as they were seen in vision, centuries later, by Jezebel's fellow-countryman, Hannibal, in the sanctuary of Gades. In the centre was Baal, the Sun-god ; around him were the inferior divinities. In front of the temple stood, on a stone pillar, the figure of Baal alone." [1]

A sanctuary was also assigned to Ashtoreth at Jezreel. Ashtoreth was worshipped under the form of an emblem, rather than of a statue. The emblem, which was sometimes of wood, sometimes of metal, was called an Ashérah, and is thought to have resembled the "Sacred Tree" of the Assyrians. It was generally set up in a temple (2 Kings xxi. 7 ; xxiii.

[1] Stanley, " Lectures on the Jewish Church," vol. ii. p. 246.

6), but may sometimes have been worshipped in the open air under the deep shade of trees. Hence the Greek translators of the Hebrew Scriptures, confounding it with its surroundings, rendered the term by ἄλσος, "grove," which the Vulgate replaced by *lucus*, whence the "grove" of the Authorized Version. Jezebel's four hundred priests or "prophets" ministered to this idol in the vicinity of Jezreel, and presented to the Israelites a form of religion which was so attractive to them, that very soon the whole people fell away from the worship of Jehovah and proclaimed themselves votaries of the two new deities, Baal and Ashtoreth.

To the corrupting influence thus introduced, the gradual declension, and ultimately the fall and destruction of the Israelite kingdom is distinctly ascribed (2 Kings xvii. 16–18). Nor did the evil stop there. The daughter of Eth-baal passed on the malign contagion of her evil genius to her own daughter, Athaliah, a daughter worthy of such a mother, who became the queen of Ahaziah, monarch of the rival kingdom of Judah, and took advantage of her position to bring Judah, no less than Israel, within the sphere of the fatal fascination. The terrible *virus* by her introduced into the Jewish state clung to it to the end, and hastened that end. Vain were the reforms of Hezekiah and Josiah. The Phœnician rites brought in by Athaliah took a firm hold on the Jewish people, and are declared by Ezekiel (chap. viii. 6–18) to have been among the chief causes of the Captivity.

For the lessons of history to have their proper

effect, it is necessary sometimes to penetrate into dark recesses, and to expose to the eye that fearful corruption which in various places has from time to time underlain the fair surface of society, like the ghastly horrors that are concealed within a whited sepulchre. When we hear of Baal-worship and Astarte-worship we are apt to suppose them very harmless and innocent things, and to wonder at the fierce denunciations which the Prophets of Jehovah hurl against their votaries. Do not all men worship one God? Are not "Jehovah, Jove, and Lord," Baal, Ammon, Zeus, Ormazd, Brahma, merely His different names in men's different languages? Alas, when a searching investigation is made into religions, it is found that they differ essentially from the root upwards—that some of them have scarcely any features in common —that, instead of all men worshipping one God, different nations worship deities as different as it is possible for thought to conceive or words to depict. What is there in common between the fearful goddess of the Thugs and—we say not the Christ—but even the "Great Spirit" of the Red Indians, or the Brahma of the Hindoos? How can there be said to be any resemblance between the fetish of the African and the "good and holy Ormazd" of the Parsee? And so between Jehovah and Baal there was the widest, wonderfullest difference. Dean Stanley, certainly no bigot, observes that "the change from the symbolical worship of the One True God, with the innocent rites of sacrifice and prayer, to the cruel and licentious worship of the Phœnician divinities, was *a prodigious step downwards*, and left traces which no subsequent reformations were able to obliterate." [1] Dr. Dollinger, one of the least sensational of the historians of religions, gives the following account of the religion of the Phœnicians as it was in the reign of Eth-baal and his successors. [2]

"In earlier times Baal had been worshipped without an image in Tyre and its colonies; but for a long time now his worship had grown into an idolatry of the most wanton character, directed by a numerous priesthood, who had their head-quarters at Tyre. . . . His statue rode upon bulls; for the bull was the symbol of generative power, and he was also represented with bunches of grapes and pomegranates in his hands. As the people of (Western) Asia distinguished, properly speaking, only two deities of nature, a male and a female, so Baal was of an elemental and sidereal character at once. As the former, he was god of the creative power, bringing all things to life everywhere, and, in particular, god of fire; but he was Sun-god besides, and as such, to human lineaments, he added the crown of rays about the head peculiar to this god. In the one quality as well as the other he was represented at the same time as sovereign of the heavens (Baal-samen), and of the earth by him impregnated. . . . The Canaanitish Moloch (king) was not essentially different from Baal, but the same god in his terrible and destroying aspect, the god of consuming fire, the burning sun, who smites the land with unfruitfulness and pestilence,

---

[1] "Lectures on the Jewish Church," vol. ii. p. 245.
[2] "Heidenthum und Judenthum," translated by N. Darnell, **vol. i.** pp. 425–429.

dries up the springs, and begets poisonous winds. When the prophet says (Jer. xxxii. 35), 'Such as in the valley of Ben-Hinnom built high-places of Baal, to lead their sons and their daughters through the fire to Moloch;' and again, 'The Jews had built high-places to Baal, to burn their children by fire as a burnt-offering to Baal' (chap. xix. 5), there is no mistaking the essential identity of the two. Besides the incense consumed in his honour, bulls also were sacrificed to Baal, and probably horses too; the Persians at least sacrificed the latter to their Sun-god. But *the principal sacrifice was children.* This horrible custom was grounded in part on the notion that children were the dearest possession of their parents, and, in part, that, as pure and innocent beings, they were the offerings of atonement most certain to pacify the anger of the deity; and further, that the god of whose essence the generative power of nature was, had a just title to that which was begotten of man, and to the surrender of their children's lives. The sacrifices were consumed by fire; the life given by the fire-god, he should also take back again by the flames which destroy being. The Rabbinical description of the image of Moloch, that it was a human figure with a bull's head and outstretched arms, is confirmed by the account which Diodorus gives of the Carthaginian Kronos or Moloch. The image of metal was made hot by a fire kindled within it; and the children, laid in its arms, rolled from thence into the fiery lap below. Voluntary offering on the part of the parents was essential to the success of the sacrifice; even the firstborn, nay, the only child of the family was given up. The parents stopped the cries of their children by fondling and kissing them, for the victim ought not to weep, and the sound of complaint was drowned in the din of flutes and kettle-drums. Mothers, according to Plutarch, stood by without tears or sobs ; if they wept or sobbed they. lost the honour of the act, and their children were sacrificed notwithstanding. Such sacrifices took place either annually on an appointed day, or before great enterprises, or on the occasion of public calamities, to appease the wrath of the god. The primitive custom is traceable in the myth of Theseus and the Minotaur. The Cretan monster with human body and bull's head, to whom young men and maidens were sacrificed, was the Moloch who had come from Phœnicia, and the overcoming of him by Theseus was the destruction of the bloody rite. Thus, too, the rape of Europa into Crete from Phœnicia, through means of the bull, was a symbol of the colonization of that island by Phœnicians. The bull on which Europa sat was the Sun-god, and she herself the Moon-goddess, Astarte.

"Another form of Baal was Melkarth, 'the city king,' tutelary god of the city of Tyre, whose worship was carried far and wide by the colonies, proceeding thence to the shores of the Mediterranean. This protector of Tyre was the Phœnician Herculas, god alike of sun and fire (whence a perpetual fire was kept up upon his altar), a race-king and hero-leader of the people's expeditions. From him have the Asiatic features of the contest with the lion, the self-immolation by fire on the pile, and others, passed over into the Greek saga of Heracles. . . .

" In the Astarte of the western Asiatics we recognize that great nature-goddess, standing by Baal's side, regent of the stars, queen of heaven, and goddess of the moon, the mother of life, and goddess of woman's fecundity.   Under the name of Astarte she was guardian goddess of Sidon, and not essentially distinct from the Baaltis of Byblus, and Urania of Ascalon.   The Greeks and Romans sometimes take her for Juno, as she was the supreme female divinity of the Asiatics ; sometimes for Aphrodite, on account of the licentious character of the worship sacred to her ; and again for Selene (Luna), for she was pictured as the goddess of the moon, with horns, representing the lunar crescent. . . .

" As highest goddess, or queen of heaven, Astarte was (as above observed) accounted by the Greeks as Hera (Juno) ; yet they also recognized in her something of Athene, Aphrodite, Selene, Rhea, Artemis, Nemesis, and the Moirai.   In fact, she came nearest to the Phrygian Cybele.   Sceptre and spindle in hand, she wore rays and a mural crown on her head, and the girdle too, an ornament only beseeming Aphrodite-Urania.   Her golden statue rode next to that of Baal-Zeus, in a chariot drawn by lions ; a precious stone, placed upon her head, illuminated the whole temple at night.   She was considered as one with Atergatis or Derceto, who was honoured under the form of a fish on the coasts of the Philistines.   A combined worship was offered to the two, Baal and the goddess. Their temple at Apheka was so exceedingly rich, that Crassus spent several days in weighing all the gold and silver vessels and precious things that were contained in it. These gifts were the combined offerings of Arabia, Babylonia, Assyria, Phœnicia, Cilicia, and Cappadocia, and therefore of all the people of the Semitic tongue. In the court of the temple there were sacred beasts in a tame state in great numbers, and also a pond containing holy fish. Priests and temple ministers were present in such numbers that Lucian counted above three hundred employed in one sacrifice; besides these there were troops of flute players, Galli, and women frenzied with inspiration. At the spring festival, called by some 'the brand feast,' by others 'the feast of torches,' which was attended by streams of visitors from every country, huge trees were burnt with the offerings suspended on them. Even children were sacrificed; they were put into a leathern bag and thrown the whole height of the temple to the bottom, with the shocking expression that they were calves and not children. In the fore-court stood two gigantic phalli. To the exciting din of drums, flutes, and inspired songs, the Galli cut themselves on the arms; and the effect of this act, and of the music accompanying it, was so strong upon mere spectators, that all their bodily and mental powers were thrown into a tumult of excitement; and they too, seized by the desire to lacerate themselves, inflicted wounds upon their bodies by means of potsherds lying ready for the purpose. Thereupon they ran bleeding through the city, and received from the inhabitants a woman's attire. Not chastity, but barrenness, was intended by this act, whereby the Galli only desired to be like their goddess. The relation which they thence-

forward occupied towards women, was regarded as a
holy thing, and was generally tolerated."

Thus terrible were the practices which Phœnicia, in
Eth-baal's time, introduced among her southern
neighbours, by whom they had been previously, if not
absolutely unknown, at least indulged in rarely and
in the deepest secrecy. Under Ahab and his sons,
Ahaziah and Jehoram, Baal worship became the State
religion of Samaria ; under Athaliah it was for a time
the State religion of Judah. The pure cult of
Judaism—the one hope of the world—contracted a
well-nigh indelible stain from the proselytizing efforts
of Jezebel, and Athaliah, and their furious persecutions ; the heavenly light passed under a thick black
cloud ; and it required prolonged convulsions through
the whole of the East, the downfall of Israel and
Judah, and the long purgation of the Captivity, to
undo the effects brought about " with a light heart "
by a royal bigot, and his cruel daughter and grand-
daughter.

VIII.

STORY OF THE FOUNDING OF CARTHAGE.

THE story which has come down to us respecting the foundation of Carthage by a body of Tyrian settlers, runs somewhat as follows :—Matgen or Mattan, the grandson of Eth-baal, who died after the short reign of nine years, left as joint heirs to his crown a daughter, Elissa, who was a maiden of great beauty, and a son, who was a mere boy of about eight or nine. Elissa being of marriageable age, was wooed and won by her maternal uncle, Sicharbas or Acerbas (the " Sichæus" of Virgil), who was one of the wealthiest and most powerful of the Tyrian nobles, and high-priest of the Tyrian god Melkarth. Within a short time of the death of Mattan a popular revolution took place. Elissa was deprived of the royal title and power, and her brother, Pygmalion, despite his extreme youth, made sole king. Desiring to possess himself of the great wealth of his brother-in-law, Sicharbas, Pygmalion ere long resolved on his assassination. Either secretly in a hunting expedition, or openly in the temple of Melkarth, where he was ministering, Pygmalion attacked Sicharbas, and slew him. Elissa, rendered intensely unhappy by the death of her husband, whom she loved with extreme ardour, made up her mind to quit the country of her birth, which had become hateful to her on account of her misfortunes, and to seek for resignation and peace of mind amid the novelties and distractions of a new and distant scene. At the same time she was anxious that the treasures which had been her husband's, and had proved so fatal to him, should not fall into the hands of her husband's murderer, and so make his triumph complete. She therefore devised a plan by which she might at once deprive Pygmalion of his expected accession of wealth, and obtain a fleet of sufficient size to convey herself, her followers, and her possessions to a remote country. Professing to her brother that she was desirous of taking up her abode in his palace, she asked him to send her a number of ships, wherein she might embark her husband's riches, her own goods and chattels, and her train of attendants and friends. Pygmalion granted her request, but sent a number of his own officers in charge of the ships, with directions to take especial care of the treasure of Sicharbas, and see that it reached his coffers. But Elissa had prepared a disappointment both for him and them. She had filled several bags with sand, and made them look as if they contained treasure, and these bags she allowed to be seen, while she carefully secreted the wealth of Sicharbas elsewhere. Then, having set sail, and reached the deep sea, she called her crew together, and announced that she was about to make an offering to the manes of her late husband. Solemnly invoking her husband by name, she required her sailors to take the bags which contained his wealth, and hurl them into the sea, while she implored him to receive, as a propitiatory offering, the valuables that had caused his death. Pygmalion's officers did not venture to interfere, or to assert their master's right to the treasure, but remained impassive while the comedy, which the princess had contrived, was enacted. At its close, she turned to them, and representing to them that by their inertness they had become accomplices in her act, and would certainly be put to death by Pygmalion, if they placed themselves in his power, she invited them to throw in their lot with her, and accompany the expedition upon which she was bent. Seeing no better plan of action, they consented ; and the fleet, instead of bearing up for Tyre, shaped its course for Cyprus, having first taken on board a certain number of Tyrian senators. In Cyprus they were joined by a high-priest of Baal, and from its shores they carried off eighty maidens, from among the votaries of Astarte, who became the wives of Elissa's adherents, and the mothers of the new colony. The prevalent north-east wind of the Levant took the fleet to the north coast of Mid Africa, and there Elissa, with her followers, founded the world-famed city of Carthage.

There can be no doubt that a great part of this tale is myth. Very little of it comes down to us from the Tyrian historians, whose fragmentary notices are curt, dry, and commonplace to a fault. The bulk is derived from Greek and Roman historians, and Latin poets and commentators upon poetry, who are never very trustworthy authorities. Modern critical historians

accept the tale so far as to believe in the existence of
Elissa and Pygmalion, in their quarrel, and in the
withdrawal of Elissa, with a body of her supporters,
to Carthage, but deny or question almost every other
portion of the story. Thus far they stand upon
tolerably safe ground. They enter on a debateable
region when they proceed further, and endeavour from
notices, which they discredit, to build up a theory of
the real circumstances of the colonization, which shall
be entitled to rank as solid and substantial history.
One of the boldest of these constructive spiders, spins
the following web out of a gluten that is very unsub-
stantial :—

"We undertake," he says, " in the following representation to separate what is matter of fact from what
is doubtful, and what is doubtful from what is
decidedly false. First then—the foundation of
Carthage sprang from the aristocratical families in
Tyre, and was brought about by means of a quarrel
between them and the party of the people under
whose influence the king was at the time. Secondly,
what the traditions, which are here unanimous, relate
concerning the immediate occasion of Elissa's emigration, and that of the aristocratical party which attached
itself to her, namely, the murder of the High-Priest,
improbable as are the details connected with it,
cannot be reasonably doubted. Thirdly, what the
traditions have preserved concerning the accompanying circumstances, under which the immigration of
Elissa and of the aristocratical families connected
with her took place, rests to a certain extent upon the
mythical dressing up of the narrative, while, neverthe-

less, other portions do not depart from that genuine historical character which belongs so remarkably to the remains of Phœnician historical literature. Fourthly, the historical foundress of Carthage, Elissa, became in the popular view, which however was not the Phœnician or Carthaginian, mixed up with the Dido or Anna, who was identical with Astarte, or rather a modification of that goddess."

Having laid down these four main points as indisputable, he proceeds to deal with the details as follows :—" After the death of Ithobaal (Eth-baal), his son Balezor (Baal-uzur), as we learn from the fragments of Menander, assumed the government. This prince reigned eight years only, and at the age of forty-five left his crown to his son Mattan, or Mutton, aged eight. Already during the minority of this king, the ambition of the parties in the state seems to have produced so much contention, that immediately upon his death it broke out openly. Mattan died in the twenty-fifth year of his reign, at the youthful age of thirty-two, and left at his death both his children, Elissa and Pygmalion, minors, as he had been. According to Menander, Pygmalion was just nine at his father's death ; according to Justin, he was quite a boy (*admodum puer*). Elissa must have been somewhat more advanced in life, since her father had assigned the kingdom to her and her brother conjointly, and had at the same time designated her as the future wife of the High-Priest of Melkarth. This dignity appertained to a brother of the king, Sichar-baal by name, whose position as High-Priest made him the first man in the state after the king, the head of the aristocracy, and at the same time the monarch's representative during his minority. However the party of the people opposed itself to the arrangements made by the deceased king's last instructions, which designed the elevation of the Priest of Melkarth to a still higher dignity, since as the queen's husband he would have been joint regent with her, at any rate during her brother's minority; but the democracy set the will aside, and made Pygmalion sole ruler, thus violating, as it would seem, the High-Priest's right of guardianship. Hereupon the rupture became open and patent between the two parties, the aristocracy, in whose interest, and by whose influence probably, the king had endeavoured before his death to alter the existing constitution, and the people which opposed itself to this encroachment. It showed itself still more definitely in the later course of the affair. For we see that, after the murder of the High-Priest, it was the higher aristocracy, which, in combination with Elissa, formed the plan of the emigration and succeeded in putting the plan into execution. . . . One may thus explain the strongly aristocratical character of the Carthaginian constitution, which bade defiance to all the storms of popular revolutionary movement ; and one may say that thus too the view, that the foundation of Carthage was the work of the Tyrian aristocracy, which emigrated on account of its wrongs, is thoroughly confirmed and established.

"The motive for the murder of Sichæus by his brother Pygmalion is said to have been the great riches of the former and the avarice of the latter; and here it is remarkable that Justin's narrative, which contains so many genuine historical particulars, represents the king Pygmalion at the commencement of his reign, which the flight of Elissa must have followed shortly, as ' quite a boy.' According to Menander Pygmalion was in his eighteenth year at the time of Elissa's emigration, which took place, according to Justin, some time after the death of Sichæus. Pygmalion then has slain the High-Priest, in order to obtain possession of his *hidden* treasures, but naturally has not by so doing obtained his end. As here the internal improbabilities of the narrative increase, so too the accounts given of the manner of the death vary : according to some Sichæus was slain at the altar, or before the image of Hercules ; according to others, he was secretly pierced with a spear at a boar hunt, and then thrown into an abyss ; while, according to a third account, he was assassinated upon a journey. These contradictions, and the internal improbabilities above alluded to, leave no doubt that all which is related concerning the occasion of the murder, and concerning the king's participation in it, belongs to the dominion of myth. Still the circumstance itself cannot have been invented. It stands in too close a connection, both as to facts and as to chronology, at once with the Tyrian history in general, and with the circumstances of the time in particular, and is also too universally attested, to be the mere product of imagi- nation. The Priest of Melkarth must thus have fallen a sacrifice in the party conflict between the people and the aristocracy, whose head he was ; and must, to draw a conclusion from the entire mass of the notices, have been secretly murdered by the opposite faction.

There could not fail to be many different accounts of the occurrence. This would follow from the kind of death, from the great importance of the fact, and from the strong feelings stirred up by party passion.

"After the murder of Sichæus, according to one account, which Justin, however, does not include in his copious narrative, the monarch appeared in a dream to Elissa, and revealed to her the bloody deed of Pygmalion. This circumstance fits in with the story, according to which Pygmalion murdered Sichæus privately while they were engaged in a hunt, and threw him into a pit, where he remained unburied; and Virgil, who represents him as slain by the hand of Pygmalion at the altar, and nevertheless as lying unburied, while Elissa gains her first knowledge of her husband's murder through seeing him in her dream, has evidently fused together two mythical notices which contradict one another. The plan of emigration which Elissa, according to this representation, adopted on the advice of her husband's ghost was, according to Justin, her own work, for the accomplishment of which she entered into an engagement with the heads of the aristocracy and with a portion of the Senate. With regard to the circumstances under which the flight was effected, there are two different accounts. According to one, whereto even Virgil makes allusion, it was customary with the Phœnicians to make purchases of grain in foreign lands out of the public revenue, and for the king to supply the gold. Elissa seized the ships which lay ready for this purpose, and at the same time sequestered the king's money which she found on board them, after which

she took hastily to flight. As Pygmalion caused her
to be pursued, she sank in the sea before the eyes of
her pursuers the money assigned for the purchase of
the grain, whereupon they gave up their pursuit.
Servius gives this account with the remark, that there
was another narrative besides with respect to the
progress of the affair. The narrative in question is
found in Justin, who relates that Elissa had obtained
the ships which she needed for her flight from Pygmalion, on the pretext that she wished to quit her
ordinary abode and to go to him, since she at the
time resided in the Island Tyre, while he lived in the
city upon the mainland. Pygmalion had readily sent
the ships, in the expectation that he might in this
way get possession of the buried treasure that had
belonged to his brother; and Elissa hereupon took
flight on board them with her treasures. At the
same time she carried away with her, not only her
fellow-conspirators, but also the royal officers, whom
she had cheated by telling them that the vessels full
of sand which she had sunk in the sea contained the
riches of Sichæus, and to whom she now pointed out
that the covetous and suspicious Pygmalion would be
sure to lay the blame of what had been done on
them, and to inflict on them a severe punishment.
Thus the men were so frightened that they too joined
Elissa and her companions.

"Both narratives have unmistakably their historical
points. The first recommends itself by the fact that
it knows nothing of the hidden treasure of Sichæus
or the avarice of Pygmalion, and consequently ignores
the equally unhistorical statement, that Pygmalion

had slain Sichæus through greed of gain. All these mythical adornments of the second narrative have evidently originated out of the first. The improved legend has seized hold of the quite accidental circumstance, that the money assigned for the purchase of grain was on board the ships, and has confused this money with the temple-treasure, whereof the High-Priest was the protector, whence it followed to assume that Elissa, when escaping, took this, too, with her. It followed to combine with the other facts of the case, the mysteriously concealed murder of the High-Priest, to which the king, who was at variance with the priestly order, must have been privy ; and thus the king was represented as an avaricious and bloodthirsty tyrant, to lend an internal probability to this combination. But, however any one may explain these traditional accessions to the narrative, at any rate the circumstance introduced into the first story of the Tyrians equipping ships at the public expense and having purchases of grain made in foreign countries, is so without design and so thoroughly credible, that by itself it would seem to establish the historical character of the story. And the other account, which Justin gives, has also its genuine historical points : for it can only have been in Phœnicia or among Phœnicians, and, as it seems to us, only through the popular conception of an historical narrative, that the story can have sprung up in the form which has been indicated. It rests, as we lately showed, on an exact local knowledge of the old Tyre as a double town— a knowledge of which a writer of the time of Alexander, when Palætyrus (which in the story figures as the royal residence) lay in ruins, would certainly not have introduced in such a way."

Such are the lucubrations of the German critic, a little condensed and cleared from ambiguities. He accepts the relationship of Elissa to Pygmalion, the joint sovereignty of the two under their father's will, the revolution whereby Elissa was dethroned, her marriage to Sicharbas, and the latter's violent death. He rejects the whole tale of Sicharbas's buried treasure, of Pygmalion's greed, and of his share in the murder. He believes that Sicharbas fell a victim to the party strife, of which he makes so much, being secretly assassinated by the democratic faction, without the king's connivance. He thinks that the whole aristocratical party, or at any rate all its leaders, left the city with Elissa, and proceeding to Carthage, founded there an aristocratic community which stood in strong contrast with the democratic Tyre. To us it seems that there are no sure grounds upon which the details of the narrative can be divided under different categories, and some pronounced to be historical facts, others doubtful, others certainly legendary. We regard nothing as certain, except that the colony started from Tyre under Elissa, a sister of the king Pygmalion, who had quarrelled with him, and regarding herself as injured sought a home in a distant country, whereto she was accompanied by a number of Tyrians, some nobles, some of lower rank, who sympathised with her in her misfortunes.

IX.

PHŒNICIA'S CONTEST WITH ASSYRIA, AND HER POSITION AS ASSYRIA'S TRIBUTARY.

THE first known contest of Assyria with Phœnicia belongs to a date not very remote from that of the founding of Carthage. When Assyria, ab. B.C. 1130, carried her arms as far as Northern Syria, and flaunted her standard on the shores of the Mediterranean Sea, she did not, so far as appears, make acquaintance with the Phœnician nation. Upper Syria was at that time in the possession of the Khatti or Hittites ; and it was with the Khatti, and Naïri, that Tiglath-pileser I. the first great conquering Assyrian monarch, contended in the region between the Euphrates and the "upper ocean of the setting sun." But when, two and a half centuries later, ab. B.C. 880–870, the second great conqueror, Asshur-nazir-pal, warred in the same distant countries, and, after reducing the Hittites of the more northern region, pressed southwards up the Orontes valley, and "occupied the environs of Lebanon," the two nations came into collision. Hitherto, it would seem, the Phœnicians, protected by the strong Lebanon range, and shut in between it and the sea, had led a peaceful life, pro voking the hostility of no great power, and abstaining themselves from any attempt to acquire an extensive continental dominion. Now, however, at length the horrors of war came upon them. Little by little the warlike people, which had its true home in the rich tract between the Middle Tigris and Mount Zagros, had spread itself over the Mesopotamian plain and the adjacent mountains on the north, had everywhere slaughtered and reduced to subjection the loose confederacies of petty tribes which opposed their progress, had crossed the Euphrates, overrun Syria and Commagene, defeated the Hittites in a hundred fights, and aimed at establishing themselves in permanent possession of the entire tract between the Euphrates and the sea. Phœnicia had to decide on the course which she would pursue. Should she resist? Trusting in the strong walls of her ancient and famous towns, and in the strong arms of the mercenaries, whom her immense resources would enable her to attract into her service, should she venture to defy the Assyrian arms ; or should she, regarding the better part of valour as discretion, submit, and make the best terms she could with the invader ?

The statesmen who presided over the councils of Phœnicia at the time determined in favour of the latter alternative. And who shall say that they were wrong ? Honour does not require a state to resist the aggressor, whatever the odds may be against the resistance being successful. Prudence must be allowed to come in, and to give her advice on a calm consideration of all the existing and impending circumstances. To understand the position of Phœnicia at the time, we must form an estimate of the greatness and military strength of Assyria, and we must balance in scales, free from any bias to either side, the relative power and resources of the two countries.

Now, Assyria was a great centralized monarchy. She had existed for little short of six centuries, and had been a conquering state for four hundred years or more. Her main attention had been turned for four or five hundred years to the training of her soldiers, and the bringing of her military system to the highest point of perfection. She had long had a standing army. She had drilled and trained and disciplined her troops with an unwearied unflagging spirit, had conceived the idea of various arms of the service, had separated the several arms, and had advanced each to a high point of efficiency. Foremost of all, both ideally and practically, was the chariot force. The chariots of Assyria in the days of Asshur-nazir-pal were to be reckoned by thousands. Cars of excellent construction were drawn by horses of great strength and swiftness, most carefully trained ; and a force was thus created, which no amount of undisciplined valour could possibly resist. The warriors, clad in coats of mail, with bronze helmets upon their heads, and their lower limbs guarded by greaves, advanced to the fight armed with spears, swords, and bows, rushed with impetuous force against their enemies, and for the most part swept them from the field. The on-coming of the Assyrians is thus described by the Prophet Isaiah : " Behold, they shall come with speed swiftly : none shall be weary nor stumble among them ; none shall slumber nor sleep ;

neither shall the girdle of their loins be loosed, nor the latchet of their shoes be broken : whose arrows are sharp, and all their bows bent ; their horses' hoofs shall be counted like flint, and their wheels like a whirlwind ; their roaring shall be like a lion, they shall roar like young lions ; yea, they shall roar, and take hold of the prey, and shall carry it away safe, and none shall deliver it. And in that day they shall roar against them like the roaring of the sea ; and if one look unto the land, behold, darkness and sorrow, and the light is darkened in the heavens thereof" (Isa. v. 26–30).

The Assyrians had moreover a trained cavalry. The chariot force was accompanied, and supplemented in respect of its deficiencies, by a certain proportion of well-armed and well-equipped horsemen, terrible especially after defeat, when they relentlessly pursued the flying masses of a scattered host, and dealt death and destruction around them. However, in the time of Asshur-nazir-pal, the cavalry force was not as yet very completely organized, nor was it very numerous ; and, though it may have augmented the alarm which was universally felt whenever Assyrian invasion was apprehended, did not constitute the main terror or the main danger.

The arm of the service next in importance to the chariot-force was the infantry. This was organized into distinct bodies of heavy-armed spearmen, heavy-armed archers, light archers, and slingers. The heavy-armed spearmen wore coats of mail, or jerkins of leather, and bronze conical helmets ; on their left arms they carried large shields of metal or wood. The heavy archers were similarly equipped, except that they worked in pairs ; one of each pair alone drew the bow, and vexed the enemy with his arrows ; the other protected him from missiles with a wicker shield, and at the same time was ready to repel hand-to-hand assailants with a short sword. The light archers had the slightest possible clothing ; they adventured themselves in the front line of battle at the beginning of an engagement, acting as skirmishers, but withdrew behind the heavy-armed when the combat became serious. The slingers, who were a distinct corps, carried nothing but their slings, from which they discharged stones, and perhaps sometimes lumps of lead against their adversaries.

When the Assyrians first appeared as belligerents in the Lebanon region, their military prestige, the numbers of their hosts, and their skill in arms were such, that the tribes of the region generally recognized them as irresistible. A general submission was made. Phœnicia, in deciding to acknowledge the Assyrian suzerainty, and to pay an annual tribute, did but bring her action into agreement with that of her neighbours, and show her appreciation of the fact, that it was hopeless to contend in arms with so formidable an adversary. Tyre, Sidon, Gebal (Byblus), and Arvad, are declared by the Assyrian conqueror to have made their submission to him in his fifth year, and to have consented to pay a tribute to the great power of Western Asia. The tribute on the first occasion consisted of "silver, gold, tin, copper, vestments of wool and linen, cloaks great and small, strong timber, ebony," and further of "the teeth of dolphins," on which the Assyrians appear to have set a high value.

The peaceful relations thus established continued, in the main, undisturbed for a century and a half, nearly. It is not quite clear whether during this space the Phœnician cities ever joined in any of those confederacies which were formed from time to time by the petty kingdoms of Western Asia to resist the continually increasing burden of the Assyrian suzerainty. On one or two occasions they may have allowed themselves to be drawn into alliances that had a promising appearance ; but they were certainly at no time very energetic members of such alliances, or very strenuous in their endeavours to shake themselves free from the Assyrian yoke. The cuneiform records for the century and a half between B.C. 870 and B.C. 727 make frequent mention of the submissive payment of tribute to Assyria by the kings of Tyre, Sidon, Gebal, and Arvad ; they nowhere speak with any distinctness of the revolt or subjugation of any Phœnician city. It is not until the time of Shalmaneser IV., the son of the second Tiglath-pileser (B.C. 727–728), that we have any clear evidence of hostilities having broken out between the suzerain power and her Phœnician vassals, or even of the latter being at all discontented with their position. It is probable that, on the whole, the establishment of the Assyrian power in Western Asia was favourable to the Phœnician land-commerce, making the passage of their caravans more safe, while it in no way interfered with their sea trade. Tyre increased in wealth and in material greatness under Assyria's wing, as may be

seen by the description of what she was, or had
recently been, given by Isaiah ab. B.C. 700.

> " Be silent, ye inhabitants of the island,
> Which the merchants of Sidon, that pass over the sea, have
> replenished.
> The corn of the Nile, on the broad waters,
> The harvest of the River, was her revenue :
> She was the mart of nations. . . .
> She was a joyful city,
> Her antiquity was of ancient days. . . .
> She was a city that dispensed crowns ;
> Her merchants were princes,
> And her traffickers the honourable of the earth " (Isa. xxiii. 2-8).

The exact circumstances under which these peaceful relations were disturbed, and hostile action taken
by Assyria against the most powerful of her Phœnician feudatories, have not come down to us in any
detail. There is reason, however, to suspect that the
primary cause of the disagreement was the ambition
of the Assyrian monarchs, and their determination to
curtail the semi-independence which they had hitherto
allowed their Western Asiatic feudatories, and to in-
corporate them absolutely into their empire. Assyria
gradually advanced her dominion by the same means
as Rome. She began with persuading or compelling
the states upon her borders to accept a semi-subject
position—one under which they paid her tribute
and helped her in her wars, but retained their own
monarchs, their own laws, and their entire internal
administration. She then, after a while, proceeded to
draw the bonds closer, to deprive the subject races of
their monarchs, and appoint Assyrian governors to rule
them instead, abolishing all distinctions between their

fresh subjects and their ancient ones, and thus fully incorporating the new provinces into the empire. A new zone of semi-independent states was then created, to be absorbed in their turn when the fitting time seemed to have arrived. The absorption of Northern Syria appears to have been commenced by Tiglath-pileser, who "added to the boundaries of Assyria" the whole of the Cœle-Syrian valley from Amanus in the north to the borders of Samaria on the south, annexing (as he tells us) at a single stroke "nineteen districts," and "appointing his generals as governors over them." Among the cities absorbed at this period we find the names of Zimirra (Simyra) and Arqa, both of which appear to have been Phœnician. The more important towns were for the time spared; but only the wilfully blind could fail to see that the evil day was but deferred a little, and that the best that was to be expected was a short respite.

Under these circumstances Phœnicia seems to have braced itself for an effort. The king of Tyre at the time was a certain Luliya, or Elulæus (as the Greeks called him), who had succeeded a Hiram about B.C. 737. Having drawn into a league with him the cities of Sidon, Akko, and Palæ-tyrus, perhaps those also of Gebal and Arvad, and thus united under his sway almost the whole of Phœnicia, he further made himself master of Cyprus, which he taxed with having revolted from him, probably because it had submitted to Assyria. At any rate Assyria took umbrage at the movement, and resolved to punish it, and at the same time to establish over Phœnicia that complete mastery, which she had not as yet enjoyed, by a great military

expedition. Shalmaneser IV., who had succeeded
Tiglath-pileser II., levied a vast host, ab. B.C. 725, and
marched with it into Phœnicia, which he overran
from one end to the other. He could make no impression, however, upon the Island Tyre, since he was
destitute of a navy, and was therefore forced to conclude peace, and retire without having effected much
by his expedition.

Foiled in war, he had recourse to diplomacy. The
Phœnician continental towns could be besieged by the
Assyrian armies, their walls destroyed by mines and
battering-rams, their streets invaded, and their inhabitants, unless they fled by sea, put to the sword. Short
of this, their territories could be ravaged, their crops
destroyed, their trees cut down, and their interests
injured in a hundred ways. Shalmaneser, in his
recent campaign, had doubtless impressed these lessons
on the cities generally. He now took advantage of
the fear which he had inspired, to draw over to his
side such of the cities as had suffered most, or such
as had any jealousy of the leadership of Tyre, and
might be expected, at a pinch, to desert her. His
representations had weight with Sidon, Akko, and
even with Palæ-tyrus. These cities and several others,
moved probably by various motives, determined to
detach themselves from Tyre, and to range themselves
on the side of Assyria. A second campaign followed,
under changed conditions. The Phœnician renegade
cities engaged to supply Shalmaneser with a navy;
and a fleet was collected and equipped, which consisted of sixty ships, and was manned by a combination of Phœnicians with Assyrians. Shalmaneser

occupied the Tyrian mainland with his host; the allied fleet put to sea, and advanced against the Island Tyre. Either the Tyrians despised their assailants, and thought a small squadron sufficient to defeat them ; or they were taken unawares, and had but a few ships in their home waters. They met the sixty vessels of the enemy with a squadron of twelve, and fearlessly engaged in a sea-fight against such odds as are almost unexampled. Yet they were successful. They charged the opposing fleet, completely dispersed it, and took five hundred prisoners. " On account of this," says the historian, and we may well believe him, " great honour accrued to all those who dwelt in Tyre." [1] The Assyrian king despaired of any immediate success, and returned to his own country, merely leaving behind him a certain number of his troops, who were instructed to cut off the Tyrians from the supplies of water, which they drew from the mainland, by occupying the embouchure of the Leontes, and the aqueducts which conveyed the waters of a famous spring—the Ras-el-Ain—to the part of the shore which was directly opposite the Island city. But Tyre, although distressed, was not intimidated. For five years the inhabitants drank only such brackish liquid as they could obtain from wells dug in the soil of their own island, eked out no doubt by the rainwater, which they carefully collected into cisterns. At the end of the five years, the attempt to coerce Tyre was relinquished, troubles having broken out in Assyria Proper, and later on in Babylonia, which taxed all the energies of the Assyrian monarchs.

[1] Menand. Ephes. ap. Joseph., " Ant. Jud." ix. 13, § 2.

It appears by the cuneiform inscriptions, that after the failure of this attempt to crush the power of Elulæus, he remained unmolested by the Assyrians for the space of nearly twenty years (B.C. 720-701). He even recovered his authority over Sidon, and held the whole tract between the Bostrenus and Mount Carmel, including the towns of Sidon the Greater, and Sidon the Less, Sarepta, Hosah, Ecdippa, and Akko, all of them strong positions and places of considerable importance. Sargon, who mounted the Assyrian throne in B.C. 722, did not care to war with him, though he made frequent expeditions into Southern Syria and Palestine, crushed the kingdom of Samaria, overran Philistia, took Ashdod and Gimzo, forced Judæa, Moab, and Edom to become his tributaries, and even carried his arms to the confines of Egypt. Sennacherib, however, Sargon's son and successor, shortly after his accession, determined to pursue a different line of policy from his father, and was scarcely well settled upon the throne before he declared war against the Tyrian, or (as he calls him) the Sidonian king, and directed the full force of the Assyrian arms against his territory. Elulæus himself retreated before the attack, despairing of successful resistance, and, embarking on board a ship, fled hastily to Cyprus. Sennacherib pressed on, and took the cities one after another with little difficulty, the inhabitants being dispirited by their king's desertion. He did not, however, venture to absorb the territory into the Assyrian dominions, or to appoint an Assyrian governor over it, but was content to place upon the throne a native monarch of his choice, and to fix afresh—probably to increase—the annual tribute which the principality was required to pay. The name of the king appointed to succeed Elulæus was Tubaal, or Tubal; there is reason to believe that he proved a faithful vassal of his foreign suzerain.

Nothing more is heard of Phœnicia in the Assyrian annals, until the accession of Esarhaddon to the ancient throne of the Ninevite kings. Esarhaddon became king of Assyria in B.C. 681. During the troubles that had followed his father's violent death, the king of Sidon, Abdi-Milkut, who had perhaps succeeded Tubal, having formed an alliance with a monarch named Sanduarri, who held the adjacent parts of Lebanon, revolted from his allegiance to Assyria, and declared himself independent. Sanduarri followed his example; and the first act of the Ninevite monarch, after settling himself on his father's throne, was to proceed against these two rebels, and to make an example of them. His attack so alarmed Abdi-Milkut, that, quitting the continent, he endeavoured to reach one of the islands off the coast, possibly the island of Cyprus, leaving his continental dominions to the tender mercies of the enemy. Esarhaddon ravaged and wasted them unrelentingly. He " swept away," he says, " the cities of the Sidonian land, removed its castles and its dwellings, and destroyed the place of its habitations," casting its buildings into the sea. He did not even allow Abdi-Milkut to escape him. Despatching vessels in pursuit of the flying monarch, he seems to have overtaken him on the open Mediterranean, and to have in this way made him a prisoner. " Abdi-Milkut, king of Sidon," he

says, " who from the face of my soldiers in the midst
of the sea had fled, like a fish from the midst of the
sea I caught him, and cut off his head." Sanduarri
was similarly treated. He fled to his " difficult
mountains "—the fastnesses of Lebanon—but was
pursued, taken, and, like Abdi-Milkut, beheaded.
The heads of the two rebel monarchs were " hung
round the necks of certain of their great men, and
" with musicians and singers," accompanied the Great
King's triumphant march homewards to his capital.

Such were the amenities of warfare at the period of
the highest Assyrian civilization. The kings of the
subject races were liable, not merely to deposition, but
to death ; and their corpses were treated with the
greatest indignity. Woe to the subject prince, who
thought he saw an opportunity of recovering his
independence if he happened to miscalculate, and to
head a rebellion which was not crowned with success!
In such a case, the reproach could no longer be made,
that " for the king's offence the people bled "—
monarchs paid the penalty of their shortsightedness,
or their over-sanguine temperament, in their own
persons. In the same spirit as that in which Joshua
slew the five kings of Jerusalem, Hebron, Jarmuth,
Lachish, and Eglon (Josh. x. 22–26), and in which
the Philistines hung the bodies of Saul and his
son, Jonathan, on the wall of Beth-shan (1 Sam.
xxxi. 8–12), the great Assyrian monarchs of the
seventh century put to death by beheading every
hostile king who could be accounted a rebel, and
exposed their bodies after death to scorn and con-
tumely.

Having slain Abdi-Milkut, Esarhaddon appears to have placed upon the throne of Southern Phœnicia a monarch named Baal, who is called "king of Tyre." Baal was at first in high favour with his Assyrian suzerain. He exerted himself to collect a fleet which should be at Esarhaddon's disposal ; and, in return, Esarhaddon, increased the extent of his dominions, assigning to him the city of Gebal, which had hitherto formed a separate monarchy, the entire district of Lebanon, and the coast tract beyond Carmel, in the direction of Philistia, as far as Dor. But Baal ill repaid his suzerain's confidence and benefits. When war was impending between Assyria under Esarhaddon, and Egypt under Tirhakah, he made overtures to the latter, accepted his suzerainty, and placed Tyre under his protection. Justly provoked by this rebellion, Esarhaddon, on his way to Egypt, in or about the year B.C. 672, made an expedition against the Tyrian monarch. Baal, it would seem, followed the example set by Elulæus, and threw himself into his island city, where he shut himself up, defying his adversary. Esarhaddon could then only act as Shalmaneser had acted. He built fortresses over against the Island Tyre, upon the mainland, and from them straitened the city for provisions and water. Tyre, however, is not said to have submitted. The Egyptian war required Esarhaddon's presence, and he hastened forward, leaving his less formidable enemy unsubdued. Baal appears to have maintained the position of an Egyptian feudatory until B.C. 668, the year of Esarhaddon's death, and of Asshurbanipal's succession.

Asshurbanipal, in his first year, as he was on his way to invade Egypt, received the submission of Baal, who probably found himself unable to resist longer the annoyance of the Assyrian occupation of the Tyrian territory upon the mainland. With Baal twenty-one other kings, including those of Judah, Edom, Moab, Gaza, Askelon, Ekron, Gebal, Arvad, and Cyprus, came into the presence of the Great King, and " kissed his feet." Asshurbanipal then proceeded into Egypt, completely defeated Tirhakah, and established his authority over the whole country. Revolt however followed, and a second Egyptian war rapidly succeeded the first, terminating in the same way, with the entire subjection of Egypt to the Assyrian yoke. It is probable that Baal mixed himself up with these transactions, and so incurred afresh the hostility of Assyria. In B.C. 664, a year or two after the close of Asshurbanipal's second war with Egypt, a great expedition was led by the Assyrian monarch against Tyre. "Against Baal," he says, " king of Tyre, dwelling in the midst of the sea, I went, because my royal will he disregarded, and did not hearken unto the words of my lips. Towers round about him I raised, and over his people I strengthened the watch. On land and sea his forts I took; his going out I stopped. Brackish water and sea water, to preserve their lives, their mouths drank. With a strong blockade, which removed not, I besieged them ; their spirits I humbled and caused to melt away ; to my yoke I made them submissive. The daughter proceeding from his body, and the daughters of his brothers, for concubines he brought to my presence.

Yahu-melek, his son, the glory of the country, who was of unsurpassed renown, at once he sent forward to make obeisance to me. His daughter and the daughters of his brothers, with their great dowries, I received. Favour I granted him ; and the son proceeding from his body I restored and gave him."

About the same time, another Phœnician city also was a thorn in the side of Assyria. Arvad, like Tyre, was a double city, partly built on the mainland, partly on a small island opposite. Assyria had still a difficulty in obtaining a naval force ; and, if she succeeded in raising one by forced contributions from the continental towns, could not trust it vigorously to exert itself. The sympathies of the Sidonians, Gebalites, &c., were with their own countrymen, and they neither enforced a blockade with any zeal, nor willingly engaged in a sea fight. Thus the *island* Tyre, and the *island* Arvad, were to the Assyrians almost unconquerable, and frequently defied their utmost efforts. Yakinlu, king of Arvad, shook off the Assyrian yoke about the same time as Baal, king of Tyre, perhaps in combination with him, and, trusting to his sea-girt fortress, declared himself independent. However, when Baal made his submission he submitted also, sent his tribute to Nineveh, and offered his daughter to Asshurbanipal as a secondary wife. The Assyrian monarch professed himself satisfied ; but within a short time he adopted a bolder course, deprived Yakinlu of his crown, and set up in his place his eldest son, Azibaal. Somewhat later, we find Akko (Acre) punished for a rebellion, the city ruined, and the male inhabitants forced into the Assyrian military service.

Thus, in the later period of the Assyrian dominion, the Phœnician cities must be regarded as dissatisfied with their position, and as taking every opportunity that seemed to offer itself, to shake themselves free from the yoke whereto they had submitted at first without much reluctance, and to re-assert independence. The Assyrians must have made their yoke intolerably grievous for the standard of rebellion to have been so often raised, and such desperate struggles adventured on, with so small an expectation of success. The hostile powers were too unequally matched. Even if all Phœnicia had been formed into a permanent confederacy, and had on all occasions acted together, the inferiority in numbers and resources would have been too marked, and the contest would, in all probability, have terminated like that between Lydia and the Ionian cities of the coast. As it was, there seems never to have been even a temporary league of all the states ; and generally each state was isolated, revolted singly, warred singly with its mighty adversary, and was crushed singly, without receiving any help from its sister communities or indeed from any quarter. The ethnic tie was too weak, the jealousies and the diversity of interests among the several states too great, to allow of their making common cause against the aggressor ; and the natural result followed that each in its turn succumbed. Though the last shadow of Phœnician independence was not wholly swept away by Asshurbanipal, Tyre, Arvad, and perhaps Gebal, being still allowed to retain their native kings, yet the substance was undoubtedly lost. The Phœnician kings, in the language of their conqueror, "submitted to perform the service " of the Assyrian monarchs, and " executed their pleasure."

The tribute which Assyria exacted from the Phœnician towns was partly a tribute in money, partly a tribute in kind. A definite sum was fixed in gold, silver, and copper, which each city had annually to pay, and which was no doubt proportioned to its resources ; but besides this, there was a certain indefinite demand for the precious products of the city and its neighbourhood, which must have been often a severer tax upon the inhabitants than the money payment. We find Arvad on one occasion compelled to furnish green paint and black paint, together with a number of the birds and fishes of the country, over and above the tribute in gold which had been imposed on it. Other cities contributed skins of buffaloes, horns of buffaloes, clothing of wool and linen, instruments and weapons, violet wool, purple wool, timber, feathers of various hues, wood for weapons, chariots and riding horses, asses trained to the yoke, lead, iron, antimony, and lapis lazuli. The severest and most detested exaction was that of royal maidens, daughters or other near relations of the kings, who were required to proceed to Nineveh, and enter the seraglio of the Great Monarch. With each such person was to be sent a dowry proportioned to her rank, and worthy of the acceptance of the " Lord of Asia."

The kings had also, from time to time, to appear

before their suzerain, either at his capital, or at some provincial town, where he had taken up his temporary abode, and, having been ushered into his presence, to prostrate themselves at his footstool, and "kiss his feet." Twenty-two kings on one occasion kissed the feet of Asshurbanipal.[1] Among others were Baal, king of Tyre, a king of Gebal, and a king of Arvad. On another occasion, eight kings, including Tubal of Sidon, Abdilihit of Arvad, and Urumelek of Gebal, kissed the feet of Sennacherib. Although this form of paying homage would not be so offensive in the eyes of Orientals as it was in those of the Greeks, who refused absolutely to conform themselves to it, yet we cannot doubt that it was disliked, and constituted a standing grievance.

The bitterest grievances, however, fell, not upon the kings, but upon the people. Assyrian armies were continually on the march, backwards and forwards, upon every line of route through Syria, harassing the inhabitants by their requisitions, their coarse speech, and their rough usage. The tax-gatherers of a foreign master are almost sure to exact more than their due. Phœnician cities had often to furnish ships for expeditions in which they had no interest or even for such as were detrimental to them. Sometimes quotas of troops were required from them to serve in the Assyrian armies. The Assyrian monarchs claimed a general right of cutting timber in the Phœnician mountains. When exaction and ill-usage drove a city to the dire extremity of revolt, the people again were the main sufferers. On them fell

[1] See above, p. 143.

the chief hardships of the siege—scant provisions, want of water, disturbed rest, suspension of industrial employments.   When at last surrender was made, it was they who principally paid the penalty.   Either their burden of taxation was increased, or else they were torn from their homes, and either deported to a distant land, or enrolled permanently in the Assyrian military service.   Their wives and daughters were made prisoners, dishonoured, and carried off into slavery.   Submission to Assyria was, at the best, a hard service ; but it was preferable to the lot of those who first submitted and then rebelled.   " The people of Akko," says Asshurbanipal, " who were unsubmissive, I destroyed.   Their bodies in the dust I threw down ; the whole of the city I *quieted*.   As for the remnant, I brought them to Assyria, and attached them to the ranks of my numerous army, spreading them over the whole."   And a punishment no less severe overtook the other cities that, from time to time, revolted.   Compassion was not an Assyrian weakness.

X.

PHŒNICIA'S RECOVERY OF INDEPENDENCE — HER COMMERCE AT THIS PERIOD.

FROM about the middle of the seventh century B.C., the power of Assyria began to decline. The Median monarchy became centralized under Cyaxares about B.C. 640, and assumed an aggressive attitude on Assyria's eastern frontier. Great hordes of barbarians, about the same time, pressed into Western Asia from the north, and carried fire and sword over Asia Minor, Media, Assyria, and a large part of Syria. The bonds which united the provinces to the central government at Nineveh became gradually relaxed under these circumstances, and the more distant ones were tempted to detach themselves altogether from the evidently moribund empire. The time at which the Phœnician cities took the decisive step, cannot be fixed with exactness; but it was probably between B.C. 640 and B.C. 630. The last Phœnician governor in the list of Assyrian eponyms belongs, apparently, to the year B.C. 637. In B.C. 633, according to Herodotus, Nineveh was actually besieged by Cyaxares, and about the same time the terrible ravages of the barbarian hordes began. It is difficult to suppose that the cities of the Syrian coast would preserve their allegiance to a power which was quite unable to afford them the slightest protection, when they were threatened severally by wandering bands of Scyths and Tartars —the armies of Gog and Magog (Ezek. xxxviii. 2–7) —who acknowledged no superior but their own chiefs, and roamed throughout all Syria, living by plunder and rapine. The instinct of self-defence must have required them to arm against this dangerous foe, and to look to themselves for the protection which they were not likely to obtain from any other quarter. Habits of independent action would be thus established : and it could not be long before the formal submitted itself to the actual, and the independence, asserted in deed, was claimed also, and declared by document or speech. On the whole, it is most probable that Phœnician independence was proclaimed about B.C. 630, and that it continued for forty-five years—from B.C. 630 to B.C. 585.

The recovery of freedom was accompanied by a great increase of prosperity ; and especially commerce received an impulse, which was felt to the furthest limits of the known world. Tyre established for herself an ascendency over the other cities, and shortly rose to the highest point of her greatness. The description which is given of her by the prophet Ezekiel about this time has been felt by all the historians of Phœnicia to be a document of priceless value, and to form the basis on which all attempts to realize the true condition of things at this period must rest. It is, therefore, here presented to the reader entire, according to the most recent version :—

"And thou, Son of man, take up a lamentation for Tyre, and say unto
    her,
O thou that dwellest at the entry of the sea,
Which art the merchant of the peoples unto many isles,
Thus saith the Lord God, Thou, O Tyre, hast said, I am perfect in
    beauty.
Thy borders are in the heart of the sea ;
Thy builders have perfected thy beauty.
They have made all thy planks of fir trees from Senir ;
They have taken cedars from Lebanon to make a mast for thee ;
Of the oaks of Bashan have they made thine oars ;
They have made thy benches of ivory,
Inlaid in boxwood, from the isles of Kittim.
Of fine linen with broidered work from Egypt was thy sail,
That it might be to thee for an ensign ;
Blue and purple from the isles of Elishah was thy awning.
The inhabitants of Zidon and of Arvad were thy rowers ;
Thy wise men, O Tyre, were in thee—they were thy pilots.
The ancients of Gebal, and their wise men, were thy calkers ;
All the ships of the sea, with their mariners, were in thee,
That they might occupy thy merchandise.
Persia, and Lud, and Phut were in thine army, thy men of war ;
They hanged the shield and helmet in thee :
They set forth thy comeliness.
The men of Arvad, with thine army, were upon thy walls round
    about :
And the Gammadim were in thy towers ;
They hanged their shields upon thy walls round about ;
They have brought to perfection thy beauty.
Tarshish was thy merchant by reason of the multitude of all kinds
    of riches ;
With silver, iron, tin, and lead they traded for thy wares.
Javan, Tubal, and Meshech, they were thy traffickers ;
They traded the persons of men, and vessels of brass, for thy mer-
    chandise.
They of the house of Togarmah traded for thy wares
With horses, and war-horses, and mules.
The men of Dedan were thy traffickers ; many isles were the mart
    of thy hands,
They brought thee in exchange horns of ivory and ebony.
Syria was thy merchant by reason of the multitude of thy handi-
    works :

They traded for thy wares with emeralds, purple, and broidereo
  work,
And with fine linen, and coral, and rubies.
Judah, and the land of Israel, they were thy traffickers ;
They traded for thy merchandise wheat of Minnith,
And Pannag, and honey, and oil, and balm.
Damascus was thy merchant for the multitude of thy handiworks ;
By reason of the multitude of all kinds of riches ;
With the wine of Helbon, and white wool.
Vedan (?) and Javan traded with yarn for thy wares ;
Bright iron, cassia, and calamus were among thy merchandise.
Dedan was thy trafficker in precious cloths for riding.
Arabia, and all the princes of Kedar, they were the merchants of thy
  hand,
In lambs, and rams, and goats, in these were they thy merchants.
The traffickers of Sheba and Raamah, they were thy traffickers ;
They traded for thy wares with chief of all spices,
And with all manner of precious stones, and gold.
Haran, and Canneh, and Eden, the traffickers of Sheba,
Asshur, and Chilmad, were thy traffickers.
They were thy traffickers in choice wares,
In wrappings of blue and broidered work, and in chests of rich
  apparel,
Bound with cords, and made of cedar, among thy merchandise.
The ships of Tarshish were thy caravans for thy merchandise ;
And thou wast replenished, and made very glorious, in the heart of
  the sea.
Thy rowers have brought thee into great waters ;
The east wind hath broken thee in the heart of the sea.
Thy riches, and thy wares, thy merchandise, thy mariners, and thy
  pilots,
Thy calkers, and the occupiers of thy merchandise,
With all the men of war, that are in thee,
With all thy company which is in the midst of thee,
Shall fall into the heart of the seas in the day of thy ruin.
At the sound of thy pilots' cry the suburbs shall shake ;
And all that handle the oar, the mariners, and all the pilots of the
  sea,
They shall come down from their ships, they shall stand upon the
  land,
And shall cause their voice to be heard over thee, and shall cry
  bitterly,

And shall cast up dust upon their heads, and wallow in the ashes ;
And they shall make themselves bald for thee, and gird them with
  sackcloth,
And they shall weep for thee in bitterness of soul with bitter mourn-
  ing.
And in their wailing they shall take up a lamentation for thee,
And lament over thee saying, Who is there like Tyre,
Like her that is brought to silence in the midst of the sea?
When thy wares went forth out of the seas, thou filledst many
  peoples ;
Thou didst enrich the kings of the earth with thy merchandise and
  thy riches.
In the time that thou wast broken by the seas in the depths of the
  waters,
Thy merchandise and all thy company did fall in the midst of thee.
All the inhabitants of the isles are astonished at thee,
And their kings are sore afraid, they are troubled in their counte-
  nance.
The merchants that are among the peoples, hiss at thee :
Thou art become a terror, and thou shalt never be any more."

                                        (Ezek. xxvii.)

Two points of this description belong to the period
whereto our inquiries have conducted us—viz., the
great prosperity of Tyre at this time, and the variety
and extent of her commercial relations. Tyre was
"the merchant of the peoples unto many isles"—there
was "none like her"—"when her wares went forth,
she filled many peoples ; she enriched the kings of
the earth with the multitude of her riches and her
merchandise." She was "perfect in beauty"—her
"builders had brought to perfection her beauty." The
rest of Phœnicia was voluntarily subject to her. The
rowers who manned her ships were, in large measure,
" the inhabitants of Sidon and Arvad ;" the "ancients
of Gebal, and the men best esteemed among her shipbuilders" were "her caulkers." Her walls were

guarded, not only by her own troops, but by those of the Arvadites and Gammadim, the latter probably the people of a town otherwise unknown to us. Senir, or Hermon, was ransacked to furnish planks for the hulls of her ships ; the tallest of the cedars of Lebanon were felled to make masts for them. The oaks of distant Bashan formed the material which she used for oars ; and the sails, which her mariners spread to the winds, were costly works manufactured in Egypt and in the Grecian islands. The choicest of her ships were fitted up with benches of "ivory inlaid with boxwood," the product of the "isles of Chittim." Altogether, she was at this time probably the fairest city of the whole earth, the Venice of the ancient world, wealthy, picturesque, influential, but sunk in luxury.

And the extent of her commerce was extraordinary. On the one side, as the exporting power of Asia, she had an enormous land traffic. From Judah and Israel she drew "wheat of Minnith, and Pannag"—perhaps millet—"and honey, and oil, and balm." From Damascus she derived the "wine of Helbon," which in after times was produced for the sole use of the Persian kings, and "white wool," the fleeces of the sheep that grazed the lands bordering the desert of Arabia. From the rest of Syria she obtained "emeralds," or, perhaps, rather "carbuncles," and "purple" (the dye of the cochineal insect ?) and "fine linen, and corals, and rubies." Arabia enriched her marts with her precious spices, "cassia, and calamus" (sweet cane), and no doubt with frankincense and other gums, and also with the bright iron sword-blades for the manufacture of which Yemen was famous, with gold and precious stones and with costly cloths for chariots. Kedar supplied her with the wool of lambs, and rams, and goats. From Mesopotamia, Assyria, and Babylonia, she drew " blue clothes and broidered work," or " wrappings of blue and broidered work "—carpets probably, and hangings, and cloaks, and garments of various kinds, esteemed for their rich colours and for the excellence of their manufacture. Armenia sent her mules and horses, which in some instances were trained for war. The nations of Asia Minor, Tubal, and Meshech, or the Tibareni and the Moschi, furnished her with vessels of bronze, and with an exhaustless supply of valuable slaves. In some cases she drew to herself by her land traffic products, which those who supplied her had probably imported by sea, *e.g.*, the ivory and the ebony, which she derived from the Dedanites, who must have got them either from Ethiopia or from India.

For the secure and continuous supply of these various commodities, she must have organized a system of caravans on the most extensive scale. Land commerce in the East has never outgrown the caravan stage. From the time when the " company of Ishmaelites came from Gilead with their camels, bearing spicery and balm, and myrrh, going to carry it down to Egypt " (Gen. xxxvii. 25) to the present age, the trade of the East has been conducted in this way for security's sake. Public conveyances do not exist ; and valuable merchandise would, as a matter of course, become the prey of robbers, unless escorted by a caravan, numerous enough and well-armed enough to bid

defiance to the robber tribes which infest almost all
Asia. If Tyre communicated with Northern Asia
Minor, with Armenia, with Mesopotamia, with
Assyria, with Babylonia, with the shores of the Persian Gulf, and with Central and Southern Arabia, and
obtained from these various quarters a perpetual
supply of the commodities which she needed for her
home consumption, or for her export traffic with her
customers, she could only have done so on the caravan
system ; and for a trade so extensive, so varied, in
some cases so remote, the system must have been
established on a scale such as has scarcely existed at
any other period. Numerous bodies of armed merchants must have started from Tyre at fixed seasons
of the year, carrying with them provisions, and in
some instances water, for many months, and provided
with large sums of money, or with commodities which
were certain to be in demand, and must have plunged
into the heart of the Asiatic continent, without reliable
maps, or anything but a vague knowledge of their
road, intending to make their way into remote and
inhospitable regions for commercial purposes, and to
return after a long absence with a goodly supply of
such merchandise as they knew that Tyre needed.
Roads, in the proper sense of the word, did not exist.
They pursued traditional routes, along valleys or
river courses, directed by native guides, who would
sometimes voluntarily mislead them ; they crossed
mountains by imperfectly known passes ; they
affronted perils and dangers of a thousand kinds ; but
they bore all, and overcame all by the force of an
indomitable will, by patience, and by the gradual

establishment of friendly relations with those whose
countries they visited. It is the glory of commerce
that it confers benefits on all those engaged in it, on
the consumer, on the producer, on the merchant who
acts as intermediary, and even on the inhabitants of
the regions, through which the line of traffic passes.
In course of time a welcome awaited the Phœnician
caravan along its entire route, some crumbs of
advantage falling by the way, wherever the travellers
made a halt. Routes became beaten ; natural
obstacles were removed, or skilfully avoided ; the
travelling became, comparatively speaking, easy ; and
the profits of trade were enhanced. Through
mountainous regions actual roads may have been
made in some places ; the narrower rivers may have
been spanned by stone arches or suspension bridges
of tough vegetable fibres and ropes, while on the
broader ones provision may have been made for the
passage of travellers by bridges of boats.

Imagine the arrival of a Tyrian caravan at Babylon. The travellers have been on the march for three
or four months. They have either toiled up the long
Cœle-Syrian valley, crossed the chalky downs about
Aleppo, and then proceeded down the course of the
Euphrates from Balis, past Tiphsach and Sirki (Cir-
cesium) and Anat and Hit, to the low flat alluvium ;
or they have taken the shorter, but far more difficult,
route, by Damascus and Tadmor, to the middle
Euphrates about Anat, and thence along the river
course, as by the former line of travel. They have
arrived weary, dusty, travel-stained. Their tents are
pitched outside the town, not far from the banks of

the river, or of a water-course derived from it, under the pleasant shadow of a grove of palms, near the northern gate of the great city. The tall necks of their camels are seen from a distance by the keen-eyed watchers of the gate-towers, and reported by them to the civic authorities, whence the secret soon oozes out and creates a bustle in the town. All are anxious to obtain some object of their desire from the long expected traders ; but especially anxious are the great storekeepers and shopkeepers, who look to the occasion for the replenishing of their stock-in-trade for the next six months, or, it may be, even for the next year. But the weary travellers must have a night's rest ere they can be ready to open their market, must unload their camels and their mules, dispose their bales of goods as seems most convenient, and prepare themselves for the fatigues of commercial dealing by a light supper and a sound sleep ensuing thereupon. How glad are the camels to have the loads removed from their galled backs, to repose their weary limbs upon the green grass or the yellow sand, and to lay their tired necks along the ground ! Not a moan is heard, scarcely a grunt, unless it be one of satisfaction. The mules, and camels, and the horses of the wealthier sort, enjoy themselves equally. We hear the tinkling of their bells, as they shake themselves, freed from all their trappings but the head-stall. Some are picketed about where the turf is richest, others contentedly munch the barley that has been placed before them in portable mangers, to reward them for the toils that they have gone through. Many prefer sleep to eating, and, leaving their food untouched,

stretch themselves upon the sward. Night falls—the
stars come out—the traders sleep in their tents, with a
stone or a bale of goods for their pillow—a profound
hush sinks upon the camp, except for the occasional
squeal of a skittish pair of mules, which have exchanged bites under cover of the darkness.

The camp, however, wakes up with the first gleam
of dawn in the eastern sky. Each man busily sets
about his proper work. Mules and horses are groomed
and are arranged in rows, with their mangers in front,
and their pack-saddles and trappings near at hand.
Bales of goods are opened, and a display made of a
portion of their contents. Meantime, the town gates
have been unclosed, and in holiday apparel a gay
crowd streams forth from them. Foremost comes the
loafers, hoping to earn an honest penny by "lending a
hand," or to make a dishonest one by filching some
unguarded article. Then follow the ordinary customers
and the petty traders whose arrangements have not
been made beforehand. The last to appear are the
agents of the great merchants, whose correspondents
at Tyre have made them consignments of goods and
sent the goods by the caravan to their destination ;
these clamour for invoices and bills of lading. But
the noisiest and the most pressing are the petty
traders and the mere chance customers, who have a
special need to supply, or covet a good bargain. With
them what a chaffering there is ! What a screaming
and apparent quarrelling ! One buyer wants a purple
robe for half its value, another a Damascene blade for
next to nothing, a third a Greek statuette for half a
shekel of silver. The seller asks at least four times

the sum that he intends to take ; the buyer exclaims, swears perhaps by the beard of his grandfather that he will not give a farthing more than he has offered ; then relents, and doubles his bid ; the seller comes down a little, but they are still " miles apart," so to speak ; it takes an hour of talking, swearing, screaming, raving, before the *juste milieu* is hit off, an agreement come to, and buyer and seller alike made happy by a conviction on the part of each that he has overreached the other.

Or let the goal of the caravan have been the city of Van, or of Urumiyeh, in Armenia. Hither the march has been through rugged tracts of scantily cultivated mountain-land, where "the steep rocks stood up," as the Assyrian writers say, "like metal posts," impracticable for carts or chariots, and wholly unsuitable for the camel. The goods have had to be carried on the backs of men, or on those of mules and asses. The rigours of a cold climate have had to be endured, and the thin silks and muslins worn on the Syrian shore to be exchanged for warm dresses of fur or leather. It has been necessary to cross snowy ridges by paths only fit for the tread of the wild goat, to drink the water of glacier torrents, and to make the unpleasant acquaintance of frost bite. But the extreme elevations are now past, and the merchants, with such of their goods as have not been lost in the passage of mountain streams, or by the slipping of mules over precipices, have descended safely into the upland plain, in which the Armenian capital, be it Van or be it Urumiyeh, is placed. Again tents are pitched, or huts are hastily erected, in the immediate vicinity of the town ; goods are unpacked and a brisk trade is carried on between the half-savage natives and the highly civilized strangers. The currency of the country is iron or copper ; silver and gold are rare, and are used only for drinking-cups, personal ornaments, and the images of the deities. But Armenia has products which enable it to pay its way, and indulge its taste for Phœnician conveniences and Phœnician luxuries. Its horses and its mules are of high repute. Though not large they are strong and sure-footed, equal to the bearing of heavy burdens, and accustomed to traverse the most difficult mountain-paths. The caravan has not long arrived before the dealers from the country districts bring in drove after drove of serviceable beasts, praise their points, make them go through their paces, and are ready to part with them for a consideration. The chaffering of horse fairs is proverbial. If at civilized and courtly Babylon there was din and confusion during the heat of the bargaining, what must have been the noise and tumult when the dealers were the rough boors of the Armenian highlands ? Whips cracking, horses neighing, mules squeaking, and men vociferating ! The result would be the acquisition by the traders of numerous long strings of horses and mules, which they would have to convey across the narrow passes, the lofty uplands, and the low plains at their base, to the marts in Cœle-Syria or to their own coast tract.

The Armenian caravans had also a further source of profit. Tubal and Meshech, the northern neighbours of Armenia, traded with Phœnicia "in the persons of men" (Ezek. xxvii. 13) ; and Armenia must, almost necessarily, have been the intermediary in this traffic. Phœnicia had from a remote period been one of the most active agents in the extension of slavery and the slave trade by her practice of systematic kidnapping on a large scale. But this practice was found subversive of legitimate commerce, since it highly provoked every people that was made the victim of it. After a time it was laid aside, and legitimate purchase in slave marts took its place. Unredeemed prisoners of war were almost universally reduced to the slave condition in antiquity ; and many nations habitually sold such captives. Some barbarous peoples were also in the habit of selling their own children into slavery. Usury laws in many places led to the enslavement, and the sale of debtors. Altogether, there was a large slave supply ; but the demand seems to have been equal to it. Phœnicia set herself to be a carrying agent in this traffic. Wherever slaves were to be got, whether from Egypt, or from Philistia, or from Meshech and Tubal, or from Thrace, or from Greece or from Mid Africa, she procured them. Her merchants bought up in every market the human commodity, which was abundantly offered for sale, and conveyed it to the regions where it was most appreciated, making a large profit on such transactions. Phœnician wealth was, no doubt, very largely derived from the traffic in slaves, and the caravans, probably did not often return from any quarter without bringing with them a slave contingent.

We must, however, always remember that the land commerce of Tyre was as nothing, compared to her sea commerce. By sea she obtained from Egypt "fine

linen with broidered work" (Ezek. xxvii. 7) ; together
with vast quantities of grain of various descriptions
(Isa. xxiii. 3). From Greece she derived blue and
purple fabrics (Ezek. xxvii. 7) ; bronzes and other
works of art ; together with a certain number of the
choicest slaves (ibid. 13). Cyprus seems to have supplied her with " benches of ivory inlaid in boxwood "
(ibid. 6). With Carthage she had always a most active
commerce. Carthage would pour into her lap the
varied spoil of Africa—skins, horns, strange animals,
leather exquisitely tanned and dyed of the most
brilliant hues, ivory, ebony, ostrich feathers, gorillas,
gold, guinea fowl. By her colonies in Southern Spain
she was supplied with abundance of silver, iron, tin,
and lead ; (ibid. 12), perhaps also with gold and copper.
The silver mines of Southern Spain were rich in the
extreme ; and the soil so abounded with the product,
that even the lead was to a large extent alloyed with
it, and the amalgam was known to the Greeks as a
peculiar metal, which they called *galena*. The iron
was of excellent quality, and when hardened into steel
produced sword blades of the finest temper, those of
Bilbilis being in Roman times as famous as in modern
those of Toledo and Bilboa. Tin abounded in the
Spanish streams, and also in places appeared on the
surface of the soil. It was sometimes black, being
found in the shape of the peroxide, but more usually
of a brilliant white colour. Whether Phœnician commerce in the seventh century B.C. went much further
afield than this, may perhaps be doubted. The
African continent outside the Straits of Gibraltar
seems certainly to have been relinquished to the
Carthaginians before this time : and so no doubt were

the Fortunate Islands and Madeira if they really ever
came within the range of the Phœnician mercantile
operations.   But there was one branch of their distant
sea-trade whereto they clung with extreme tenacity and
which, at a date long subsequent to the seventh century, they prevented even the Romans from sharing.
This was the trade for tin with the Scilly Islands and
the coast of Cornwall, already mentioned in an earlier
section, which was one of the main sources of the
Phœnician wealth, tin being found in a few places
only, and being largely required for the hardening of
copper into bronze by almost all the races inside the
Pillars of Hercules, with which the Phœnicians had
dealings.   Tyre, at the height of her greatness, sent
her ships year by year through the stormy Atlantic to
the British Islands, to fetch a commodity which has
largely flowed back to the country of its birth as an
ingredient of the precious bronzes that are to be seen
in English collections.

XI.

PHŒNICIA'S CONTEST WITH BABYLON.

PHŒNICIAN independence, established about B.C. 630, on the decline of Assyria, was first seriously menaced by Egypt. As Assyria sank in power, Egypt rose ; and even Psamatik I. had hopes of pushing his dominions beyond the bounds of Egypt into Syria, and perhaps dreamt of renewing the glories of the Thothmeses and Amenhoteps. But his Syrian expeditions, which were directed against Gaza and Ashdod, effected little ; and it remained for his son, Neco, to attempt conquests of a more important character. Apparently, Assyria " died hard ; " and from B.C. 630 to B.C. 610, or even later, Western Asia was in a state of trouble and disturbance, the grasp of Assyria upon it being relaxed, and that of Babylon not having been as yet firmly laid upon the *disjecta membra*. Under these circumstances there seemed an opportunity for Egypt to step in ; and in B.C. 609 or 608 Neco, the son of Psamatik I., having recently ascended the Egyptian throne, made an expedition into Syria with the object of re-attaching to Egypt the entire tract between the " Torrens Ægypti " and the Euphrates. At first success crowned his efforts ; Josiah, king of

Judah, who had ventured to oppose him, was defeated and slain at Megiddo ; Palestine was conquered, and placed under a tributary king (Jehoiakim) : Syria was overrun, and the Egyptian dominion established over the entire region extending northward from Egypt to Amanus, and eastward to the Euphrates and Carchemish. This tract remained under the government of Neco for three years (B.C. 608–605). Phœnicia must have submitted herself. She probably accepted a position similar to that which she had occupied in her first submission to Assyria, becoming dependent and tributary, but retaining her native kings, the administration of her own laws, and the municipal government of her towns.

This condition of things was, however, of very short duration. In B.C. 605 Nabopolassar, king of Babylon, having finally crushed the Assyrians, sent his son Nebuchadnezzar, at the head of a large army into Syria, with the object of recovering the tract, whereof Neco had made himself master, and of attaching to the Babylonian Empire all that portion of South-western Asia, which had, before her disasters began, acknowledged the dominion of Assyria. A great and decisive battle was fought near Carchemish between the Babylonians and the Egyptians in the spring of that year, in which the latter were completely defeated. The Egyptian army broke up and dispersed. Nebuchadnezzar made a triumphal progress through Syria, receiving everywhere the submission of the several states, and causing them to swear allegiance to Babylon. The Phœnician cities, it is expressly declared, were among those which submitted themselves; but here again we may understand, that they accepted that condition of qualified subjection, whereto they had been so long accustomed, and which under ordinary circumstances, was a necessity of their position. Babylon became suzerain over them, as Assyria had been for centuries; but their internal independence was guaranteed, their tribute fixed, and the monarch who made the submission left in possession of the throne.

Nebuchadnezzar was about to press on into Egypt for the purpose of further chastising Neco, when he received intelligence of his father's death, and felt that his presence was required at the capital. Sending, therefore, the heavier part of his forces, with his prisoners, including many Phœnicians, by the usual route, through Cœle-Syria and by way of Aleppo and Balis, to Babylon, he himself with a few light troops took the direct way across the desert, which occupied comparatively speaking a short time. He was fortunate enough to find his arrival waited for, and consequently ascended the throne without difficulty. The "Chief of the Chaldeans" had taken the direction of affairs in his absence, and had kept the throne vacant for him, so that he had not to dispute it with any pretenders.

Syria, however, and all the western part of the empire, had been left in a very unsatisfactory and unsettled condition. Phœnicia, Judæa, Edom, Moab, Ammon, were discontented and longed to resume the complete independence which they had enjoyed for a few years, while the struggle between Assyria and Babylon remained undetermined. Egypt was enraged at her defeat, and brooded sullenly over the idea of revenge. There can scarcely be a doubt that she fomented the dissatisfaction of the petty princes, and stirred them up to rebel against Babylon before her yoke should be firmly riveted upon them. The kings of Tyre, Sidon, and Judæa seem to have been among the first to listen to her suggestions. As early as B.C. 602—three years after his submission (2 Kings xxiv. 1)—Jehoiakim, king of Judah, revolted from Nebuchadnezzar, and proclaimed himself an independent monarch. Ithobalus (Eth-baal II.), king of Tyre, followed his example a few years later. Nebuchadnezzar appears to have been too busily engaged at home to be able at first to give much of his attention to these distant matters. He contented himself for some time with letting loose upon Jehoiakim the hostile tribes of the neighbourhood—"bands of the Syrians, and bands of the Moabites, and bands of the children of Ammon" (2 Kings xxiv. 2), who, assisted by a few "bands of the Chaldees," ravaged the Judæan territory at their pleasure. When, however, about B.C. 599, the revolt of Tyre was announced to him, he saw the danger of permitting the spirit of disaffection to spread further, and roused himself to a great effort. Summoning his allies, Medes and others, to his aid, he levied a vast army, consisting (we are told) of ten thousand war chariots, one hundred and twenty thousand cavalry, and one hundred thousand infantry, with which he marched into Syria, and laid siege at once to Tyre, Sidon, and Jerusalem. Sidon was probably the first to fall. The "princes of the north," *i.e.*, of Gebal, Arvad, and the neigh-

bourhood, came to her aid (Ezek. xxxii. 30); but
to no purpose. Sidon was taken by assault, a fearful
carnage occurring in her streets (ibid. xxxviii. 23);
and the northern princes, "all of them," together with
"all the Zidonians," went down with the slain, killed
in the *mêlée*. The siege of Tyre was then begun
(B.C. 598); but the city resisted vigorously, and Nebuchadnezzar, leaving the bulk of his army to invest it,
proceeded in person against Jerusalem, which submitted
to him. Jehoiakim was deposed, perhaps put to death,
and his son, Jehoiachin, a lad of eighteen, made king;
three months later, however, he too offended the Babylonian monarch, who carried him off to Babylon, and
made his uncle, Zedekiah, tributary monarch in his
place.

Meantime the siege of Tyre was pressed. It is
always to be remembered that the great Phœnician
capital was a double city, consisting of two towns,
locally distinct, but politically united, one on the
mainland, called in later times Palæ-tyrus, the other
on an island off the coast. Nebuchadnezzar's first
attack was, naturally, on the continental town. Against
this he "came up from the north, with horses and with
chariots, and with horsemen and companies, and much
people" (Ezek. xxvi. 7). He "made forts against
Tyre, and cast up mounts against her, and lifted up
the buckler against her. He set his battering-engines
against her walls, and with his axes he broke down
her towers. By reason of the abundance of his horses,
their dust covered her; her walls shook at the noise
of the horsemen, and of the waggons, and of the
chariots, when he entered into her gates, as men enter

into a city wherein is made a breach. With the hoofs of his horses he trod down all her streets ; he slew her people with the sword, and the pillars of her strength went down to the ground. He made spoil of her riches, and made prey of her merchandise ; he broke down her walls, and destroyed all her pleasant houses ; and her stones, and her timber, and her dust, he cast into the waters" (ibid. vers. 8–12). Manifestly, every mode of attack known at the time, every weapon of assault, was employed against the doomed city. Movable towers were brought up to her walls ; mounds were raised against them, and battering-rams emplaced upon the mounds, whence they were worked with deadly effect against the weaker upper defences. Archers plied their arrows unremittingly, each defended by a companion who "lifted up the buckler to protect him ; " axes were used to split open the gates, and destroy the foundations of the towers. The horsemen and charioteers waited for an effectual breach to be made, by which they could pour into the town. How long this siege of the continental Tyre lasted, we cannot say ; probably for a very considerable time, since it is more likely that "heads were made bald and shoulders peeled " (Ezek. xxix. 18) in the siege of the continental town than in the blockade of the island fortress. Jerusalem ultimately resisted the Babylonians for two years ; Samaria resisted the Assyrians for three. The mainland Tyre may have held out for four or five. At length, however, the besiegers worked their will ; a practicable breach was effected, and the Babylonian troops, exasperated by the long resistance offered them, poured headlong into the town. Horse, and foot, and even chariots occupied the streets, and the carnage was prolonged and terrible. We hear of no prisoners being made. A certain number of the defenders may have taken ship and escaped by sea, and others may have hid themselves till night, and then crept to the shelter of the neighbouring mountains ; but the greater part, of the males at any rate, fell in a massacre where no quarter was given, and perished with the city which they had striven, but striven in vain, to save from capture.

Still the island fortress survived, and could not even be attacked without much preparation and much difficulty. Unless the besiegers formed the conception, which was afterwards carried out by Alexander the Great, of attaching the island to the mainland by a mole, it was requisite that the attack should be made wholly by sea. All the methods of land warfare would have been inapplicable, and the second siege would have had to be commenced under conditions completely changed from those which had prevailed during the first. One writer only—a writer who lived nearly a thousand years after the event—states that Nebuchadnezzar anticipated Alexander, and that his attack on the Island Tyre was by means of a mole, from which his machines shook its walls.[1] But the universal silence of history on so important a point for a thousand years is an adverse argument that can scarcely be overcome ; and the existence of a broad and deep channel in Alexander's time is a strong proof that, up to that date, no mole had ever even

[1] Jerome, " Comment. in Ezek. xxvi. 7."

been attempted. For the conditions are such that if once the channel is filled up, it is scarcely possible that it should be re-opened. The currents on either side wash up, at different seasons of the year, so much mud and sand that, let once a nucleus of resistance be formed, and the channel necessarily silts up, the isthmus becoming continually higher and broader. The present broad tract connecting the original island with the shore is probably twice the width of that dam which Alexander constructed. And it continually grows with time. If Nebuchadnezzar had in B.C. 585 constructed a dam, Alexander in B.C. 332 would have had little to do but to erect his engines upon it.

Probably the conception of a mole or dam between the shore and the island never occurred to the Babylonian monarch. There was no precedent for the construction of any such work. So far as history gives us information on the subject, it would seem that the possibility of joining an island to the continent by means of a mole first suggested itself to the monarch who bridged the Hellespont and cut through the peninsula of Athos, the magnificent Xerxes, who, however, made but a half-hearted effort to carry out his purpose.[1] Alexander was the first who not only conceived, but succeeded in accomplishing, such a work, in which, however, he experienced such difficulty that nothing less than his indomitable energy and stubborn will could have overcome it.

The real trust of Nebuchadnezzar was, no doubt, first, in his ability to collect a powerful fleet from the other Phœnician cities, which had already submitted

[1] Herod. viii. 97.

to him ; and, secondly, in the pressure which he could exert on Tyre by the occupation of all her territory except the island. Arvad and Gebal had, apparently, surrendered themselves on the capture of Sidon. Akko had probably followed their example, together with most, or all, of the minor towns. The fleets of these cities would be at Nebuchadnezzar's disposal, and though they might not serve with any ardour against their sister state, would, if manned in part by Babylonians, probably blockade the island effectually. There would follow the usual difficulties with respect to water and provisions. These were borne for the long period of eight or nine years ; but at length, in the twentieth year of Nebuchadnezzar, and the thirteenth year of the siege (B.C. 585), the Island Tyre must have capitulated, surrendering herself upon terms. Her surrender, though not distinctly stated by any historian, is implied, first, in the very fact of the termination of the siege, for it is inconceivable that the great Babylonian monarch, then at the zenith of his power, should have submitted to be baffled by a little knot of merchants established on an isle not a mile long ; and, secondly, by the position which she thenceforth occupied towards Babylon, which was evidently one of dependency. She became an object of hostility to Egypt, Babylon's rival, which sought to injure Babylon through her ; and she drew her kings from the hostages which she was compelled to send to the Babylonian Court. Her prestige and her commerce dwindled ; she was not allowed to rebuild her suburb upon the mainland (Palæ-tyrus), which remained in ruins to the time of Alexander ; and she lost for a time the leading position among the Phœnician cities, which seems to have passed to Sidon.

It was inevitable that, in a contest where a single city, however " ancient, spirited, wealthy, and intelligent," was pitted against an empire which counted its population by tens of millions, the city should succumb, and no doubt there were many at the time, who, like the Greek historian in treating of a later occasion,[1] taxed the Tyrians with " foolish wilfulness " for daring to offer resistance to a power whose strength was so overwhelming. But the credit of nations is not best maintained by always consulting expediency, and shrinking from every struggle in which they may seem to be overmatched, and to have no chance of bringing their resistance to a successful issue. " There is a time for all things "—and, among other things, for making a heroic, desperate, stand against over-whelming odds. Tyre would not have increased her reputation by a timid submission to either Nebuchadnezzar or Alexander. She holds the position which is hers in the Valhalla of nations, by the courage and constancy and heroic stiffness which she exhibited in times of danger, and in defiance of vastly superior strength. Her thirteen years' siege by Nebuchadnezzar is an element in her greatness and her fame ; and would have been ill exchanged for a tame submission to the menace of an overbearing power, which would have been encouraged to trample on her all the more by a manifestation of tameness and subserviency.

[1] Diod. Sic. xvii. 40.

XII.

THE CIRCUMNAVIGATION OF AFRICA, AN EPISODE IN PHŒNICIAN HISTORY.

DURING the transition period, while it was uncertain whether Babylonia or Egypt would emerge from the troubles of the time in the better position, Phœnicia, with the prudence that is inculcated by commercial pursuits, strove to stand well with both parties. Neco, king of Egypt, almost certainly received aid from Phœnicia in the construction of those two fleets with which he navigated the Mediterranean and Red Seas. We cannot assert that the Phœnicians dug his great canal for him, though they afterwards were so much more at home in canal-digging than any of the other Oriental nations, when Xerxes set his maritime subjects to excavate the canal of Athos. But, at any rate, it is clear that in the flourishing times of Neco, before his defeat at Carchemish, the Phœnicians looked upon him with a very friendly eye, and were willing, even at a considerable cost to themselves, to render him a service. He was not in a position to exercise any authority over them; but they, of their own accord, consented to undertake on his behalf an enterprise of such danger and difficulty that many critics refuse to believe in its conception, and there-

fore much more in its execution, at the time assigned
to it.   But, what so sceptical a writer as Mr. Grote
admits and accepts, will scarcely be rejected by the
more candid criticism of the present day.   Neco,
according to the positive statement of Herodotus,[1]
anxious to procure a water-communication between
the Red Sea and the Mediterranean, and having
failed in the construction of a canal between the Nile
and the head of the Gulf of Suez, whereby such a
communication might have been effected, resolved to
attempt the circumnavigation of Africa for the
accomplishment of his purpose.   Feeling the need of
employing bold and skilful mariners, he sought the
aid of the Phœnicians, and engaged the services of a
select band of Phœnician sailors, to whom he committed the task of accomplishing the perilous enterprise.   The sailors took their departure from a port
on the Red Sea, and coasting along its shores, passed
the Straits of Babelmandeb, and entered upon the
Southern or Indian Ocean.   Still hugging the land,
they proceeded south-eastward, past the Somauli
country, Zanzibar, Mozambique, and Zululand, till
they reached the Cape of Good Hope, when they
commenced their return journey, coasting the western
side of Africa, and finally reaching Egypt by way of
the Straits of Gibraltar and the Mediterranean.   It
took them nearly three years to accomplish the voyage,
since they were insufficiently provisioned, and found
it necessary each autumn to effect a landing on the
coast, to plough up a tract of ground, sow it with
grain, and await the ripening of the corn in the ensu-

[1] Herod. iv. 42.

ing spring. On their return to Egypt, they recounted a tale, which, says Herodotus, "others may perhaps believe, though I certainly do not, that in sailing round Africa they had the sun on the right hand," *i.e.*, to the north.

The reality of this circumnavigation, and the general credibility of the narrative, have been the object of much doubt and criticism. But there seems to be no reason why the physical difficulties should not have been overcome by a people accustomed to affront the dangers of the open Atlantic. The statement with regard to the length of time occupied by the voyage, supplemented by the account of an annual sowing and reaping of a corn crop—itself no improbable arrangement—accords well with the circumstances. The ships would, of course, have hugged the shore, and therefore have greatly lengthened the voyage. They would have been careful to lie by, whenever the weather was stormy, or even threatening. They would have proceeded slowly and leisurely, understanding that there was no need to hurry, and that what was desired was, that they should effect their purpose, not that they should accomplish it within a certain time. "We may take for granted that the reward consequent upon success was considerable" (Grote), and hence that there was but little temptation to "turn tail," and hurry back as soon as any difficulties began to be experienced. Though the inhabitants of the coast would have been savages, and perhaps generally cannibals, yet they were not disinclined to commercial dealings, as appears from the "Voyage of Hanno," as well as from the organized "dumb trade" established by the Carthaginians on the western seaboard. We can quite understand their allowing the Phœnicians to land, and plough up a tract of ground, and sow it with corn, and stay three or four months till the corn was ripe, and reap it and carry it away with them. The stay of the mariners would have considerably benefited the natives through the continual exchange of commodities ; and the legacy of a piece of reclaimed land, cleared of stumps and thorns, would have been of value.

The principal argument, however, in favour of the actual circumnavigation having been effected lies in the story told by the mariners on their return, which Herodotus discredited. They said that, in sailing round Africa, they had had after a time the sun on their right hand. "This phenomenon," as Mr. Grote remarks, "observable according to the season even when they were within the tropics, could not fail to force itself on their attention as constant, after they had reached the southern temperate zone." It was a phenomenon not within the cognizance of any Greek of the time of Neco, or even of the age of Herodotus, nor probably of any Phœnician or Egyptian. Abstract reasoners might argue, that, as the sun lay towards the south, if a traveller proceeded far enough, he would get beyond the sun, and have his shadow thrown to the southward ; but practical men are not likely to have indulged in such speculations. The phenomenon observed by the Phœnicians on this voyage would never have been regarded as possible by rough sailors, if they had not witnessed it. Their tale was incredible to their contemporaries, and to many succeeding generations of men. It was not until about the time of Augustus, that correct views began to be entertained about the motions of the earth and sun, and the direction of the shadows in the southern hemisphere came to be known and understood by the better educated. In the time of Neco, when the report was made by the Phœnicians to their employers, no such knowledge existed anywhere with respect to the movements of the great mundane bodies ; and the phenomena which they reported were naturally disbelieved and rejected. But the fact of their making the report is evidence to us of their having actually experienced the phenomenon, and so of their having reached the southern latitudes, in which alone it would press itself on their attention. That they accomplished the entire voyage, and did not, like the later navigator, Sataspes, despair of success and return by the way by which they had gone, is sufficiently evidenced by the fact, which is beyond all doubt or cavil, that, having started from a port on the Red Sea, they returned to Egypt by way of the Mediterranean.

This feat is one that deserves to be recorded in any history that treats of the ancient Phœnicians. It is doubtful whether the enterprise was ever repeated until nearly the close of the fifteenth century, when Vasco di Gama revolutionized the commerce of the world by doubling the Cape from the West. The Carthaginians in the time of Herodotus seem to have asserted that they also had been successful in making the voyage ; but their claim was not in any satisfactory

way authenticated.   It is doubtful whether their unsupported assertion merits belief ; it is certain that in
their subsequent commerce they made no practical
use of the Cape route, which became a mere tradition
of the past, and was by many regarded as a fable.
The legitimate conclusion is, that the practical difficulties of the voyage, with the resources at the command
of the ancient navigators, though not insuperable, were
very great, sufficient to deter any traders, not stimulated by a royal commission and the expectation of
royal bounty, from attempting it. " Without any doubt
the successful Phœnician mariners," as Mr. Grote
remarks,[1] " underwent both severe hardship and great
real perils, besides those still greater supposed perils,
the apprehension of which so constantly unnerved the
minds of even experienced and resolute men in the
Unknown Ocean.   Such was the force of these terrors
and difficulties, to which there was no known termination, upon the mind of the Achæmenid Sataspes
(upon whom the circumnavigation of Africa was imposed as a penalty ' worse than death ' by Xerxes in
commutation of a capital sentence), that he returned
without having finished the circuit, though by so doing
he forfeited his life."   The Phœnicians were braver—
they persevered, and by so doing added another leaf
to the unfading laurel crown, which the voice of
history awards them for their daring and intrepidity.

[1] " History of Greece," vol. ii. p. 462.

XIII.

PHŒNICIA UNDER THE BABYLONIANS.

THE state of things established by Nebuchadnezzar's reduction of Tyre in B.C. 585 continued for the space of nearly half a century. Tyre was depressed, both internally and externally. Externally she seems to have sunk into a condition inferior to that of Sidon, which appears as the dominant power of Phœnicia in the war wherein Apries, king of Egypt, strove to become master of Syria. She had to suffer the indignity of attack, and probably defeat by sea, at the hands of Egypt, which she had herself greatly helped to become an important naval power. Internally, she suffered a revolution, about twenty years after her capture by Nebuchadnezzar, whereby her ancient line of kings was brought to an end, and a government by judges (*suffetes* or *shophetim*), as at Carthage, substituted in its stead. The change implied a diminution of the central authority, and a rise in its place of either an oligarchic or a democratic party. The early judges had but short periods of office. After Baal, the son of Eth-baal, had reigned for ten years, Ecnibaal, the first judge, held the chief authority for no more than two months. His successor, Chelbes, succeeded in maintaining himself in power for ten months, when he had to give way to Abbarus, who united the chief sacerdotal with the chief civil authority, but failed to fix himself firmly in his seat, holding office only three months. Something more nearly resembling fixity of tenure was then established, Mytgen and Gerastartus conjointly bearing rule for six years, but with the interruption of a year, during which a certain Balator reigned as king. At the expiration of the joint judgeship of Mytgen and Gerastartus, the monarchy was formally restored, and the Tyrians sent an embassy to Babylon, requesting that a certain Merbal, who had been detained there as a hostage for the fidelity of the Tyrian state, should be allowed to return home to be their king. The petition was granted, and Merbal having returned to his native city, enjoyed the sovereignty over it for four years. At his death, which seems to have been natural, the people were so satisfied with his rule, that they determined on repeating the experiment which had proved so great a success. They sent to Babylon for a second hostage, a certain Hiram, brother of Merbal, and made him king in his brother's place. Hiram reigned twenty years, and survived the Babylonian monarchy, which was crushed by Cyrus the Great after he had held the Tyrian throne for fourteen years.

If we accept the dates which Josephus reports as those given by the Tyrian historians, we must suppose that Ithobal, or Ethbaal II., continued to reign for eleven years after his loss of independence, and was succeeded by Baal, probably his son, in B.C. 574. Nebuchadnezzar was still king of Babylon, while

Apries had (in B.C. 588) succeeded his father, Psamatik II., as monarch of Egypt. The feud between the
two powers was still raging, and Apries, about B.C.
570, determined on an invasion of Syria both by sea
and land, with the object of aggrandizing his own
country at the expense of the Babylonians. Herodotus tells us that his fleet engaged that of Tyre, while
his land army attacked Sidon. Diodorus adds that
he defeated the combined navies of Phœnicia and
Cyprus in a great sea-fight, after which he took Sidon,
and made himself master of the entire Phœnician
seaboard. The condition of affairs called for some
great effort on the part of the Babylonian monarch,
unless Babylon was altogether to lose her prestige
and sink into the position of a secondary power.
Accordingly, in B.C. 568, Nebuchadnezzar made the
effort which circumstances required, and, collecting
all the forces of the empire invaded Egypt with a
large army. His campaign may be traced in the
Book of the Prophet Jeremiah. He entered Egypt
at Migdol (Jer. xlvi. 14), took Daphnæ and Memphis,
and ascended the Nile valley, carrying all before him.
The "hired men" of Egypt "in the midst of her"
(verse 21) were "like fatted bullocks—they were
turned back and fled away together ; they did not
stand, because the day of their calamity was come
upon them, and the time of their visitation." The
Nile valley was ravaged from end to end : "the multitude of No"—*i.e.*, of Thebes—"was punished"
(verse 25) ; and all Egypt lay at Nebuchadnezzar's
mercy. One check was received by his forces, near
Syêné ; but otherwise his triumph was continuous

and complete. His actual antagonist appears to have been Amasis, Apries, the monarch against whom he had taken arms, having been deposed from power by his subjects, but allowed to retain the title of king and to inhabit the royal palace. Some obscurity hangs over the secret history of the time; but it seems probable that Nebuchadnezzar required the execution of Apries before he would negotiate with Amasis, and that Amasis, to conciliate him, consented. The deposed monarch was certainly put to death, and Amasis became sole king, reigning however as a Babylonian vassal, and not as an independent monarch.

Phœnicia, which had been the occasion of the quarrel between Babylon and Egypt, was well satisfied with the result of the struggle. She had learned that nothing was to be hoped for from the "bruised reed," on which if a man leant, it would pierce the hand that trusted it. The little states between Mesopotamia and Egypt suffered least, when one great power or the other was manifestly in the ascendant. Nebuchadnezzar's campaign of B.C. 568 secured Western Asia an interval of profound peace, which lasted for thirty years. At Tyre, Baal held the throne till B.C. 564, when "Judges" were substituted for kings by the will of the Tyrian people. But this constitutional change was distasteful to many, and was not lasting. After the space of about eight years, during which the chief authority had changed hands repeatedly, the Tyrians reverted to their old form of government, and with the approval of the Babylonian monarch of the time, probably Neriglissar, placed the

crown on the head of a certain Merbal, whom they
sent for from Babylon. Merbal reigned four years,
probably from B.C. 556 to B.C. 552. He was contemporary with three Babylonian kings, Neriglissar
(Nergal-sar-uzur), Laborosoarchod (Lakhab-basi-
kudur), and Nabonidus (Nabu-nahid), the last of whom
ascended the throne in B.C. 555. On the death of
Merbal, in B.C 552, the Tyrians set up as king his
brother Hiram, who reigned till B.C. 532, thus surviv-
ing Nabonidus, and witnessing the great revolution,
by which the dominion of Western Asia passed from
the Babylonians to the Persians. It appears from a
cylinder of Nabonidus, that Syria and Phœnicia continued faithful to Nabonidus until the very last year
of his struggle with Cyrus, when they deserted what
was clearly the losing side, broke out in revolt, and
asserted their independence. It speaks well for the
treatment of these distant dependencies by the
suzerain state, that they clung to her, even in her
decadence, for so long. Neither Tyre, nor any other
Phœnician town, can have had much to complain of
under the Babylonian rule, or we may be sure that
revolt would have broken out, when the troubles of
Babylon began, which was at least as early as B.C.
546.

XIV.

PHŒNICIA UNDER THE PERSIANS.

THE conquest of Babylon by Cyrus involved, in the estimation of the conqueror, his succession to the entire dominion which had been held by the Babylonians. Considering Judæa to have passed under his sway, he issued a commission authorizing Zerubbabel, the legitimate descendant of the old Jewish kings, to re-occupy Jerusalem and the adjacent districts with as many of his countrymen as he could induce to follow him. Claiming sovereignty over Phœnicia, he granted the Jews a large quantity of Phœnician timber, which was to be cut for them in Lebanon, and conveyed to Joppa, whence the Jews were themselves to transport it to Jerusalem (Ezra iii. 7). The Phœnicians do not appear to have overtly disputed this claim. They had revolted from Babylon, and regarded themselves as independent; they had made no formal act of submission to Cyrus; but it suited them well to supply the timber which the Jews needed, provided however that they received in return its full value. The Jews were, on their part, quite willing to purchase the timber, and to pay for it, as Solomon had paid for the timber which he

obtained from Hiram, by supplying Phœnicia with a
fixed amount of corn, and wine, and oil. So matters
remained under Cyrus. The Persian king did not
press Phœnicia for any definite act of submission to
his rule ; and the Phœnicians were content to show a
most friendly spirit towards the Jews, newly located
in their neighbourhood. They had formerly lived for
the most part on amicable terms with both the
Israelite kingdoms, and were probably well satisfied to
renew an ancient amity and to re-establish an ancient
commerce.

It was impossible, however, that things should long
remain on this indefinite footing. Amasis, king of
Egypt, was encouraged by the uncertain condition of
affairs in Western Asia, to lay claim to Cyprus, which
had once been an Egyptian dependency. He sent an
expedition thither, and succeeded in occupying the
island. This act was a challenge to Persia, since it
implied a claim to a share of the spoils of Asia, left
a prey to the first comer by the collapse of Babylon.
Whether Persia had, or had not, any previous designs
against Egyptian independence, she could not but
accept the challenge thus thrown out to her, and
resolve at once to pit her strength against that of the
ancient kingdoms of the Pharaohs, and see which
would prevail in the encounter. To have done less
would have been to expose herself to continual encroachments on the Egyptian side, and to a gradual
loss of territory, which would have weakened her
considerably, when the time of trial ultimately came,
as it was sure to do. *Principiis obsta* is a good
maxim, alike in foreign wars and in times of civil

disturbance.   Persia adopted the principle, and Cambyses had scarcely succeeded in establishing himself on his father's throne (B.C. 529) when he determined on a great expedition against Egypt.

To secure success it was necessary to have the command of the Mediterranean.   Egypt, which had recently conquered Cyprus, must have possessed a powerful fleet, while the Persians had no navy at all of their own to oppose to it.   The subjected Greeks of Asia Minor might have been compelled to furnish a certain number of ships ; but such a fleet as they could have supplied would· have been quite insufficient to cope with the combined Cypriots and Egyptians.   Cambyses was forced either to invade Egypt at a great disadvantage or to procure such a naval power as would be able to hold the Egyptian navy in check, if not even to sweep it from the Mediterranean waters. The large army about to invade Egypt along the shore needed the support of a fleet to convey its provisions, its water, and its heavy baggage.   The blockade of the Nile was requisite in order to secure the surrender of Memphis.   Cambyses grasped the essential points of the situation, and made it his first business after his father's death and his own accession, to obtain the naval strength without which he could not count confidently on victory.

There was but one power in the world which could furnish it.   Phœnicia possessed a fleet at once more numerous, better appointed, and better manned than the Egyptian.   If Phœnicia's cordial good-will, and energetic co-operation could be enlisted on the Persian side, the whole difficulty would disappear, and the success of the expedition would be certain. How Cambyses approached the Phœnicians, what arguments he employed in his negotiations with them, whether he trusted to persuasion alone, or whether he employed also the gentle stimulant of menace, we have no means of determining. All that is certain is that no force was actually used. Phœnicia was induced, by means at which we can only guess, to submit to Persia, and take up the position of a dependency, retaining (of course) that qualified independence which is implied in the continued government of each town by its own king, and which may be regarded as involving also municipal freedom, and the exclusion from the cities of Persian garrisons. It is quite possible that other favours were granted, as a light taxation, of which we seem to have some evidence in the account which Herodotus gives of the organization of the satrapies, an exemption from land service, an assured position at the head of the Persian fleet, and an enjoyment on occasions of the sunshine of the royal presence. Sidon was under the Persians a royal residence, and in its immediate neighbourhood was probably situated the " paradise," or hunting-park, which the Achæmenian monarchs certainly maintained in some portion of the Tyrian province.

The adhesion of Phœnicia, with its entire good-will and to its entire satisfaction, had a further most important consequence. Cyprus, which was closely connected with Phœnicia ethnically, and had been during long ages almost always connected with it politically, revolted from Egypt on learning that Phœnicia had accepted a position of dependence upon Persia, and voluntarily offered her submission to the Achæmenian king. It was, we may be sure, gladly accepted; and the result followed that, while Egypt now, in regard to her navy, stood isolated and alone, Persia, which until Phœnicia joined her, had been almost destitute of any fleet, united in one under her standard the maritime strength of three great naval powers—Phœnicia, Cyprus, and Asiatic Greece—and thus obtained the complete command of the Eastern Mediterranean, where Egyptian vessels no longer dared to show themselves. The combined fleet of Phœnicia, Cyprus, and the Greeks of Asia, was probably three times as numerous as any that Egypt could place on the Mediterranean waters, and was superior in equipment, and in the quality of the sailors who manned it.

Thus strengthened and supported, Cambyses made his expedition, and, so far as Egypt was concerned, met with complete success. His fleet accompanied his land army along the coast, ascended the Nile, blockaded Memphis, and forced it to surrender after a short siege. The whole country then submitted itself; and it might have been expected that the Persian monarch would return, satisfied with what he had achieved, to his own land. But it soon became apparent that he had wider views. Instead of at once setting out on his homeward march, he " took counsel with himself," says Herodotus, " and planned three expeditions. One was to be against the Carthaginians, another against the Ammonians, or inhabitants of the Oasis of Ammon, and the third against the long-lived Ethiopians, who dwelt in the country lying south of

Egypt, and reaching to the Southern Sea." With two of these we have no present concern, since it was not proposed to employ the Phœnicians in carrying them out ; but one was of vital moment to the future of the Phœnician nation, and, had it taken place, would probably have affected deeply the general course of civilization in the world. If the Phœnicians had consented to execute the will of their despotic master, and had been unnatural enough to engage in a hostile expedition against their own offspring, either the two powers would have wasted each other's strength in a prolonged and fierce struggle, or Carthage must have succumbed. In the former case the Phœnician influence generally, both in the West and in the East, would have been greatly diminished ; in the latter, which we regard as the more likely result, all that civilizing influence which in later ages Carthage exercised in the Western world, and not least upon Rome herself, would have come to nought. The West would have grown up without that leaven of Aramaic ideas which in point of fact penetrated classicism, and prepared the way for that fusion of Oriental with Occidental conceptions which was ultimately produced by Christianity.

Fortunately for the world, and much to their own honour, thePhœnicians, when Cambyses issued orders to his fleet to sail against Carthage, refused to obey. They were bound to the Carthaginians, they said, by solemn oaths, and, even apart from that consideration, it would be a wicked act on their part to make war upon their own children. Cambyses did not usually allow his commands to be disputed, or listen very patiently to reasonings directed to proving them such as ought never to have been issued ; but for once he appears to have exercised self-restraint, to have acknowledged that there was some validity in the objections made by his Phœnician subjects, and to have desisted from his purpose without making any attempt to compel their obedience. His undisputed mastery of the continent would have enabled him to put a severe pressure on most of the Phœnician towns by actually occupying them, and even on Tyre and Arvad by seizing their territories upon the mainland ; but he was either ashamed or afraid of resorting to such high-handed measures. The submission of the Phœnicians to Persian rule had been a voluntary act ; it was recent, and the memory of it was fresh in men's minds ; a dim and faint public opinion existed even in Persia, as now in Russia, and the Great King himself could not always venture to defy it. Moreover, if Phœnicia had revolted, her revolt might have been followed by that of Cyprus, and then he would have lost his navy, and his hold on Egypt would have been rendered insecure, so that a fear of the material results may have also influenced him. There can be no doubt that he exercised a wise discretion in not pushing matters to an extremity, since he at once avoided an immediate peril, and attached the Phœnicians to Persia by a sentiment of affection, which continued without any serious abatement for above a hundred and fifty years.

In the troubles that ushered in the reign of Darius Hystaspis Phœnicia appears to have taken no part. She lay remote from the scene of conflict, and had no interest in the religious differences which arrayed the Magians against the Zoroastrians. Her attention was no doubt turned once more exclusively to commerce ; and she must have rejoiced in the increased facilities for land communication furnished by the Persian system of post-routes, and in the stimulus given to trade by the establishment of a metallic currency through all parts of the Persian Empire. Hitherto, so far as we know, the only states which had enjoyed such a currency were Lydia and Argos. The Persian coinage of darics, both gold and silver, on a large scale effected a revolution in commercial transactions throughout the East, and led to the adoption of money as a general medium of exchange in all parts of the civilized world. Phœnicia must have greatly profited by a change so favourable to the increase of mercantile transactions, and must at the same time have derived considerable advantage from the establishment of lines of road, with post-houses, and relays of horses, at intervals, open to the private trader no less than to the courier of the government.

Among the earliest acts of Darius, after he had crushed the rebellions which crowded upon him during his first six years, was to establish over the whole of the empire a uniform system of finance and government. The entire territory was divided into satrapies, under civil governors or satraps, who were to see to the tranquillity and prosperity of their several provinces, and to collect from each a fixed revenue, which was to be transmitted to the Court. Phœnicia, together with Syria and Cyprus, formed the fifth of the twenty satrapies into which Darius originally divided

his dominions, and paid its quota of an annual contribution to the Persian treasury, which amounted to
three hundred and fifty talents, or about £84,000 sterling.   The Phœnician share of this contribution can
scarcely have exceed one half, in which case we may
regard the nation as exceedingly lightly taxed.   The
incidence of taxation would scarcely have exceeded
one shilling and eightpence a head, whereas in
modern communities the incidence is generally from
ten to twenty times as much.

   Phœnicia, moreover, notwithstanding the introduction of the satrapial system, which in idea substituted
for local varieties of government a uniform state
arrangement, retained her own private administration
of her affairs by native monarchs, which probably excluded the jurisdiction of the Syrian satrap, not only
from the Phœnician towns, but from the territories.
Thus to the Phœnicians under Persian rule the burdens and disabilities involved in subjection were
extremely slight.   They consisted mainly—(1) In the
relinquishment of the right of making peace and war
with other nations, or of communicating with them
diplomatically ; (2) in the obligation to pay annually
a fixed quota to the revenue ; and (3) in the obligation
to contribute to any great expedition in which the head
of the empire was engaged such an amount of force
as was fairly proportioned to that furnished by the
other subject nations.

   It was probably a matter of agreement, from the
first, that the Phœnician contribution should be entirely naval.   Without venturing to maintain that a
definite commercial proportion was assigned per-

manently for the contingents of the several states, we
may give some idea of the estimation in which
Phœnicia was held by stating that, when the full
force of the empire was called out, the burden that
fell upon the Phœnician cities was that of furnishing
three hundred triremes, while Egypt was called upon
to furnish no more than two hundred, Cyprus one
hundred and fifty, Cilicia, Ionia, and the Greeks of
the Hellespont one hundred each, Caria seventy, the
Æolian Greeks sixty, Lycia fifty, Pamphylia thirty,
the Dorians of Asia the same number, and the
islanders of the Ægean under twenty. Thus, out of
a total of twelve hundred triremes, which formed the
maximum strength of the Persian navy, Phœnicia
contributed a full fourth ; and, with her dependencies,
Cyprus and Cilicia, not much short of half.

Moreover, the Phœnician vessels were at this time
excellently equipped and armed. Xenophon makes one
of his characters say of a Phœnician ship during the Persian period : " I think that the best and most perfect
arrangement of things which I ever saw was when I
went to look at the great Phœnician sailing vessel : for I
saw the largest amount of naval tackling separately disposed in the smallest stowage possible. For a ship, as
you well know, is brought to anchor, and again got
under way, by a vast number of wooden implements,
and of ropes, and sails the sea by means of a quantity
of rigging, and is armed with a number of contrivances
against hostile vessels, and carries about with it a
large supply of weapons for the crew, and, besides,
has all the utensils that a man keeps in his dwelling-
house, for each of the messes. In addition, it is loaded

with a quantity of merchandise, which the owner
carries with him for his own profit. Now all the
things which I have mentioned lay in a space not
much bigger than a room that would conveniently
hold ten beds. And I remarked that they severally
lay in such a way that they did not obstruct one
another, and did not require any one to look for them,
and yet they were neither placed at random, nor en-
tangled one with another, so as to consume time
when they were suddenly wanted for use. Also I
found the captain's assistant, who is called ' the look-
out man,' so well acquainted with the position of all
the articles, and with the number of them, that even
when at a distance he would tell where everything lay,
and how many there were of each sort, just as one
who had learned to read could tell the number of
letters in the name of Socrates and the proper place
for each of them. Moreover, I saw this man, in his
leisure moments, examining and testing everything
that a vessel needs when at sea; so, as I was surprised,
I asked him what he was about, whereupon he replied,
' Stranger, I am looking to see, in case anything should
happen, how everything is arranged in the ship, and
whether anything is wanting or is inconveniently
situated; for when a storm arises at sea, it is not possible either to look for what is wanting, or to put to
rights what is arranged awkwardly.'" [1]   Xenophon
evidently considered the arrangement and stowage of
the Phœnician ships as superior to that of the vessels
of his own countrymen; and the advantages in these

[1] Xen., " Œconom." viii. pp. 11-16.

respects were probably indicative of a general superiority.

After the part which she took in the Egyptian expedition, Phœnicia appears to have been first called upon to lend her assistance to the Persian Government, when Darius, half persuaded by his queen, Atossa, to attempt the conquest of Greece, resolved to send the Crotoniat Democedes, with a small squadron, to survey the Hellenic shores, and report how far Greece was assailable. Democedes and his Persian escort were sent down to the Phœnician coast, with orders to take ship at Sidon, and thence proceed on their exploration. At Sidon, they "fitted out two triremes and a trading vessel," loading the last named with " all manner of precious merchandise," according to instructions received from the Persian Court. They then set out on their expedition, which had a disastrous issue, but from no negligence or fault of the Sidonian mariners.

About twenty years later (B.C. 498), the Phœnicians were called upon to lend their aid to their suzerain under extremely critical circumstances. The Greeks of Asia had revolted. They had received assistance from Eretria and Athens. Sardis had been burnt. Caria and Caunus had made common cause with the rebels, and thrown off the Persian yoke. The flames of war had burst out in Cyprus, where the population was half Greek, half Phœnician, and except Amathus, all the cities, whatever their nationality, had taken up arms against Persia. The Great King was deprived entirely of his northern fleet, that on which he placed his greatest reliance, and which had alone accom-

panied him in his expedition against Scythia, and
guarded for him the Bosphorus and the Danube. Had
Phœnicia failed him under these circumstances, had
she stood aloof and declined to take part in the conflict, still more had she followed the example of her
Cyprian kinsmen, and gone over to the enemy, Darius
must, it would seem, have suffered a great calamity—
he must have lost the command of the sea, and
possession of the greater part of Western Asia. The
only ships remaining to him would have been those of
Egypt, Cilicia, Lycia, and Pamphylia, none of them
naval powers of first-class rank, and all of them more or
less disaffected. The struggle would then have become
at least as critical as was, a century later, that against
Evagoras, which shook the Persian power to its basis.

As it was, Phœnicia did not fail him—she does not
appear even to have hesitated. An ample fleet was
put at the disposal of the Persian generals, which
transported a large Persian army from Cilicia to the
shores of Cyprus. A double battle was fought near
Salamis, in which, though the Ionian Greeks defeated
the Phœnicians by sea, yet the land force which the
Phœnician fleet had conveyed to the island gained so
complete a victory over the Cypriots that the back of
the rebellion was broken ; the Ionian fleet retired and
dispersed ; Persia was left mistress of the situation,
and succeeded shortly in trampling out the flames of
revolt in Cyprus, Caria, and Caunus. By the year
B.C. 495, the fifth of the war, nothing remained for
her but to take vengeance on the Ionian Greeks, who
had set the rebellion afoot, and especially to punish
Miletus, which had been its head and front.

Miletus, however, and Ionia were determined to die hard. The full naval force of all the Ionian cities was collected in the harbour of Miletus, the mustering-place being a small island called Ladé which lay in front of the town. The entire fleet amounted to three hundred and fifty-three triremes. The crews, though not of a race from which severe work or steady endurance of hardships could be expected, were trained sailors, well accustomed to the sea, and were full of confidence owing to the recent success of a portion of their number against the Phœnician squadron at Salamis. If Persia was to be victorious over so numerous and so well-manned a fleet, a great effort must be made, an overwhelming force must be collected. Phœnicia alone, if her full contingent was three hundred vessels, could not be counted on to contend with success against the combined Ionian navies, since by herself she would be outnumbered. Egypt therefore, and Cilicia, and even Cyprus, though so recently reduced, were called upon to send squadrons proportionate to their respective strength, and by these means a force was got together, which amounted, according to Herodotus, to six hundred triremes, or nearly double the Greek strength. The contribution of Phœnicia to the combined Persian fleet was probably somewhat less, though not much less, than one-half ; we are told that " of all the naval states they showed the greatest zeal ; " and, not unnaturally, the doings of the fleet are in a general way ascribed to them, though it was really a joint armament contributed by four of the subject nations.

The battle of Ladé, which shortly followed the

collection of the two fleets, though a very decisive victory for Persia, does not add much to the reputation of the Phœnicians either for courage or for good seamanship. Where numbers are very unequal, the side which preponderates can gain but little honour by winning the day. Besides which, in the present encounter, the weaker party lay under the additional disadvantages of divided leadership and divided counsels. A portion of the Ionian fleet drew off and sailed away as soon as the battle began ; those who remained were disheartened, and did not know where the treachery would end. The only ships which appear to have made a stout resistance were those of the Chians, one hundred, and those of the Phocæans, three in number. " The Chians," we are told, "when they saw the greater number of the allies betraying the common cause, scorned to imitate the base conduct of those traitors, although they were left almost alone and unsupported, a very few friends continuing to stand by them ; notwithstanding this, however, they went on with the fight, and often cut the line of the enemy, until at last, after they had taken a large number of their adversaries' ships, they ended by losing more than half their own." [1]   The three vessels of the Phocæans supported the resistance of the Chians until evidently all was lost, when they made their way out of the fight, carrying off with them three of the enemy's ships, which they had captured. The victors had the material advantages, but the vanquished obtained the honours, of the conflict.

[1] Herod. vi. 15.

After the battle of Ladé (B.C. 494) the Phœnicians were employed by the Persians in the reduction of the islands of the Ægean, and of various cities on the European shores of the Propontis and the Straits. Miltiades narrowly escaped being captured by one of their vessels as he fled from the Chersonese. Metiochus, his son, actually fell into their hands, was conveyed to Susa, and lived and died a Persian !

From this time till Xerxes began his preparations against Greece, we have no definite information as to the relations of the Phœnicians to. the Persians. It may be assumed as highly probable that they furnished the greater portion of those fleets, with which Mardonius in B.C. 492, and Datis and Artaphernes in B.C. 490, made their expeditions against Greece ; but the fleets were certainly not composed of Phœnician vessels exclusively. Persia drew her armaments from her subjects generally, and the ordinary rule was that the maritime states conjointly should furnish the fleets.

When, in B.C. 485, Xerxes, having determined on the Greek expedition, began to prepare the way for it, there were two especial tasks, on which we know that he employed the services of the Phœnicians. One was the cutting of a ship-canal through the isthmus which joins Mount Athos to the mainland, and the other the construction of a double bridge of boats across the Hellespont, which should form the basis of a solid causeway. In both works, the Phœnicians distinguished themselves. At Athos they showed their superior knowledge of engineering by making their portion of the cutting twice as wide at the top as it was required to be at the bottom, and then

sloping the banks at the proper angle, which prevented them from falling in, a misfortune which was
experienced by the workmen of all the other nations
employed on the task. At the Hellespont, where
they were employed in friendly rivalry with the
Egyptians, though they exhibited no superiority of
intelligence, they constructed a work so firm and
strong that it effectually served its purpose, and
enabled the Great King to march his huge army
from Asia into Europe without experiencing the
slightest difficulty.

On another occasion during the expedition, they
had an opportunity of exhibiting before the eyes of
the entire fleet and army the matchless excellence of
their ships. Xerxes, when he reached Abydos, took
a fancy to test the relative merit of the several contingents to his fleet, and ordered a regatta to be held,
open to all-comers. The ship which won the race
was one of those contributed by Sidon ; and thenceforth the king, when he had occasion to embark and
trust himself to the winds and waves, invariably went
on board a Sidonian vessel.

In the sea-fights also, the Phœnicians, though they
could not avert defeat, showed much gallantry. Con-
tributing one-fourth of the entire Persian fleet, they
naturally had the lead in every engagement. Their
first exploit was the capture of an Æginetan trireme,
which had been stationed, to keep a look-out, off
Sciathus. Later on, at Artemisium, they failed to
come to the front, being out-done by the Egyptians,
who bore off the palm of valour. At Salamis, however, there is reason to believe that they held the

foremost position. It was no fortuitous arrangement which opposed them to the Athenians, the flower of the hostile navy. Beyond a doubt they began the combat, and for a time forced the Greeks to beat a retreat. The entanglement of a Phœnician with an Athenian trireme brought on the general engagement. When victory declared itself on the side of the Greeks, the Phœnician vessels continued to make a desperate resistance. A large number of them were sunk; several were taken; comparatively few emerged from the battle uninjured, or indeed without serious injury. Their leaders had a right to exclaim—"All is lost except our honour;" but unfortunately, and to the deep disgrace of Xerxes, this consolation was not, in the hour of their distress, allowed them.

The Great King had contemplated the battle from a marble throne placed on the Attic coast over against Salamis. The hurry-skurry and confusion was such that it was impossible for him — an excited and timorous spectator — to distinguish and estimate aright the conduct of the various contingents. He could only see—and he saw with disappointment and fury, that the general result had gone against him, and that his fleet was completely defeated. As the Phœnicians were the nucleus and chief strength of the fleet, it was natural for him to lay the blame of the defeat chiefly upon them. He therefore, in a moment of rage, put to death a number of their officers, and (according to one authority) so threatened the others, that their fears and resentment were aroused, and, when night fell, they quitted the fleet, retired to the Attic shore, and thence sailed away to

Asia. It is certain that we hear no more of any service rendered by the Phœnicians to the Persians for fifteen years, though the war with the Greeks continued, and Persia had, of necessity, to maintain a fleet in the Ægean. No Phœnicians took part in the battle of Mycale ; none are mentioned as engaged at Sestos, or Byzantium, or Eïon, or Doriscus, or even Phasêlis ; it was not until B.C. 465, fifteen years after Salamis, that Phœnicia, finding the southern coast of Asia Minor, and the island of Cyprus, threatened, consented once more to employ her naval force in the service of her suzerain, and resumed her old position at the head of the Persian fleet in the great action at the mouth of the Eurymedon. Once more, she was unfortunate. The confederate Persian navy was completely defeated by Cimon, son of Miltiades, with the loss of two hundred ships out of a total of three hundred and fifty. A further squadron of eighty galleys, entirely Phœnician, which had failed to effect a junction with the other ships before the great battle, was attacked by Cimon on the open sea in the afternoon of the same day, and swept from the ocean.

From this time for about seventy-five years, till the star of Persia began to show signs of setting, Phœnicia lived the life of a submissive subject state, paying her tribute regularly, and rendering effective aid to the Persians in all their naval enterprises, which were numerous, and sometimes of great importance. It was his command of a Phœnician fleet amounting to nearly a hundred and fifty vessels, which enabled Tissaphernes to play so influential a part in Asia Minor during the later years of the Peloponnesian War.

It was the presence of their fleet at Cnidus which turned the scale between Athens and Sparta, enabling the Athenians to recover the naval supremacy which they had lost at Ægospotami. It was the appearance of a Phœnician fleet in Greek waters, which, in B.C. 393, gave an opportunity to the Athenians to rebuild their long walls, alarmed Sparta for her own safety, and extorted from her fears in the succeeding year the agreement known as "the Peace of Antalcidas." Persia owed to her Phœnician subjects the glory of recovering complete possession of Asia Minor, and of being accepted as a sort of final arbiter in the internal quarrels of the Greeks.

It seems, however, that not long after the conclusion of the peace of Antalcidas, which secured Phœnicia from attack on the part of the Greeks, she began to waver in her allegiance. The example of successful revolt is contagious. Egypt, after a long period of subjection, had thrown off the Persian yoke, about B.C. 406 or 405,[1] and had established her independence under a native sovereign. In B.C. 392 or 391, Evagoras, a Cypriot Greek, having made himself master of the Cyprian Salamis by defeating and putting to death the despot in possession, who was a Tyrian, named Abdemon, followed the example of Egypt by declaring himself independent of Persia, and proceeded to strengthen himself by alliances and conquests. Having reduced under his sway almost the whole of Cyprus, and concluded treaties with Athens, Egypt, and Cilicia, he seems to have conceived the hope of attaching Phœnicia to his side, and with this object made an expedition into Syria and

[1] See the "Story of Egypt," p. 385.

Palestine. According to Isocrates, he took Tyre by assault; but it is reasonably suspected that his successes roused a general spirit of disaffection, and that "the surrender of Tyre was a voluntary defection." [1] Tyre, at any rate, embraced his cause, and sent him a contingent of twenty triremes. Several other Phœnician cities gave in their adhesion. An Arabian chieftain furnished him with some light troops. Hecatomnus, prince of Caria, secretly supplied him with money. Open war with Persia began about B.C. 390, and lasted about ten years, at the end of which time the bold Greek was compelled to make his submission, but retained his Cyprian sovereignty. Upon this, Phœnicia, no doubt, returned to her former allegiance; but the tie which had united her to Persia was sensibly loosened, and henceforth her fidelity became questionable.

The Persian power was now manifestly on the decline. The expedition of the younger Cyrus, and the return of the Ten Thousand under Xenophon, had made patent to all the internal weakness of the empire. The campaigns of Agesilaus had shown how open Asia Minor was to attack by an enterprising enemy. The long contest with Evagoras, a mere petty prince, had been a further evidence of decay, approaching to dissolution. The failure of the attempt to reduce Egypt in B.C. 375 had been felt as an encouragement to rebels everywhere. About B.C. 366, fresh troubles broke out in Asia Minor, which led on (in B.C. 362) to a general revolt of the western provinces, and to the war known as "the war of the satraps." In this struggle Phœnicia took part,

[1] Kenrick, "Phœnicia," ch. xiii.

first entering into alliance with the revolted governors, and then welcoming the army of Tachos, king of Egypt, when it marched into Syria. Had Tachos been a bold prince, the Persian Empire might very probably have been at this time broken up; but he hesitated, he procrastinated, finally he retreated into his own country, without striking a blow, and Persia, using the arts, with which she was now familiar, of bribery and treachery, succeeded in crushing the satrapial rebellion, and in once more imposing her yoke upon all the allies excepting Egypt.

Tranquillity remained untroubled for about the space of ten years. Then, however, Artaxerxes Ochus, the Persian king, having determined on a vigorous effort to reduce Egypt once more to subjection, the south-western provinces were again thrown into a ferment. The first attack of Ochus upon Nectanebo II. having failed through the good generalship of two Greek commanders in the Egyptian service, Phœnicia and Cyprus again detached themselves from the Persian cause, and threw in their lot with Egypt. Sidon, which had been continually increasing in wealth during the Persian period, took the lead, and, having united Phœnicia under her headship, proclaimed a war of independence. The Persian garrisons, which held most of the Phœnician towns, were either massacred or expelled. An embassy was sent to Memphis, and a formal alliance concluded with the Egyptian king. Substantial aid was promised by the Pharaoh, who shortly afterwards redeemed his promise by the despatch of 4,000 Greek mercenaries under the command of a Rhodian, named

Mentor, a general of consummate ability.   Tennes, the Sidonian monarch, in conjunction with Mentor, gave battle to the Persians, in B.C. 351, and succeeded in inflicting a severe defeat on the two satraps who had been commissioned to attack them, Belesys, satrap of Syria, and Mazæus, satrap of Cilicia.   But this defeat only stirred up the Persian monarch to greater efforts.   Collecting an army of 340,000 men, who were to have the support of three hundred triremes and five hundred transports or provision-ships, he set out in person from Babylon, and marched upon Syria.   Meanwhile Tennes had greatly strengthened the fortifications of Sidon, surrounding the town with a triple ditch, and raising the height of the walls considerably.   He had also collected a fleet of a hundred ships, including a number of quin-queremes, the first which we hear of the Phœnicians possessing.   He had, no doubt, well provisioned the town ; and, had he possessed sufficient resolution, might have made a defence that would have rendered his name memorable in history.   But the force which Ochus brought into Syria appeared to him irresistible. Tennes despaired of success, and with a cowardice and a treachery that are quite unpardonable en-deavoured to purchase his own life from the Persian king by betraying into his hands, first, one hundred of the principal citizens, and then the main defences of the city.   The hundred citizens were immediately slain with javelins.   Five hundred others, who issued from the town with boughs of supplication, and made an appeal to the mercy of Ochus on behalf of their fellow-citizens, shared the fate of the hundred delivered up by Tennes. The Persian monarch was inexorable, and refused to grant any terms or make any promises. Hereupon the Sidonians, understanding that their fate was to be death or slavery, took a desperate resolution. They had already burned their ships before their city was invested. They now resolved, rather than fall into the hands of Ochus, to destroy at once themselves and their town. Each citizen shut himself up with his family in his own house, and then applying the torch consumed with fire himself, his family, and his dwelling. Forty thousand persons are said to have perished in the conflagration! Sidon became a heap of ruins, which Ochus sold for a large sum to speculators, who hoped to reimburse themselves by the riches which they knew must lie among the ashes. One only satisfaction comes to us bound up with this hideous tale of perfidy and suffering. The traitor, Tennes, gained nothing by his treachery. Ochus, having obtained from him all that he wanted, with cynical cruelty, instead of rewarding his desertion, punished his rebellion with death. He seems, however, to have allowed him to be buried in a tomb, which he had previously prepared for himself in the vicinity of Sidon.[1]

Eighteen years elapsed between the destruction of Sidon and the downfall of the Persian power at Issus. During this space Sidon was rebuilt, and became once more a flourishing city. It may be suspected that the king under whom Sidon recovered itself was the Esmunazar, whose sarcophagus, discovered in the year 1855, has furnished the longest extant Phœnician

[1] See below, p. 307.

15

inscription. Esmunazar describes himself as King of the Two Sidons, son of Tabnit, King of The Two Sidons, and grandson or great-grandson of a former Esmunazar, also King of the Two Sidons." The form of his sarcophagus fixes his reign to the fourth century B.C., while the Tabnit, who was his father, may be identical with the unhappy Tennes. If the identity be allowed, we must suppose that Esmunazar was allowed to succeed his father, notwithstanding the latter's execution, and held his crown under Persia for the space of fourteen years. He rebuilt, he tells us, the Temple of the Gods, the Temple of Baal-Sidon, and the Temple of Ashtoreth, in the sea-side Sidon — which was the city destroyed by its inhabitants ; he also built, or re-built, a temple of Esmun in some unknown locality, and a sanctuary in Lebanon, upon a river which he calls "the Purple-Shell River." He entertained hopes of an extension of Sidonian dominions to the south, where he coveted the fertile corn-lands of Dor and Japhia in the plain of Sharon. As such a change could only have been brought about by the good-will of Persia, we may conclude that he cultivated amicable relations with his Persian suzerain, whatever may have been his secret sentiments.

Acquiescence in Persian rule seems indeed to have been the general characteristic of the period. The reign of Ochus was a decided "revival." Persia had under him shown an unexpected strength ; Egypt had submitted to her; rebellion elsewhere had been scotched; no fresh troubles broke out. Perhaps there was in the air a sort of general expectancy of coming extensive change, which caused men to wait and reserve themselves for the crisis that might any day arrive. At any rate, the Phœnician communities, exhausted by the efforts which they had recently made, elected to remain quiet, to resume their old relations to the Persian crown, and to discharge in an exemplary way all their obligations. The interval between B.C. 351 and B.C. 333 was a time of repose and peace for the Phœnician cities generally, which, whatever their feelings, exhibited no dissatisfaction with their position under the Persian sway, and made no attempts to alter it.

XV.

ALEXANDER AND THE PHŒNICIANS—SIEGE AND DESTRUCTION OF TYRE.

THE design of Alexander to invade Asia was known beforehand to the Asiatics. A wise policy would have dictated the collection in the Propontis and the Northern Ægean of the largest possible fleet, the keeping a careful watch on Alexander's movements, and the making of every practicable effort to intercept his heavily laden vessels when they put to sea. Mentor of Rhodes, the best strategist on the Persian side, urgently recommended that this course should be taken. He maintained that, if the whole naval force of Persia were brought up, including the entire Phœnician fleet, the Persian king would have complete command of the sea, that the Greek troops under Parmenio and Attalus, which had already crossed the straits would be able to effect nothing, and that the war might easily be transferred into Macedonia, where Alexander might be made to tremble for his hereditary dominions. The advice appears to have been sound, and at any rate to have deserved a trial. Alexander's genius was so unique, and Asiatic unreadiness and ficklencss so great, that success might not have been achieved, even had the policy been adopted. But the final catastrophe would certainly have been delayed, and it is just possible that the entire course of history would at this point have been altered.

The counsel of Mentor was, however, not followed. Alexander was allowed to cross the Hellespont with an army of 35,000 men ; and the war became a land war, the movements of the fleets becoming, comparatively speaking, unimportant. Phœnicia, which might have played a grand part in the struggle between Europe and Asia, was not brought to the front, was called upon for no great effort, was suffered to drop into a quite secondary position. The fact was, that the Persian land-commanders were jealous of Mentor and of the navy. They expected to defeat Alexander by land, and did not want the glory of his discomfiture to be carried off by a Rhodian. They despised nautical matters, and had no conception of their importance. Perhaps they distrusted the Phœnicians, who had so lately been in arms against them, and were not sure that a Phœnician victory was a thing greatly to be desired.

Thus, between B.C. 336, the date of Alexander's accession, and B.C. 333, the year of the battle of Issus, Phœnicia played a part purely negative ; was faithful to Persia, but did her no good ; held aloof from Alexander, but in no way impeded his designs ; was a spectator, rather than an actor, in the drama that was being played before the eyes of men ; waited passively, like Deïaneira on the banks of Acheloüs, to see how the struggle would end, and to learn which of the two combatants was to be her master.

But, with the complete defeat of the army of Darius Codomannus on the plain of Issus, in November, B.C. 333, the circumstances were wholly changed. The flight of Codomannus beyond the Euphrates, and the entire dispersion of his vast army, left the whole of Syria and Phœnicia open to Alexander, and called on the various Phœnician cities immediately to determine what course they should take. Alexander let it be soon seen that he was not about to pursue his flying enemy, or to push his conquests for the present into the heart of the empire. He regarded it as of the utmost importance to detach from Persia the sources of her naval power, Phœnicia and Egypt, and was resolved, before proceeding further, to subject and attach to himself these provinces, in order to secure his communication with Greece, and render Persia powerless in the Ægean. He therefore, immediately after Issus, sent Parmenio with a strong force to secure Damascus, and, a few months later, began his own march southward along the Phœnician seaboard.

It does not appear that the Phœnician cities exchanged any common counsel, or in any way acted in concert. The resolution of Alexander perhaps took them by surprise. They may have expected, almost to the last moment, that he would march eastward in pursuit of his flying adversary. But, in fact, after a short pause, Alexander, towards the beginning of winter, broke up from Issus, and took his march southward. Having crossed the Orontes, and the ridge which terminates in Mount Casius, he entered the Phœnician low country, and found himself in the

vicinity of Marathus. Marathus at this time formed
a part of the dominion of the Aradian prince, Gerostratus (Ger-astartus ?), who was absent from home,
serving with his naval contingent among the Persian
fleet in the Ægean. Gerostratus was, however, represented during his absence by his son, Strato, who
had remained behind to administer the government.
Strato, under the circumstances, deemed it best to
make an unqualified submission, and meeting Alexander on his march, offered him a crown of gold, at
the same time surrendering to him, not only Marathus
and the adjacent towns upon the mainland, but also
the island of Aradus, which lay off the Syrian coast.
The next place reached was Byblus, anciently Gebal,
which formed a separate sovereignty under a prince
named Enylus, who, like Gerostratus, was serving
with the Persian fleet under Pharnabazus and Autophradates. Left to itself, Byblus followed the example of Marathus and Aradus, submitting itself
unhesitatingly to the Macedonian power, whereto it
could certainly not have opposed any effectual resistance.

Sidon was now approached, Sidon, recently the
queen of the cities, and, according to the tradition,
the original parent of them all, and the founder of
Phœnician prosperity. If any city made a stand for
independence, Sidon, in consideration of its ancient
glories and its recent position, might have been
expected to have done so. But Sidon was embittered
against the Persians by the remembrance of the bloody
and perfidious proceedings which, about eighteen years
before, had marked the recapture of their city by the

army of Ochus. Sidon was rejoiced at the prospect of Persia's downfall, and hailed with satisfaction a change which she expected would be for her advantage. While Alexander was still at some distance, the Sidonians sent envoys to meet him, and invite him to enter their town. The Macedonian monarch readily complied with their request, and Sidon passed quietly into his hands. As, however, Strato the king was serving on board the Persian fleet, and was reputed to have Persian leanings, Alexander deposed him from his sovereignty, and commissioned Hephæstion to select a successor and place him upon the throne. The choice of Hephæstion is said to have fallen upon a certain Abdalonymus (Abd-alonim), who belonged to a distant branch of the royal family, but was so poor that he followed the occupation of a gardener.

It only remained that Tyre should follow the example of its sister (or mother) city, and make an unqualified submission, for Alexander to feel that the subjection of Phœnicia was accomplished, and that he might turn his whole attention to the conquest of Egypt. But here difficulties sprang up. Tyre was willing to continue on the same terms under Alexander on which she had existed and flourished for nearly two hundred years under the Persians. As her king, Azemilchus, was absent, serving in the Persian fleet like the other Phœnician princes, the community chose a deputation, composed of the most eminent men in the city, including the eldest son of the sovereign, and sent it to meet Alexander, to present him with a crown of gold,

together with other valuable gifts, and a quantity of
supplies for his army, and to declare formally that
the Tyrians were prepared to do whatever Alexander
commanded. The Macedonian made what seemed
a gracious reply. He commended the good disposition
of the city, accepted the presents, and desired the
deputies to announce to their government that he
would shortly enter their city for the purpose of offering
sacrifice to Hercules. The Greeks had long identified
their own Hercules, or Heracles, with the Phœnician
Melkarth, whose temple in the Island Tyre was
greatly venerated and of the highest antiquity. The
Macedonian kings claimed to be descended from
Hercules, and thus the wish to sacrifice to him was
natural, and might be regarded as doing the city an
honour. But the Tyrians saw in the proposal a design
permanently to occupy their island city, which the
Persians, it would seem, had never garrisoned. They
were not prepared to place themselves so absolutely
in the power of Alexander, and they therefore, after
deliberating on his message, sent a reply to the effect
that in all other things they would conform to his
wishes, but that they would not admit within the
walls of their island town either Macedonians or
Persians—the king, if he wished to sacrifice to
Hercules, might do so without visiting the island,
since there was another temple of Melkarth in Palæ-
tyrus upon the opposite shore, which was (they said)
even more ancient and more venerable than the
island shrine. Any resistance to his will always in-
censed Alexander. On hearing the answer of the
Tyrians, he showed himself violently angry, and at

once dismissed the ambassadors with fierce menaces, declaring that if they would not open their gates to him he would break their gates down.   Still the Tyrians did not yield to send a softer answer, but made up their minds for resistance.

For this decision they have been charged by a Greek historian with foolish and headstrong rashness, and with bringing their fate upon their own heads. It is not, however, altogether clear that, antecedently, their conduct could have been pronounced imprudent. Alexander, at the time that he threatened them, possessed no naval force worth taking into account; and though the Phœnician towns upon the mainland, and even Aradus, had fallen into his power, it was not certain that their squadrons, which were serving under Autophradates in the Ægean, would elect to desert the Persian cause, and embrace the Macedonian. Even if they did, it was reasonable to expect that they would not act with much vigour against their own kindred.   The inclination of Cyprus also, which possessed a considerable fleet, was uncertain.   And, supposing the worst, supposing that Marathus, and Aradus, and Byblus, and Sidon, and even Cyprus, should give in their adhesion to the conqueror, and unite against a community which was of their own blood, and had generally made common cause with them in the past, was it so certain that they would be able to effect anything ?   Tyre had once defeated the combined navies of the rest of Phœnicia with a squadron of thirteen ships.   Why might she not repeat her victory ?   And even if she were blockaded and reduced to an extremity, what might not be

expected from her powerful colony Carthage, whose
fleets at this period occupied almost the whole of the
Mediterranean? Would Carthage allow the extinction
of her mother city? According to Curtius, the
Tyrians were not left to conjecture upon this question. A Carthaginian embassy visited Tyre just
about the time that Alexander made his demands,
bent upon taking part in a certain annual ceremony
which the colony and the mother city celebrated
conjointly. The ambassadors, on hearing of the
strait in which the Tyrians were placed, gave their
voice in favour of a bold policy, bidding the citizens
to resist and stand a siege, and promising them that
very soon the Carthaginian squadrons would come to
their relief.

As for expecting that Alexander would adopt the
course which he actually pursued, would patiently
sit down before the place, and set to work to construct
a mole which should join their island city to the
mainland, there is no reason to suppose that they
had any, even the slightest, inkling or suspicion of it.
Such a method of attack did not enter into the
known military resources of the time. Once only
had the conception presented itself to the mind of a
powerful commander, one who had at his disposal an
inexhaustible supply of human and animal labour,
one, moreover, who had already bridged the sea and
turned a peninsula into an island, the fantastic
Xerxes, and even then the attempt had not been
seriously made and had very soon been given up.
The Tyrians cannot be blamed for not having anticipated a proceeding for which there was no precedent

in past history, and the successful carrying out of
which they may well have deemed impossible. Their
island was separated from the shore by a strait nearly
half a mile wide in the narrowest part. The channel,
though shallow at first, rapidly deepened, and, where
it washed the walls of the city, reached a depth of
eighteen or twenty feet. Moreover, there were strong
currents in the channel, and, when the south-west

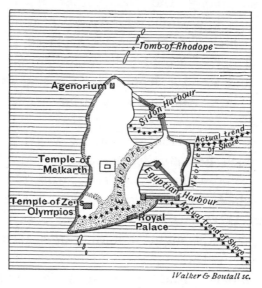

Walker & Boutall sc.

THE TYRE OF ALEXANDER'S TIME.

wind blew, the sea rushed through it with great force,
so that it became dangerous to navigate. Probably
the Tyrians as little feared being captured by means
of a work of the kind which Alexander constructed,
as Constantinople has ever dreaded being taken by
means of a mole thrown out from Asia into the
Bosphorus.

Moreover, there might have seemed to be a good

prospect, that Persia would not suffer a city of so much importance to be captured without making a strenuous effort to save it. Alexander's entire force in Phœnicia and Syria did not amount to as many as fifty thousand men. These troops were already to some extent divided and scattered, having to hold the important towns of Marathus, Sidon, Byblus or Gebal, Damascus, and others, so as to prevent surprises, besides occupying the mainland opposite Tyre. As time went on they would have to scatter more widely in order to obtain provisions. Persia might have been expected, at least, to have hung upon the skirts of Alexander's army, to have harassed him by a guerilla warfare, and to have made it difficult for him to carry on a siege. The Tyrians are not likely to have known how complete had been the collapse of the Persian army in the battle of Issus, nor are they likely to have at all gauged the depth of Persian imbecility and lack of initiative. Enterprising themselves, vigorous, daring, and full of resource, it was scarcely possible for them to anticipate the apathy which came over Darius after Issus, or to imagine that, when a province was threatened which was of the most vital importance to Persia, and which might fairly be called the most valuable part of her dominions, no effort at all would be made for its deliverance, but the Great King would calmly sit down and employ himself in devising proposals of peace, while his active adversary was making himself master of cities and a territory which carried with them the dominion of the sea, and, in the contest or empire which was being waged, would more than half decide the battle.

Thus resistance was determined on. A message was probably sent to Azemilchus the king, requiring him to quit the combined Persian fleet, which was cruising in the Ægean, and to hasten home with the squadron which he commanded, to assist in the defence of the capital. Triremes and light vessels were collected from various quarters. The walls of the town were provided with engines of war for throwing stones and darts on any vessels that might approach them ; arms were distributed to all capable of bearing them ; fresh arms were forged, fresh machines constructed, and every possible preparation made to meet and resist attack. But, as yet, the assailants had no navy, or none that they could venture to oppose to the Tyrian fleet, which held complete command of the sea ; and thus, for a while, there was a pause, neither adversary being able to strike a blow at the other.

Alexander now took his resolution. With that dogged determination to overcome difficulties which characterized him, and which was one main cause of his success, he resolved on the construction of a solid mole—two hundred feet wide—across the strait, from the mainland to the islet, whereby he should actually join it to the continent, and so be able to bring up his engines to its walls, and to press the siege in the usual way. Having requisitioned the services of several thousands of labourers, he began the work where it was easiest, in the shallow water near the shore. Here piles were driven at intervals into the soft mud, which formed the sea bottom at this point, and stone, rubbish, boughs of trees, and whatever material came to hand was precipitated into the water, from the shore and from boats, to fill up the intervals between the piles, and make a solid structure. The work was, comparatively speaking, easy at first, for the water was shallow, the shore at hand, and the Phœnician ships unable to approach near enough to do the labourers employed much harm. There was a plentiful supply of materials in the near vicinity, for Palæ-tyrus, which stretched along the shore for several miles opposite the islet, was partly in ruins, partly deserted by its inhabitants, and the crumbling houses and walls were easily pulled down, and the stones conveyed to the edge of the mole, as it advanced. Wood for the piles was cut in Libanus, and perhaps in Anti-Libanus, where the working parties suffered occasional losses from the attacks of the neighbouring Arabs. The Tyrians also occasionally effected landings, and cut off bodies of labourers who were bringing up stone. Progress, however, was tolerably rapid until the deeper water was reached, when the difficulties of the undertaking began to show themselves, and it was only by the most strenuous efforts that any further perceptible advance could be accomplished.

The current which ran through the channel was perpetually working its way amidst the interstices of the mole, washing holes in its sides and face, and loosening the entire structure. When a storm came, the waves broke over the top of the work, and increased the damage. The deepening of the water required continually more and more material to be provided, while, even when "mountains" were thrown in, the sea absorbed them and appeared no shallower.

The Tyrians were also enabled, after a time, to bring their ships close to the mole, and to attack with missiles the men engaged in pushing the work forward, so distracting their attention, and causing them to seek safety in hasty retreat. The Macedonians, on their side, met these attacks by suspending sails and curtains of hide between their workmen and the Tyrian ships, to intercept the missiles, and by the construction of two lofty wooden towers on the most advanced part of their mole, from which projectiles could be discharged at the ships which approached the nearest.

When matters were in this position, the Tyrians resolved on an attempt to burn the new works, which greatly incommoded them, and at the same time to do serious injury to the mole. They fitted up one of their largest horse transports as a fire-ship, stowing the hold with dry brushwood, and other combustible materials, while on the prow they erected two masts, each with a projecting arm, from which a cauldron was suspended, filled with bitumen and sulphur, and everything else that could kindle and nourish flame. By loading the stem of the vessel with stones and sand, they succeeded in depressing it, and correspondingly elevating the prow, which was thus prepared to glide over the mole and bring itself into contact with the towers. All the fore part of the vessel was piled up with torches, resin, and other inflammable matter. Watching an opportunity when the wind blew straight from the seaward, they manned the oars, spread the sails, and ran their fire-ship at full speed upon the mole, igniting the combustibles at

the prow of the vessel as they drew near, and at the
same time transferring the oarsmen from the fire-ship
into boats, which dropped astern with the utmost
alacrity. Entire success attended the enterprise.
The two towers, and all the more important siege
works, which had been brought forward to the most
advanced part of the mole, were at once in a blaze,
and, as no means of extinguishing the flames had
been provided, were in a short time consumed. The
occupants of the towers were either burnt to death or
made prisoners by the Tyrians as they attempted
in vain to save themselves by swimming. "The
cauldrons swung round from the masts, scattered
their contents over the mole ; the Tyrian triremes,
anchoring just beyond the reach of the conflagration,
kept off by their flights of arrows all who attempted
to quench it ; and the townsmen, manning their small
boats, set fire to all the machines which the flames
from the fire-ship had not reached, and pulled up the
stakes which formed the exterior face of the mole.
The labour of the Macedonian army for several weeks
was lost ; a heavy sea accompanied the gale of wind
which had favoured the conflagration, and penetrating
into the loosened work, carried the whole into deep
water." [1]

So far Alexander, great as was his military skill,
and stubborn as was his determination, had done
nothing towards effecting his purpose. On his return
from an expedition against the Arabs, who had ventured to annoy his wood-cutters in the Anti-Libanus
he found, says Curtius, scarcely any traces of his mole

[1] Kenrick, "Phœnicia," pp. 418.

remaining. He had, therefore, to begin a new work, which he made broader than the former one ; and, instead of taking it straight across the channel in a direct line from east to west, he inclined it at an angle from north-east to south-west, so that it should face the prevalent wind, and not have its flank exposed to the wind's action. He also gave orders for the construction of new machines, to replace those which had been burnt. Again the solid structure, composed of wood, stone, rubbish, and earth, was pushed out from the shore and advanced into the sea even more rapidly than before. Whole trees, with their branches still attached, were dragged to the water's edge, and thrown into the strait, solidified into a mass with stones and mud, and then followed by another layer of trees, which was treated in the same way. But the Tyrians had a device to meet the new tactics. Their divers plunged into the sea at some distance, and secretly approaching the work under water, attached hooks to the projecting ends of the boughs, and dragging the trees out by sheer force, brought down in this way large portions of the superincumbent mass.

It had by this time become apparent to Alexander, that all his efforts would fail, unless he could dispute with the Tyrians the mastery of the sea, and either destroy their navy or at least keep it in check. Accordingly, he determined to bring up whatever vessels he possessed, and to make every effort to obtain additional ships from all quarters. For this purpose he repaired in person to Sidon, and arrived opportunely just as the squadrons of Sidon, Aradus, and Byblus, which had quitted the fleet of Autophradates, on hearing that Alexander was master of their respective cities, sailed into the port. Conjointly the squadrons numbered eighty vessels, and Alexander had no difficulty in persuading the captains to embrace his cause, and even to take service under him against Tyre. Soon afterwards there joined him ten ships from Rhodes, ten from Lycia, and three from Soli and Mallus. From Macedonia came a single penticonter, fit emblem of Macedonia's naval weakness. Alexander might still have hesitated, uncertain whether his fleet was strong enough to engage the Tyrian; but a few days later the princes of Cyprus, having heard of Alexander's occupation of Phœnicia, and resolved to side with him rather than remain faithful to Darius, brought to Sidon, and placed at his disposal their powerful fleet of one hundred and twenty ships. This raised the number of his vessels to two hundred and twenty-four, " comprising the most part and the best part of the Persian navy." It put a stop to any hesitation, and made him determine to put to the test, as soon as possible, the relative strength of the Tyrian fleet and of that which he had now succeeded in gathering.

First, however, his ships required the completion of their equipments for immediate active service, and some practice in nautical manœuvres. Alexander allowed them eleven days for these preparations, and then, having placed on board a strong body of his best soldiers, whom he hoped to utilise in the encounter, if the Tyrians would "fight fair," and not make the combat one of tactics and manœuvring, he set sail for Tyre in order of battle, leading in person the right division of the fleet, which, advancing from the north, held the open sea, and so affronted the greater danger. Craterus and Pnytagoras of Salamis led the left wing. Their approach was quite unexpected by the Tyrians, who had received no information of the great accession to his naval strength, which Alexander had received : they saw with astonishment the advance towards them of a fleet more powerful than their own ; they marked with wonder the perfect order of the approach, and the precision of all the movements ; and they took the resolution, to decline the battle that was manifestly offered them, to remain in port, and block with vessels the mouths of their harbours. Alexander sailed up close to the mouth of the Sidonian harbour, but, seeing the precautions taken, refrained from making any general attack ; the ardour of his Phœnician captains was, however, such, that some of them could not be restrained from charging the outermost of the Tyrian triremes, three of which were sunk, the crews escaping by swimming. Having passed the night with his whole fleet sheltered under the lee of his mole, on the next morning he divided it into two bodies ; the Cyprian ships, with the Admiral Andromachus, were allotted the task of keeping watch on the northern or Sidonian port, while the rest of the fleet, passing on through the narrow channel which separated the mole from the island, took the supervision of the southern or Egyptian harbour, near which, at the south-western corner of the mole, Alexander's own tent was pitched.

The fate of Tyre was now certain, unless the Tyrians

could summon up courage to risk a naval engagement, and could recover the mastery of the sea out of the hands of their adversary. Alexander's workmen, no longer impeded in their labours by the attacks of the Tyrian ships, rapidly completed the mole, and brought it up to the walls of the town. Its towers were advanced close to the walls, and were armed with more formidable and more numerous engines. Other engines, the work of Cyprian and Phœnician artists, were placed on board horse-transports and the heavier class of triremes, and with these demonstrations were made against the walls north and south of the mole, while the main attack was delivered from the mole itself. Every device for assault and defence known in ancient warfare, was brought into play on both sides. The Tyrians had lowered into the sea huge blocks of stone, which kept Alexander's ships at a distance, and prevented them from plying the battering-ram ; these blocks the Macedonians endeavoured to weigh up by means of cranes ; but the unsteadiness of their ships prevented them from having sufficient purchase, a difficulty which they thought to meet by anchoring their vessels. But the Tyrians sent out boats well protected from missiles, and rowing under the sterns and prows of the Macedonian galleys, cut the cables by which they were moored. Alexander upon this, appointed armed boats to watch the cables, but the Tyrians employed divers, whose movements could not be seen, and the cables were cut as before. At last, the Macedonians bethought themselves of using chains instead of ropes, and so got the better of the divers. Finally, they succeeded in fastening nooses round the blocks, and by dragging from the mole, bore them off into deep water.

The time had now arrived, when the Tyrians themselves felt that nothing but a naval victory could save them. As Alexander had divided his fleet, it was open to them to choose their adversary, and to contend separately either with the Cypriote, or with the the Greco-Phœnician squadron. They determined to attack the Cyprians, and to make every effort to take them by surprise. Some time previously they had spread sails before the mouth of the harbour, so that their proceedings inside it could not be overlooked. When the day appointed for the attack came, they selected thirteen of their best vessels— three quinqueremes, three quadriremes, and seven triremes—and waiting till the hour of noon, when the Cyprian sailors would be at their midday meal, and Alexander was gone to his tent on the opposite side of the mole, they secretly and silently placed on board their ships picked crews, and picked men-at-arms, and issued from the harbour in single file, rowing without noise or splash, and not uttering a word, until they were close upon the enemy. Then the boatswains set up the customary cry, and the rowers cheered, and the oars were plied with vigour ; and a fierce onset was made upon the Cypriote fleet, which was taken wholly unawares and thrown into the utmost confusion. The ships of Pnytagoras, king of Salamis, and Androcles, king of Amathus, and also those of Pasicrates, a Thurian, were borne down and sunk in the first charge ; others fled, and were chased, and ran themselves on shore. A general panic pre-

vailed ; **and** the entire Cyprian fleet would probably
have been destroyed, had not Alexander returned from
his tent after a shorter absence than usual, and set to
work to prevent such a disaster. It would seem that a
portion of the Cypriote fleet was lying off the north
shore of the mole, with their crews disembarked. Alexander manned these vessels as rapidly as possible, and
sent them, as fast as they could be got ready, to station
themselves opposite the mouth of the Sidonian harbour, and prevent the egress of any more vessels. He
then crossed the mole to its southern shore, and
manning as many as he could of the ships which lay
there, he took them round the island into the northern
bay, where the Tyrian and Cyprian fleets were still
contending. The people in the town saw the movement, and made frantic efforts to signal it to their
sailors, but in vain. The noise and confusion were
such that their signals remained unperceived till too
late. When at last the sailors understood the situation
and took to flight, Alexander was upon them. A small
portion of the squadron only re-entered the harbour ;
the greater number were either disabled or captured
before they could pass the mouth. The crews, however, and the men-at-arms, who were on board, jumped
into the water, and saved themselves by swimming to
the near and friendly shore.

The last chance was over—the last effort had failed
—but the Tyrians would not give in any the more.
They still met every attack upon the walls with a
determined resistance, and with a fertility of resource
that was admirable. To deaden the blows of the
battering-ram, and the force of the stones hurled from

the catapults, leathern bags filled with sea-weed were let down from the walls at the points assailed. Wheels set in rapid motion intercepted the darts and javelins thrown into the town, turning them aside, or blunting, or sometimes breaking them. When the towers erected upon the mole were brought close up to the defences, and an attempt was made to throw bridges from them to the battlements, and thus to pass soldiers into the city, the Tyrians flung grappling-hooks among the soldiers on the bridges, which caught in the bodies of some, mangling them terribly, dragged their shields from others, and hauled some bodily into the air, dashing them against the wall or upon the ground. Masses of red-hot metal were pre-pared and hurled against the towers and against the scaling-parties. Sand was heated to a glow and showered upon all who approached the foot of the walls : it penetrated through the joints of the armour, and caused such intolerable pain, that the coats of mail were torn off and flung aside, whereupon the sufferers were soon put *hors de combat* by lance thrusts and missiles. The battering-rams were attacked by engines constructed for the purpose, which brought sharp scythes, attached to long poles, into contact with the ropes and thongs used in the working them, and cut them through. Further, wherever the wall showed signs of giving way, the defenders began to construct an inner wall, to take the place of the outer one, when it should be demolished.

In sieges, however, it is accepted as a tactical axiom, that the attack has the superiority over the defence. Alexander, after one or two failures, organized a general assault, from which he anticipated success, and which succeeded. As the wall opposite the mole was so strong that no impression could be made on it, he had for some time concentrated his efforts on the battering of the sea-wall north and south of the mole. It was known that a considerable impression had been made on the southern side of the town, where the wall had collapsed and a portion had sunk into the sea. Alexander fixed on this as the point where his chief effort should be made. Giving orders to his main fleet to attack both harbours, and at the same time sending a number of vessels to make a circuit of the town and menace the defenders at all points, he took the command of the southern assault in person. Having first enlarged the breach considerably by means of the ships that carried battering-rams, he drew these ships off, and advanced to the attack with two vessels only—vessels provided with boarding-bridges, and carrying the *élite* of his army—one, that of Admetus, which he manned with the Hypaspists, the other, that of Cœnus, having on board a portion of the phalanx. He himself accompanied the Hypaspists. The conflict was short when once the bridges were thrown across and rested on the breached wall, affording the soldiers a firm and stable footing. Admetus, indeed, who was the first to quit the bridge, fell pierced by a lance at the moment when he alighted on the wall, but he encouraged his followers to advance, and in a short time they had driven the defenders from the breach, and were in full possession of it. Alexander mounted among the first, and seeing the royal palace near, directed his soldiers to make for it, as affording ready access to the rest of the city.

Meanwhile, the Phœnician fleet in Alexander's service had broken through the obstacles by which the entrance to the southern harbour was closed, and attacking the ships inside had either crippled them or driven them ashore. The Cyprians had at the same time sailed into the northern or Sidonian harbour, which seems not to have been blocked, and held the north-eastern portion of the city at their mercy. The outer circuit of the walls was thus occupied in three places ; and it might have been expected that resistance would have ceased. But the spirit of the Tyrians was not yet daunted. Some, shutting themselves up in their houses, mounted to the roofs, and thence flung down stones and other missiles upon the heads of the Macedonians in the streets. Others threw themselves into a sacred building called the Agenorium, and barricading the entrances, made a desperate defence, though attacked by Alexander himself, till at length they were overpowered and killed almost to a man. Some, despairing of escape, committed suicide. There was a general carnage in the streets and squares, the Macedonians being exasperated by the length of the siege, the stubbornness of the resistance, and the fact that during the siege the Tyrians had publicly massacred, perhaps sacrificed, a number of their prisoners upon the battlements. Eight thousand are said to have been slain in the *mêlée ;* two thousand others, taken prisoners with arms in their hands, were crucified on the sea-shore by order of Alexander. The women, children, and slaves were sold to the number of thirty thousand. Those who escaped consisted of a certain number of the women and children who had been given a refuge by the Carthaginians before and during the siege ; a few hundred males, they could scarcely have been more, whom the Sidonians spared and secreted on board their ships ; and a small body of noble and official personages, who, together with the king, Azemilchus, and some Carthaginian sacred envoys, had taken refuge in the Temple of Melkarth, when the town was stormed. These persons were spared. It would have been more just, if the resistance of Tyre was regarded as a crime, to have visited the offence upon the king and the members of the government, and not upon the two thousand unfortunates, whose blackened corpses, disfiguring the Phœnician sea-shore for months, attested the cruelty rather than the power of the conqueror.

To celebrate his success, Alexander, before marching on against Egypt, entered Tyre in sacred procession, with his soldiers in their full armour, and mounting to the Temple of Melkarth, offered his much-desired sacrifice to Hercules. At the same time his fleet defiled before the temple as part of the ceremony, which was followed by gymnastic games and a torch-race. As memorials of his triumph, he consecrated and gave to Hercules the battering-ram which made the first impression upon the walls, and a Tyrian ship, used in the service of the god, which he had captured in the course of the siege. He then quitted the city, which was half-burnt half-ruined, and almost wholly without inhabitants, content, as it would seem, with his work, having trampled out the only spark, which the East had shown him, of independence.

The siege had lasted seven months, from the middle of January to the middle of July, B.C. 332. For a time Tyre ceased to be a city ; but the advantages of the site, and the energy of the people, who flocked back to it after Alexander's death, raised it again, within no long space, to the position of a wealthy and flourishing community.

XVI.

PHŒNICIA UNDER THE GREEKS AND ROMANS.

ON the division of Alexander's Empire, it was the unhappy fate of Phœnicia to become a chief seat of the struggles between the various sovereigns, known as his " successors," and especially between the two great monarchies of Syria and Egypt, ruled respectively by the Seleucidæ and the Ptolemies. Phœnicia was the battle-field on which Ptolemy Lagi contended with Laomedon and Antigonus; Seleucus with Demetrius Poliorcetes; and Antiochus the Great with Ptolemy Philometor. Tyre, which recovered itself after about eighteen years, and became once more the leading city of Phœnicia, was captured by Antigonus in B.C. 315, by Ptolemy Lagi in B.C. 307, by Demetrius, the son of Antigonus, in B.C. 301, and a second time by Ptolemy Lagi in B.C. 287. Sidon and Akko passed half a dozen times from the possession of Egypt into that of Syria, and again from the possession of Syria into that of Egypt. Ultimately, about B.C. 198, the preponderance of Syria was established, and the fortunes of Phœnicia were thenceforth attached to the kingdom of the Seleucidæ. There is reason to believe that the Phœnicians were willing adherents of the

Syrian cause ; they entertained a jealousy of Egypt, where the rising importance of Alexandria threatened their commerce ; and the Seleucidæ, appreciating the important services which they were capable of rendering, granted them privileges, which they had never enjoyed while they were under the dominion of the Ptolemies.

Among the chief of these was the privilege of striking their own coins. Autonomous coins of Sidon are found bearing a date as early as B.C. 299, when Phœnicia was attached to Egypt ; but the regular series of such coins does not begin till the time of Antiochus Epiphanes (B.C. 175–164), when the coins of Tyre appear with two legends, one Greek and the other Phœnician, coins issued from a local mint, at once acknowledging suzerainty, and claiming a certain qualified independence.

Another sign of favour, belonging to about the same period, is the presence of the Syrian king at the Phœnician capital, on occasion of the great quinquennial festival, and apparently at other seasons also. Alexander's games and sacrifices had taken firm root in the half-Grecized city which had sprung up on the ruins of the former town, and every fifth year there was held at Tyre one of those festive assemblies, in which the Greeks took so much delight, where the offering of sacrifices was combined with gymnastic contests and other amusements. Epiphanes attended the festival of B.C. 175 (2 Macc. iv. 18), and three years later again paid a visit to the city, where he remained for some time, hearing and determining matters of importance (2 Macc. iv. 44–50).

On this latter occasion the Tyrians ventured upon an act, which cannot but have displeased their mighty sovereign, though it does not appear to have drawn down upon them any punishment. Antiochus had made arrangements to hear, while he was at Tyre, a very serious complaint which had been brought against the Jewish High-Priest, Menelaus, who had plundered the Temple of a number of its holy vessels, and was said to have sold some of them to Tyrians (2 Macc. iv. 32). The Sanhedrim, by appointment, sent three representatives to Tyre to take charge of the case against Menelaus, and press the accusations against him before the king. Hereupon, Menelaus, finding that his conviction was certain, if the trial took its regular course, bribed an influential courtier, Ptolemy, the son of Dorymenes, to intercede with Antiochus on his behalf, and by his influence to obtain his acquittal. This Ptolemy easily accomplished, since justice was commonly bought and sold at the Syrian Court ; and there would have been nothing remarkable about the business, had not Antiochus taken it into his head, that, in so grave a matter, some one must be punished, and, therefore, as he had acquitted the guilty, proceeded to condemn the innocent. The three Jewish officials, whose only crime it was to have made the charges which their government had commissioned them to make, by the orders of Antiochus suffered death. Hereupon, in order to mark their sense of the iniquity of this sentence, the people of Tyre decreed to give their bodies honourable burial (2 Macc. iv. 44–50).

About seven years later B.C. 166–5, Phœnician

cupidity seems to have prevailed over Phœnician sense of justice, in another case wherein the Jews were vitally concerned. Epiphanes, on quitting Syria for the East, which required his immediate presence, gave it in charge to Lysias, one of his generals, to proceed into Judæa with what was thought to be an overwhelming force, and entirely destroy the Jewish state. He was first to overcome all resistance, and then to sell for slaves the whole Jewish population, after which he was to repeople the land with strangers (1 Macc. iii. 34–36). The rate of sale was fixed at something under £3 a head (2 Macc. viii. 11)—a price which naturally attracted the slave merchants. We are not expressly told that the traders, who flocked in to buy, were Phœnicians, but only that they were the inhabitants of the "cities upon the sea-coast"— it is, however, almost certain that the bulk of them must have been Phœnicians, since the trade of the Syrian coast was almost wholly in Phœnician hands, and no other merchants of the time would have had such a command of the slave-market as to be willing to purchase slaves by the hundred thousand. It would seem, therefore, that the expectation of securing an enormous profit, tempted the Phœnicians to make themselves accomplices of Antiochus in his iniquitous designs against the Jewish nation—"the merchants of the country, hearing the fame of the Syrians, took silver and gold very much, with servants, and came into the Syrian camp to buy the children of Israel for money" (1 Macc. iii. 41). The result was not what they had expected. Judas Maccabæus completely defeated the vast army of Nicanor, and severely handled the merchants, taking from them as lawful prize a large part of the money which had been intended for the purchase of the captives (2 Macc. viii. 25).

After this, Phœnicia for a while almost disappears from history. She was an integral part of the kingdom of the Seleucidæ, and, though treated with favour, could take no separate action, but was politically merged and sunk in the sovereign state. Her population became more and more Grecized, but still the old Semitic nationality underlay the veneer of Hellenism, and in certain respects showed itself. The coins continued to have Phœnician, as well as Grecian, legends. The trading instinct was as strongly developed as ever, and both Tyre and Sidon had an extensive commerce through the whole of the Syrian period, though the unsettled state of Syria, and the East generally, must have greatly crippled their land-trade, while the rivalry of Alexandria and of Rhodes tended to thwart and impede their maritime enterprize. The Grecizing spirit prevailed especially among the higher orders, and the literary classes. Greek names were commonly borne by men of letters, *e.g.*, Theodotus, Dius, Philostratus, Boëthus, Hermippus, and the like ; the literary works produced were chiefly written in Greek ; and Greek philosophy was studied in the schools of Sidon. By the time of Christ, the language even of the common people seems to have become Greek, for the woman with whom He conversed, when He " went away into the borders of Tyre and Sidon," though " a Syro-Phœnician by race " (Mark vii. 26), was a Greek ('Ελληνὶς) in language.

17

The kingdom of the Seleucidæ came to end in B.C.
83, and for a short time Phœnicia fell under the rule
of Tigranes, the Armenian monarch contemporary
with Lucullus and Pompey, and enjoyed an interval
of comparative tranquillity. War, however, broke
out afresh in B.C. 69, when Tigranes was attacked by
the Romans, and dispossessed of his Syrian principality, which, after a brief hesitation, Rome attached
to her dominions, reducing it into the form of a province under a pro-prætor or a proconsul.

Under the Romans, Tyre, Sidon, and Tripolis enjoyed at first the privilege of being "free cities."
This involved municipal independence, the government of the towns by their own freely elected council
and chief magistrates. Hence we find Julius Cæsar
writing a letter respecting Hyrcanus to the "Magistrates, Council, and Demus of Sidon." Hence, too,
when Antony (B.C. 36) made over to Cleopatra the
government of Palestine and Cœle-Syria as far as the
river Eleutherus, he did it with certain reservations with
respect to the Phœnician cities, whose ancient liberties
were to be respected. Augustus is said (B.C. 20) to
have cancelled these liberties, moved to do so by the
fact that the Phœnicians had embraced the cause of
Antony ; but there is some doubt as to the extent
of the punishment which he inflicted, since Strabo,
writing shortly after the time when the revocation is
supposed to have taken place, speaks of Tyre as still
enjoying its former semi-independence. The position
occupied by the two chief Phœnician cities towards
Herod Agrippa in A.D. 44 (Acts xii. 20–23) implies
their continued possession of a certain separateness

and modified autonomy, since Agrippa could not
have ventured to quarrel openly with towns which
were part and parcel of the Roman state, for to do
so would have been to quarrel with Rome. The
embassies of the two States to the court of Herod at
Cæsarea, their deprecation of his anger, and anxiety
to propitiate him, are indicative of their still occupying the half-subject, half-independent position which
Rome certainly allowed them when they first submitted to her sway.

The date which we have now reached brings us
close to the time when Tyre certainly, and the other
Phœnician cities probably, became acquainted with
the religion brought into the world by Christ, and to
a certain extent adopted it. Phœnicia is mentioned
(Acts xi. 19) among the places which received the
Gospel from some of those persons who were " scattered abroad" upon the death of Stephen. In St.
Paul's third missionary journey (A.D. 57?), on his
return from Greece and Asia Minor to Palestine, he
happened to land at Tyre on his way to Jerusalem,
and found there a "church" established, with which
he remained seven days (ibid. xxi. 3–6). The converts
consisted of men, women, and children. They showed
much regard for the Apostle, being anxious that he
should not go up to Jerusalem, where they knew that
afflictions awaited him, and when he departed escort-
ing him out of the city to the harbour, and there
kneeling down on the shore with him and joining in
prayer. There was a sharp contrast between the
religion of Christ, with its unbloody commemorative
sacrifice, its pure and almost austere ceremonies, its

simple ritual but strict discipline, and the lax, sensuous, nature-worship of Phœnicia, with its impure orgies, its bloody rites, its occasional human sacrifices, and its elaborate ceremonial; but the Tyrian Church flourished and took firm root in the course of the first two centuries, and by the end of the second we find it under its own bishops taking a prominent part in the Paschal Controversy, which then agitated the East. Among the Tyrian bishops known to us were Cassius (about A.D. 198), Marinus (A.D. 253), Methodius (A.D. 267), and Tyrannion (A.D. 310). In A.D. 334, under Constantine the Great, Tyre was selected as the seat of a council in which charges of cruelty, impiety, and use of magical arts were brought against Athanasius, who, as the bishops assembled were chiefly Arians, was condemned and deprived of his see. This condemnation being ultimately reversed, the Synod of Tyre came to be regarded as unorthodox, and Tyre itself suffered in general estimation in consequence.

The growth of Christianity was, of course, gradual in Phœnicia, as elsewhere. During the first three centuries after the Christian era heathenism continued side by side with Christianity in the Phœnician towns, and still more in the country districts, having the advantage that it was closely allied with the civil power, while Christianity was a religion which the law condemned, and which from time to time was persecuted. But, in spite of this disparity, Christianity continually gained on its rival, and early in the fourth century it became apparent that, unless severe measures were taken, heathenism must succumb. Hence the violent persecutions of Diocletian, Galerius, and others. In Phœnicia the repression of Christianity was undertaken by Maximin, who induced the heathen inhabitants of Tyre and other cities to send deputies to his presence with petitions that the Christians might be exterminated. Professedly in compliance with these petitions, Maximin, in A.D. 311, commenced a general persecution of the Christians throughout the East, in which Phœnicia suffered severely. His death, however, two years later, put an end to the troubles ; and the accession of Constantine to the dominion of the whole Roman world was the introduction of a new era of toleration, peace, and prosperity.

Parallel with the growth of Christianity in the Phœnician towns, but commencing somewhat earlier, was a development of Phœnician literary activity which is very remarkable. Strabo informs us that in his day (about B.C. 40 to A.D. 18) there was a philosophical school at Sidon which was familiar with the works of Aristotle. He himself studied Aristotle in conjunction with one of these philosophers named Boëthus, and was acquainted with his brother, also a student of philosophy, by name Diodotus. Tyre had boasted even earlier two Stoic philosophers—one called Antipater, who was intimate with the younger Cato, and known, by reputation at any rate, to Cicero ; and another called Apollonius, who wrote a work about Zeno, and compiled a table of the authors who had written on the subject of the Stoical philosophy, and of the works composed by them. Towards the close of the first century Byblus began to rival Tyre

and Sidon as a literary centre, producing first Heren-
nius Philo, better known as Philo Byblius, and then
his pupil, Hermippus. Philo published a work which
he called a Phœnician history, and professed to have
translated from a Phœnician original. This original
he attributed to an early native writer, whom he
called Sanchoniatho ; but the fragments of the work
which remain seem to show that Philo either composed it himself or at any rate greatly corrupted it.
The main portion which has come down to us is a
cosmogony rather than a history, and may be compared with the cosmogonies of Hesiod, Berosus, and
Apollodorus. It has not much literary merit, but deserves attention as perhaps embodying some genuine
Phœnician ideas. Hermippus, the disciple of Philo
Byblius, contemporary with Trajan and Hadrian, was
a critic and grammarian. Though he studied under
Philo, he was a native of Berytus, which in the third
century became noted as the seat of a school of law,
and for several hundred years furnished the eastern
portion of the Roman Empire with pleaders and
magistrates. Nearly contemporary with Hermippus
must have been Marinus of Tyre, the first really
scientific geographer. Marinus, taking advantage of
the great stores of geographical and hydrographical
knowledge accumulated by the Phœnicians, and
further making diligent use of the works of Greek
and Roman travellers, substituted maps mathemati-
cally constructed according to latitude and longitude
for the itinerary charts which had been in use previously. Ptolemy of Pelusium founded his great
geographical work wholly upon the labours of Mari-

nus, whom, according to his own account, he followed
throughout, except where he had detected him in an
error. Another author of about the same period was
Paulus of Tyre, a rhetorician, who so pleased the
Emperor Hadrian by an oration which he delivered
before him at Rome, that Hadrian conferred on Tyre
the title of "Metropolis," together with the dignity
which the title implied. A little later (A.D. 160–190)
flourished Maximus, also of Tyre, a sophist and Pla-
tonic philosopher, many of whose works are still
extant. He is said to have been among the instructors of the Emperor M. Aurelius, and he appears
certainly to have taken up his residence at Rome in
the reign of Aurelius's son and successor, Commodus.

About the year, A.D. 250, Origen took up his abode
at Tyre. He was far advanced in life, and seems to
have removed to Tyre in order to be out of the way
of persecution. The precaution, however, did not
avail ; he was thrown into prison on account of his
religion, and for some months exposed to much bodily
suffering. It may have been at this time, or it may
have been earlier, that Porphyry, the Neo-Platonist,
attended his teaching. Porphyry was a native of
Tyre, and had originally borne the Phœnician name
of Malchus, *i.e.*, Malik, "king," but being desirous of
ingratiating himself with the Greeks and Romans,
and of sinking his Asiatic origin, he took the Hellenic
and more sonorous appellation of Porphyrius, purple
being the *royal* colour. Indefatigable in his efforts
to become acquainted with learning of all kinds, he
wandered from place to place in order to study under
the most eminent teachers, heard Origen in the East,

was for many years a pupil of Longinus at Athens, and finally came to Rome, about A.D. 262, and joined the Neo-Platonic school of Plotinus. Porphyry was a most determined opponent of Christianity. He wrote a life of Pythagoras on the model of Philostratus' life of Apollonius of Tyana, representing him as having worked stupendous miracles, and as having communicated the gift to Empedocles, Epimenides, and others, which was intended as a covert attack upon the obnoxious religion ; and he likewise directly impugned the Christian doctrines in a work which ran to twenty-one books. This last-mentioned work was answered by Methodius, Bishop of Tyre at the time, but is said to have had a considerable effect in checking the advance of Christianity among the educated classes.

From the latter part of the third century the literary activity of Phœnicia declines. Berytus continued eminent for two centuries longer as a school of Roman law and jurisprudence, but otherwise we find no further signs of intellectual stir or life among the people. With Porphyry the list of ancient Phœnician writers terminates, for even " William of Tyre " (A.D. 1167–1188) was not a native of that city, but of Jerusalem. It will be observed that there was little to distinguish the Phœnician authors of the Greco-Roman period from the rest of their literary compeers. As authors, they for the most part gave no signs of their nationality, but wrote just as the other literary men of their time. It may be doubted if many of them were even acquainted with the Phœnician language, which seems to have gone completely out of use by the first century after our era. The only writers who can be thought to have been exceptions were Marinus of Tyre and Philo of Byblus. Philo distinctly claims to have translated his work from a Phœnician original ; and, whatever we may think of that pretension, we must certainly allow that his work shows a considerable knowledge of the Phœnician language. Marinus must, it would seem, have got the bulk of his facts from Phœnician geographers, whom he must have read, apparently, in the original. But the other learned men who have been enumerated—Boëthus, Diodotus, Antipater, Apollonius, Hermippus, Maximus, Paulus, Porphyry— were Greeks in feeling, perhaps generally Greeks in blood, whom accident had caused to be born in cities that were once Phœnician.

XVII.

PHŒNICIAN ARCHITECTURE.

OF Phœnician architecture, in the ordinary sense of the term, that is to say, of their temples, palaces, courts of justice, even of their ordinary residences, we know next to nothing. Some ambitious efforts have been recently made to restore the plans, and even the façades, of Phœnician structures ; [1] but the attempts, which rest almost wholly upon conjecture, are unsatisfactory, and the buildings themselves do not belong to Phœnicia Proper. From the accounts which have come down to us of the original Temple of Jerusalem, which was the work of Phœnician artists, we may, perhaps, conclude, that the main material which they employed in building was wood—chiefly fir-wood and cedar, which Lebanon could furnish in inexhaustible abundance—and that in general stone was only employed for the substructions of their edifices—substructions, which, however, were sometimes of remarkable size and grandeur. This feature of their architecture will account, to a certain extent, for the extraordinary dearth of remains of ancient buildings in Phœnicia, since wooden structures would necessarily

[1] See Perrot and Chipiez, " Histoire d'Art dans l'Antiquité," vol. iii. pp. 393-5.

SHRINE AT MARATHUS.

crumble and disappear in the course of a few centuries, even if they were not, as they may have been in most cases, destroyed by fire. It is certainly most remarkable that, in Phœnicia Proper, there have not hitherto been discovered even the substructions of any considerable temple. No doubt it is true, that the worship was, to a certain extent, and especially in the earlier

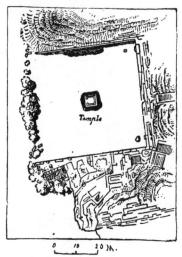

times, an open-air worship ; and, when this phase of the religion passed away, a small cell, open on one side to the winds of heaven, sufficed as a shrine before which the faithful could offer their prayers and sacrifices. The *Maabed* of Amrit or Marathus is a specimen, almost complete, of this earliest kind of temple. In the living rock a quadrangle, 192 feet long by 160 broad, has been cut

GROUND PLAN OF SHRINE AT MARATHUS.

and smoothed into a nearly flat area. In the middle of this space has been left a portion of the natural rock, a block some twenty feet square and ten feet high. Upon this cubical mass, which is one with the floor of the enclosure, has been built of separate stones, a small shrine or tabernacle, fifteen feet long by twelve feet broad and fourteen feet high.[1] The walls are made of three layers of hewn stone, and the roof of a single block. The only

[1] See the woodcut, p. 251.

external ornament is a fillet and cornice along the four sides of the roof, and the only internal one a slight vaulting of the otherwise flat stone by which the chamber is covered in. No steps or staircase leads up into the chamber, and it is difficult to understand how it was entered. Perhaps it was built merely to contain an image of a deity, before which worshippers in the court below prostrated themselves. Two other very similar shrines were discovered by M. Renan, in the neighbourhood of the *Maabed*, and are figured in his great work.[1]

But shrines of these limited dimensions could not long satisfy a nation which had access to the grand edifices of Sais, Tanis, Bubastis, and Memphis, and which was possessed by a spirit of rivalry and imitation. We are told that Hiram, the friend of David and Solomon, not only took part in the constructing of the great Temple at Jerusalem, but also himself erected at Tyre more than one temple of considerable size and magnificence. Unfortunately, no remains of these structures exist at the present day. We may conclude, however, from the example of Solomon's Temple, that they were mainly of wood, but built upon a stone basis ; and that the stone basis was of that solid character which marks all the efforts of the Phœnicians in that material. They laid their courses of stone horizontally in colossal blocks, rough hewn in the main, but smoothed and carefully bevelled at the edges, a style of building which, more markedly than any other, pushes into notice the size of the blocks, their variety, and the harmonious arrangement of

[1] " Mission de Phénicie," Planches, pl. ix.

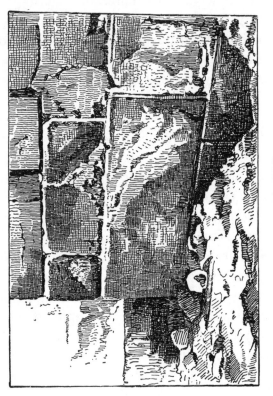

WALL OF GEBEIL.

their sutures or vertical divisions. The grandest specimen of this style, which remains to us, is in the substructions of the Temple of Jerusalem, recently uncovered and measured by the employés of the Palestine Exploration Fund. Here the stones imposed upon the native rock have in some instances a length of thirty-nine and a depth of seven feet, while the courses are for a considerable height formed of blocks almost equally massive. In Phœnicia Proper there are bases of walls which exhibit almost exactly

WALL OF TORTOSA.

the same character, as those at Gebeil and Tortosa, which have been figured by Renan and Perrot.

With respect to the plan of temples, we have little to guide us, with the exception of one or two ground-plans of edifices thought to be temples, in places outside Phœnicia Proper, but known to have been occupied by Phœnician colonists. The Temple of Paphos in Cyprus, explored by M. di Cesnola, is the most remarkable of these specimens. This temple has a double *enceinte* or *peribolus*, both of them oblong squares, the outer one 700 feet long by 630 feet broad, the inner 224 feet by 165. The two periboli are symmetrically placed, and were of the usual colossal masonry, some of the stones measuring about sixteen feet by eight. The material used was a bluish granite, not to be found in the country, which can only have been brought either from Eygpt or from Cilicia. It is thought that both the inner and the outer peribolus were internally screened by porticos, which kept off the sun and rain from the worshippers. This was certainly the case with the Temple of Byblus, whose porticoed court is represented on the coins.

COIN OF BYBLUS ENLARGED.

It is doubtful whether the Temple of Paphos had any cell or shrine. The conjecture has been made, that all which the inner court contained was a stélé or cippus, of the conical form usual in Phœnicia, with perhaps an altar in front. These cippi, called by the Greeks βαιτύλια or κίονες, were special objects of Phœnician worship, serving the place commonly

occupied by images, and regarded with extraordinary
veneration. They were generally said to have " fallen
from heaven ; " and some of them may have been
actual aëroliths ; but the form assigned to them in
the representations is too regular for this to have been
their general origin. They represented, probably, the
same object as the phallus, and were regarded in the
same way, as symbols of the generative power in
nature, and so of Baal, who was that power personified.

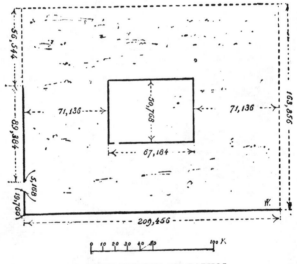

PLAN OF TEMPLE AT PAPHOS.

The walls of towns in Phœnicia had the same
massive character as the foundations of temples. In
some cases the stones were bevelled, but in others
they were merely squared blocks of a vast size, emplaced one upon another in regular courses, and kept
in position by their own weight. The wall of which
the remains are most striking is that of Aradus, now
Ruad. M. Renan calls it "that extraordinary wall

WALL OF ARADUS.

which formerly surrounded the whole island, and which served at once for a defence against the enemy and against the waves. This wall is erected," he says,[1] " upon the outermost ranges of the rocks in such a way as to impend over tolerably deep water. It is composed of quadrangular prisms nine feet three inches in height, and from thirteen to sixteen feet long, sometimes without art and even with a sort of strange negligence, the joints of the stones being in some cases exactly imposed one over the other, sometimes, on the other hand, with an extreme care and attention. The courses are at times regular, small blocks being used to fill in the apertures, and a perfect junction of the parts being in this way effected, but at times the arrangement of the blocks is without any strict or rigorous order, with the exception that they are always laid horizontally. The predominant idea of the constructors has been to utilize in the best way possible the finest blocks. Brought to the spot from the neighbouring quarry, the block has in a certain sense determined its own place. It has been given the best possible position without being required to sacrifice any portion of its mass ; and then the gaps about it have been closed up with smaller materials. . . . One observes no cement. The courses, which in some places number five or six, rest upon a foundation of rock artificially scarped. I do not think that there is anywhere else in the whole world a ruin that is more imposing or of a more marked character. There can be no doubt but that here we have a remnant of the ancient Arvad, a work truly Phœnician

[1] " Mission de Phénicie." pp. 39, 40.

and one which may be used as a criterion for distinguishing other constructions of the same origin.
It is wholly made of the stone of the island itself
which has been extracted from huge quarries, inter-
posed between the present town and the old wall."

The next in importance of the Phœnician monuments remaining to us, and the only other which have
an architectural character, are their tombs.   The
" tomb of Hiram " has been already described.   Four
monuments of a more or less similar character exist
on the Syrian mainland opposite Aradus, in the near
vicinity of Amrit.   Two are known as "the Mêghâzils."
They stand near together on a low hill, at some little
distance from the coast, between the Nahr Amrit and
the Nahr Kublé.   The more striking of the two has
been described as a " real masterpiece in respect of
proportion, elegance, and majesty." [1]   It consists of a
basement storey, which is circular, and flanked by
four stone lions, whereof the effect is admirable,
with a second story of a cylindrical shape, and
a third similar one of smaller dimensions, crowned
by a dome or half-sphere.   The whole, except the
basement-storey or plinth, which consists of four
blocks, is cut out of a single stone.   The double
cylinder is decorated round the summit of each
of its parts, with a row of carved crenellations
standing out about four inches from the general
surface.   The lions, whose heads and fore-quarters
alone project from the mass of the base, are roughly
carved and seem to have been left unfinished ; but
the mouldings, and the general dressing of the stone,

[1] " Mission de Phénicie," p. 72.

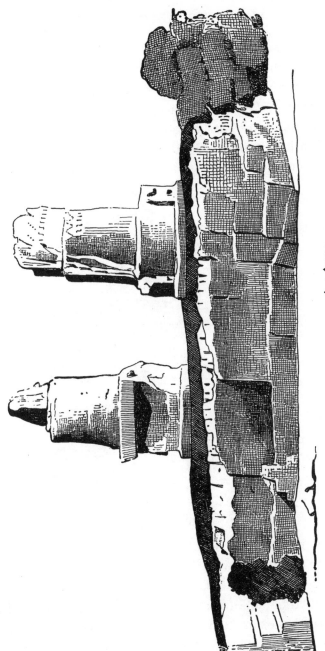

VIEW OF THE TWO MÊGHÂZILS.

have been executed with much care. The entire
height of the monument is thirty-two feet.

The monument stands over a tomb-chamber, and
was erected, we may be sure, to the memory of some
illustrious king or chieftain. The access to its
sepulchral chamber was at a little distance. A flight
of fifteen steps led down to a descending passage

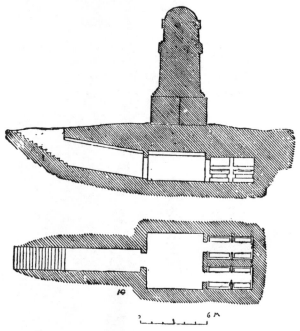

PLAN AND SECTION OF TOMB AT AMRIT.

about twenty-five feet long, which opened into a
square chamber, twenty feet each way, and nine feet
in height. From this, at the further end, opened out
two further chambers, still in the same direction,
containing each four *loculi* or niches for coffins.
Both the chambers and the niches were excavated in
the solid rock.

TOMB AT AMRIT.
(*Sepulchral Monument, restored.*)

Another, companion, monument stands on the same platform with the one above described, at the distance of a few yards. The design of it is less happy. " It is composed, first, of a cubical block with a salient band at top and bottom ; secondly, of a monolithic cylinder about thirteen feet high and twelve feet in diameter ; thirdly, of a five-faced pyramidion. The base is rough, the stone apparently left as it came from the quarry, and the work as a whole looks unfinished." The entire height is about the same as that of the companion monument.

The third of the Amrit tombs is much simpler than either of the Mêghâzils, and much smaller. It consists of a square monolith, resting upon a double base, and crowned with a sort of cornice, above which rises a second block, squared below and shaped like a truncated pyramid above. The entire height was originally about twenty feet, but the apex of the pyramid is gone, and the present height does not much exceed fourteen feet. The monument stands directly over its sepulchral chamber, which is reached by a flight of fourteen steps and a descending passage, and has the peculiarity that the entrance to it is covered by a ridge roof cut from a single block, and supported laterally by a course of huge stones.

The fourth of the Amrit monuments, which is called the *Burdj-el-Bezzak*, is of somewhat a different character. It is megalithic rather than monolithic, being built of large blocks in courses, the number of the existing courses being five ; and, instead of covering a sepulchral chamber or chambers, it has its

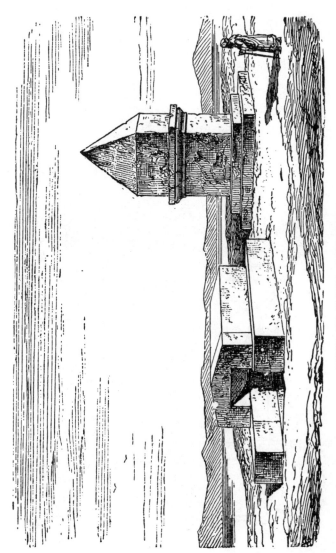

TOMB AT AMRIT, DESTROYED.

TOMB AT AMRIT.
(*Exterior view of the Burdj-el-Bezzak, restored.*)

sepulchral chambers within it. These are in number two, and are at different levels, one parallel with the blocks of the lowest course, and the other with those of the second and third courses. The stones of the lowest course are bevelled, but the others are dressed plainly ; they are laid without cement, and are in some cases sixteen feet in length. The building was originally crowned with a cornice of the ordinary

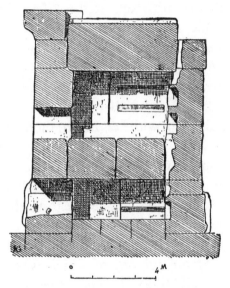

SECTION OF THE BURDJ-EL-BEZZAK.

character, above which rose a low pyramid, about sixteen feet in height. The height of the existing remains is thirty-seven feet ; and thus the monument, as originally constructed, must have had an elevation of at least fifty-three feet. This is considerably more than that of any other of existing Phœnician buildings.

Phœnician tombs were more usually mere excavations in the solid rock, or in the chalky ground common in the country. They consist of one or more chambers, generally on a level, but sometimes one above another, in which are sarcophagi. The chambers are mostly square, and connected one with another by doorways. A single square doorway gives access to them. The following description of the great sepulchre recently discovered near Beyrout (Berytus), will give some idea of the general character of such tombs as are excavated. "The chamber on the eastern side of the deep square shaft (which is truly orientated) contained two sarcophagi in white marble. One of these is perfectly plain ; the other is ornamented with sculptures of the richest and most beautiful kind. The chamber itself is surrounded by an arcade, adorned with eighteen mourning figures in relief, dressed in Greek costume, each in a different pose. The southern chamber had two sarcophagi, one in black marble, plain ; and the other in white, with splendid sculptures. The western chamber had one sarcophagus, in white, mummy-shaped. But this chamber proved to be the vestibule to another, containing four sarcophagi, one of which was the richest and finest of all those found. The walls of this chamber also are richly decorated. The chamber on the north had two plain, mummy-shaped sarcophagi. On removing the *débris* which covered the ground, two other chambers were found, one on either side, on a lower level. One of these contained a small tomb; the other, four white marble sarcophagi. Under the eastern chamber also was found another, containing a sarcophagus of black stone, in which were the teeth, bones, and hair of a woman. All these tombs had been violated by breaking a corner of the coffin lid. But, in carrying out the works for the removal of the sarcophagi, a chamber was found, in which at first nothing was remarked but two fine bronze candelabra, each about five feet in height. The flooring of this chamber, however, on examination, proved to consist of a bed of great stones laid with the utmost care. Beneath these was a second bed, and then a third; and, under all, thus carefully covered up and hidden away, a great monolith, covering an opening in the rock. In this deep chamber was found a splendid sarcophagus in black stone, resembling that of the King Esmunazar, in the Louvre. It was also, which is more important, provided with an inscription in Phœnician, eight lines in length. The inscription is supposed to read as follows: ' I, Tabnit, Priest of Ashtoreth, and King of Sidon, son of Esmunazar, Priest of Ashtoreth and King of Sidon, lying in this tomb, say—" Come not to open my tomb; there is here neither gold, nor silver, nor treasure. He who will open this tomb shall have no prosperity under the sun, and even in the grave shall not find repose." ' [1] There seems to

---

[1] Another version of the inscription runs thus: " I, Tabnit, Priest of Ashtoreth, and King of Sidon, son of Esmunazar, Priest of Ashtoreth and King of Sidon, lying in this tomb, say: ' I adjure every man, when thou shalt come upon this sepulchre, open not my chamber, and trouble me not, for there is not with me aught of silver, there is not with me aught of gold, there is not with me anything whatsoever of spoil, but only I myself who lie in this sepulchre. Open not my chamber, and trouble me not; for it would be an abomination in the sight of Ashtoreth [to do] such an act. And if thou shouldest open my chamber, and trouble me, mayest thou have no posterity all thy life under the sun, and no resting-place with the departed."

have been little else of importance found in these chambers—some gold buttons, a coin or two, some collars, rings, and bracelets, two bronze candelabra, and a few terra-cotta lamps exhaust the list, so far as can at present be learnt."

Where the soil was wanting in firmness and solidity, another kind of tomb seems to have been in use, at any rate in Phœnician colonies. A pit was dug to the depth of from forty to fifty-five feet, and at the bottom a sepulchral chamber was constructed of finely-cut stones, generally of a great size. Some were twenty feet in length, nine feet in width, and three in thickness; and the average size was sometimes as much as fourteen feet long, seven and a half wide, and two thick. The stones fitted admirably, so that often it is difficult to discern the joints of the masonry. The chambers were roofed in two ways: sometimes the roof rose in the form of a gable, three or four sloping slabs rising from the side walls, meeting at the ridge, and supporting each other; sometimes it was flat, the slabs being laid horizontally, and reaching from end to end. A second chamber, occasionally, opened out from the first; and a third, and even a fourth has been found, in a few instances. The chambers invariably contain sarcophagi, which are sometimes very richly ornamented.

The following remarks of M. Renan on the general character of Phœnician architecture may fitly conclude this section:

"The foundation of Phœnician architecture is the carved rock, not the column, as with the Greeks. The wall replaces the carved rock, without entirely

SEPULCHRAL CHAMBER AT AMATHUS.

SEPULCHRAL CHAMBER AT AMATHUS.

losing its character. Nothing conducts to the belief
that the Phœnicians ever made use of the keyed
vault. The principle of monolithism which ruled the
Phœnician and Syrian art, even after it had adopted
much from the Greek, is the very contrary of the art
of the Hellenes. Grecian architecture starts from
the principle of the division of blocks of stone into
small pieces, and avows this principle boldly. Never
did the Greeks derive from Pentelicus blocks of a size
at all comparable to those of Baalbek and of Egypt;
they saw no advantage in them; on the contrary,
they saw that with masses of this kind, which are to
be used entire, the architect has his hands tied; the
material, instead of being subordinated to the design
of the edifice, runs counter to the design. It would
be impossible to construct the monuments upon the
acropolis of Athens with such blocks as were employed in Syria. In Greece the beauty of the wall is
a primary object; and the Grecian wall derives its
beauty from the joints of the stones, which follow
symmetrical rules, and correspond with the general
lines of the edifice. The stones of a wall built in
this style have all of them about the same size,
and this size is determined by the general plan; or
at any rate, as in the masonry which is called
pseudisodome, the very inequality of the courses has
a law of symmetry, which it follows. The architrave,
the metopes, the tryglyphs, are made of several
blocks, even when it would have been easy to unite in
one and the same block several of these parts of the
architecture. Such facts as we remark frequently in
Galilee, where three or four distinct architectural

members are formed out of a single block of stone, would have seemed monstrous in Greece, since they are the negation of all logic. In the Greek style every stone has its individuality, for its represents one member of the order, and it is unnatural to make several members out of a single stone. The principle of Greek construction is by no means, as is the case at Amrit (Marathus), to get out of the block that has been dragged from the quarry, the very utmost that is possible. Every stone is submitted beforehand, and by the very plan of the architect, to a cutting previously determined according to its place in the edifice; the workmen diminish it, if it is too large, unlike the Phœnicians, who leave it all its superfluities. Absolute master of his materials, the Greek architect pushes his art to a delicacy, which has been universally neglected elsewhere. The Syrian and Phœnician architects, and even those of Egypt, are at the command of their material; the stone does not submit to the shape which the artist's thought would impress upon it; it continues to be with them mere rock, more or less; that is to say, undetermined matter. This is the reason why the Grecian architects never made, what we meet with at every step in Phœnicia, at Jerusalem, in Persia, at Petra, in Lycia, in Phrygia, architectural work in the living rock.

"Vast walls in which the courses are of colossal size, brought from the quarry in some sort ready made—so that the characteristic mark of a building made with care was that 'no sound of hammer or saw was heard during its erection (1 Kings vi. 7)—such was the essential character of Phœnician monuments. The somewhat coarse nature of the Syrian stone did not allow the delicate elaboration of bases, friezes, capitals, which by their contrast with the smoothness of the walls, form one of the principal charms of the Grecian architecture. The ornaments which we discovered were very fine and very elegant, but stood out in very low relief. Moreover, one may doubt if they belonged to the early epochs of Phœnician art. In the edifices erected by Solomon, the ornamental parts were, for the most part, in wood or metal. The employment of marble and of Egyptian granite always seems to me in Syria the sign of a later age. The column, when used, appears to have had a certain heaviness; the walls were of the most massive character. It is easy, moreover, to explain how it has happened that these ancient colossal constructions have generally disappeared. Such constructions were in no way suited for the wants of those more refined conditions of society which succeeded to the civilization of the Canaanites; thenceforth they became nothing but quarries open to the sky, from which it was found convenient to borrow the blocks wanted for the edifices which were required to satisfy the new needs."[1]

[1] Renan, "Mission de Phénicie," pp. 822-824.

XVIII.

PHŒNICIAN MANUFACTURES AND WORKS OF ART.

THERE were four principal manufactures in which the Phœnicians excelled the other nations of antiquity ; and, though the limits of our knowledge with respect to each and all are narrow, it may perhaps be expected that the present work should contain some account of the results which modern research has reached with respect to the crafts in question. They were the manufacture of the famous purple dye which was the especial boast of Tyre ; the production of a glass, which was peculiarly characteristic of Sidon ; the weaving of fabrics suitable for garments and furniture ; and the elaboration of works in metal of a superior quality. It is not too much to say, that, while the wealth and prosperity of Phœnicia depended very greatly, perhaps mainly, on her carrying trade, her fame and reputation were chiefly sustained by the excellency of her productions under these four heads.

For the purple dye which acquired so great a celebrity, Phœnicia was primarily indebted to the bounty of nature in scattering abundantly along her coast the somewhat rare shell-fish which yield the precious liquid wherefrom the dye is obtained. The molluscs alluded to are indeed spread tolerably widely over the shores of the Eastern Mediterranean ; but it was only on the rocky part of the Syrian coast, between the "Ladder of Tyre" and Haifa, near Mount Carmel, that they reached the perfection of which they are capable, and yielded the beautiful tints that the whole world agreed in admiring. The

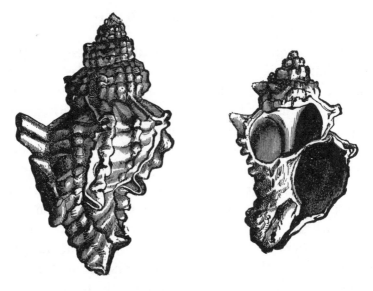

SHELL OF THE MUREX TRUNCULUS.

shell-fish included two distinct species—one known to naturalists as the *Purpura pelagia* or *Murex trunculus;* the other as the *Purpura lapillus* or *Buccinum lapillus.* The chief characteristics of the two molluscs have been given in a former chapter ; but some further account of their habits may be here added. The Buccinum is found on rocks in the vicinity of the shore, and in comparatively shallow water ; the Murex prefers a greater depth, whence its name of *pelagia ;* in modern times it has been dredged from a depth of twenty-five fathoms. Both molluscs are oviparous. The female in spring deposits on the mud or sand at the bottom of the sea a number of minute eggs enveloped in a species of mucus, which by contact with the salt water coagulates and assumes a membranous structure. The male then fecundates the eggs, which gradually undergo a transformation within their respective cells, expanding and then hardening into shell-fish like those which produced them. The membranous structure containing the eggs is compared, by Aristotle, to a honey-comb, but more resembles the nest of the humble-bee. While the process of egg-laying is going on, the molluscs are at their worst in respect of their dye-producing faculty, partly because the eggs contain a considerable quantity of the colouring matter, and partly because the animal is generally weakened and exhausted by the process of reproduction.

The colouring matter is contained in a *sac,* or vein, which begins at the head of the animal, and follows the tortuous line of the body as it twists through the spiral shell, being larger in some, and smaller in other specimens. The matter is a liquid of a creamy consistency, and, while in the *sac* or vein, is of a yellowish white colour; on extraction, however, and exposure to the light, it becomes first green, and then purple. No one has yet been able to discover what purpose it is designed to answer in the economy of the animal; but certainly it is not naturally exuded so as to colour and cloud the water, as sepia is by the cuttle-fish.

The season for collecting the purple dye was the end of the winter, or the very beginning of spring, just before the molluscs would naturally have set to work to lay their eggs. The ordinary mode of capturing them was the following : " A long rope was let down into the sea, to which were fastened at intervals baskets, constructed like those used at the present day, with openings into which the fish easily entered, but could not return, and baited with mussels or frogs, on which the Murex seized with avidity. Being taken from the shell, the *sac* was extracted while the animal was yet alive, as the colouring matter soon changed its quality after death ; or if killed, it was with a single blow, as protracted death injured the colour.   The Buccinum being smaller, the *sac* was not extracted, but the body crushed with the shell, and both thrown in together.   Salt, in the proportion of twenty ounces to one hundred pounds, was then thrown upon it.   After a maceration of three days the pulp was placed in a vessel of lead (brass or iron being carefully avoided, lest these metals should communicate a tinge to the dye), and caused to simmer at a moderate heat by a pipe brought from a distant furnace.   The animal matter which adhered to the *sac* was removed by repeated skimmings ; and at the end of ten days the liquor had become clear, being so reduced in bulk that a hundred amphoræ, or eight thousand pounds, of the pulp produced only five hundred pounds of the dye. At this stage of the process the colour of the fluid should be dark rather than red.   Wool in the fleece, carefully washed, was then dipped into it, to ascertain its strength, and heat again applied till the due strength was attained."

The dye produced by the Buccinum alone was considered to be of inferior quality. It was red, rather than purple, and could not be depended on for endurance. Two hundred pounds of the Buccinum dye was worth no more than a hundred and eleven pounds of the Murex. The Murex, if used alone, produced a dull and dark purple, which was not in favour. It was customary therefore to apply both dyes separately ; and the best and most highly prized colour was that which was given by first applying the dye of the Murex, and then super-adding an immersion in that of the Buccinum. The tint produced in this case was a dark, rich purple, "the colour of coagulated blood, but when held up to the light showing a crimson hue."

It is suspected that another kind of shell-fish, the *Helix ianthina*, was also used by the Tyrians for dyeing purposes ; but this is not stated by the ancients. The *Helix ianthina* has a small shell, not more than three quarters of an inch in diameter, and of a very delicate material. It is a spiral, but of only about three twists, and very unlike the representations of the Buccinum. The fish is found abundantly on the Phœnician coast, about Tyre and Beyrout (Berytus), and is remarkable for throwing out a quantity of purplish liquid when approached, in order (like the cuttle-fish) to conceal itself, which it does effectually, since the water becomes completely clouded all around it. The hue is rather violet than actual purple, and it was perhaps this dye which the

Romans called "conchyliata," and the colour of which they compared with the amethyst.

The rough account which Pliny gives of the Tyrian method of dyeing omits all mention of those more refined processes, which the dyers regarded as secrets of their trade, and on which the superiority of their method over that of others no doubt mainly depended. Among these secrets was probably the employment of mordants to fix the colours permanently and prevent them from washing out. The alkali furnished by a certain kind of sea-weed, found principally on the coast of Crete, was certainly employed in fixing some dyes, and may have been among those known to the Phœnicians, and used by them in the manufacture of their purple fabrics ; but we have no distinct evidence of its actual use. Again, the exposure of the dyed cloths at certain stages to certain degrees and kinds of light was an important factor in the production of peculiarly esteemed hues, and the rules to be observed in this respect would likewise, as far as possible, have been kept secret. Tyrian purple was imitated at various other places, in antiquity, as on the coast of Lacedæmon, in Cythera, at Tarentum, Aquinum, and Ancona in Italy, on the North Coast of Africa, and in the Canary Islands ; but nowhere did the imitations attain to the excellence of the original. The Tyrian dyes continued to be celebrated by poets and affected by priests, senators, and emperors up to the date of Phœnicia's conquest by the Saracens (A.D. 633–638). Even after the Mahometans were installed in power the manufacture continued, and " Tyrian purple " is mentioned among the articles of luxury imported into Lombardy from the East by the Venetian merchants in the time of Charlemagne (A.D. 768–814).

How the Tyrian dyes were originally discovered is a matter, not for dogmatism, but for conjecture. The popular tradition upon the subject will scarcely at the present day be regarded by any as historical. According to this, Hercules, the tutelary deity of Tyre, was one day walking along the Syrian shore, in company with a native nymph called Tyrus, with whom he was in love, and followed by a favourite dog. The dog found a specimen of the *Murex trunculus* lying on one of the rocks, with its head protruded from its shell, whereupon he seized it and devoured it, colouring his mouth with the juice. When Tyrus saw the beauty of the tint, she fell into such an admiration of it, that she told Hercules she must positively refuse his suit until he brought her a garment of the same lovely hue. Thus stimulated, Hercules set himself to collect a number of shell-fish similar to the one which his dog had eaten, and, having extracted from them their colouring fluid, succeeded in obtaining enough to dye a robe, which he presented to the nymph, and thereby gained her consent to become his spouse. How Hercules obtained his shell-fish out of the deep water in which they ordinarily live, or managed the dyeing process, we are not told; nor is any information given us with respect to the discovery of the colouring matter of the Buccinum, as essential as that of the Murex for the production of the true Tyrian dye; so that the story scarcely goes upon all-fours, or satisfies an in-

282 PHŒNICIAN MANUFACTURES AND ART.

quiring mind. But it is perhaps worth something. Dead murices and buccina, thrown up by the sea, may have disclosed their colouring matter as they lay upon the shore, or even have stained the mouths of the creatures that fed on them, whether dogs or birds. Primitive peoples are always fond of bright colours, and the red and purple hues, once noted, would be soon applied, either to stain the bodies or the clothes of those whose attention had been arrested by them.

As Tyre was specially noted for the manufacture of the purple dye, so was Sidon for the manufacture of glass. The discovery was said to have been made by accident. Some merchants, who had brought a cargo of natrum, which is the subcarbonate of soda, to the Syrian coast, where it was used for soap, went ashore at the mouth of the river Belus for the purpose of cooking their provisions. Having lighted a fire on the sand, they looked about for some stones to prop up their cooking utensils, but finding none convenient for the purpose, they fetched from their ship several blocks of the natrum, and supported their cooking-pots upon them. The heat was such as to fuse some of the natrum, which, uniting with the silicious sand upon which it rested, produced a stream of glass. The circumstance is quite a possible one, and there is no reason why glass should not have been invented a dozen times over in a dozen different places. Its manufacture appears to have been known in Egypt, before the Phœnicians settled in the tract afterwards called Phœnicia; and it is perhaps most probable that the Sidonians derived their acquaintance with the art from that country, with which in the early times they were very friendly. Egypt possessed in abundance both the alkali needed in her Natron Lakes, and the silica in the desert sand, which is of very fine quality, whereas Syria has no natrum, nor any convenient substitute for it. What Syria did possess was an inexhaustible supply of fine white silicious sand, free from all admixture of clay, and peculiarly suitable for glass-making; but she had always to import her alkali, either from Egypt or from some other quarter.

The most ancient of the objects in glass, which have a claim to be regarded as of Phœnician manu- facture, are a remarkable kind of beads, found in tombs and elsewhere in almost all parts of Europe, in India and other regions of Asia, and in some parts of Africa, especially upon the Ashantee Coast, where they are known as " Aggry " beads, and are much prized by the natives. They are of opaque glass, generally coloured, and patterned, the colours and patterns being very various, and the beads showing often various degrees of skill in the manipulation. It is thought that the Phœnicians manufactured this kind of bead very early for commercial purposes, and used it in the bartering transactions which they carried on with the uncivilized inhabitants of all the regions to which their trade extended. The fashion once set was followed by other nations ; and " Aggry " beads continued to be made during the Middle Ages, and are even now to a small extent manufactured at Venice.

Glass was, however, chiefly applied, in Sidon as

elsewhere, to the construction of vessels such as
bottles, vases, drinking-cups, bowls, and the like.   It
was seldom employed in large masses, but was very
delicately fashioned and coloured with metallic oxides,
exquisite objects of a small size being produced,
chiefly by means of the blow-pipe.   Occasionally,
patterning was effected by cutting or grinding with a
wheel, while sometimes the surface was engraved with
a sharp tool.   Cylinders of coloured glass were also
made as ornaments of houses or temples ; these were
either solid or hollow ; in the latter case, a lamp
might be introduced into the interior and a dazzling
effect accomplished.   The great difficulty with the
artists of the time was to produce perfectly clear and
transparent glass ; but the Sidonians battled with
this difficulty so far successfully as to cast round
plates of glass which were made into mirrors by covering the back with a thin sheet of metal.   The extent
to which Phœnicia carried the artistic manipulation of
glass is, and must probably always remain, uncertain,
since glass objects are scarcely ever inscribed, and the
best connoisseurs are unable to determine, with a
large number of the specimens in museums, whether
they are of Phœnician, or Greek, or even of Egyptian
manufacture.   So excellent a judge as Winckelmann
confesses his inability to draw the line between Greek
and Phœnician art in this department ; and it is quite
possible that many of the more artistic objects,
commonly set down as Greek in museum catalogues,
are really the product of the best Sidonian glass-
works.

The woven fabrics which the Phœnicians produced

from their looms were, in the early times, either linen or woollen, in the later frequently of silk. Raw silk was imported into Phœnicia by the Persian merchants, and was there dyed and woven into stuffs, which were sometimes of silk only, sometimes of silk intermixed with linen or cotton. These fabrics were held in high esteem, and much sought after by the traders of all countries, but perhaps rather on account of their colours than of any special skill shown in the weaving process. Sidon, however, had a distinct reputation for the excellence of its embroidery from a very ancient date, and the broidered robes of Sidonian sempstresses found a ready market in all the chief resorts of pleasure and luxury.

For metallurgy Tyre and Sidon were, in the remoter times, about equally famous. It was a Tyrian artist who constructed for Solomon those magnificent works in bronze which were among the chief glories of the Temple at Jerusalem, the two pillars called Jachin and Boaz, each nearly forty feet high, elaborately ornamented, and the " molten sea," or great laver, fifteen feet in diameter, supported on the backs of twelve oxen, arranged in four groups of three. It was the same artist who fashioned for the same king "the altar of gold, and the table of gold whereon the shewbread was set, and the ten candle-sticks of pure gold, with their lamps and flowers, and the tongs of gold, and the bowls, and the snuffers, and the basins, and the spoons, and the censers of pure gold, and the hinges of gold both for the doors of the inner house, the most holy place, and for the doors of the house, to wit, of the temple" (1 Kings

vii. 48–50). On the other hand, they were Sidonian artists whose works in silver Homer celebrated as "most beautiful"—"the most beautiful in all the world;" and it is to Sidon and not to Tyre that Strabo ascribes especially the manufacture of drinking-vessels in gold and silver.

As with objects in glass, so with those in metal, it is difficult to lay down positively that any extant specimens are Phœnician. There seems, however, to be much probability that the series of bronze dishes, carefully embossed and engraved, which Sir Austen Layard discovered at Nimrud, and which are represented in the Second Series of his "Monuments of Nineveh," are examples of early Phœnician workmanship, belonging to the eighth or ninth century, B.C. One of them has a Phœnician legend, and two others exhibit a scarab, or beetle, which is pronounced to be "more of a Phœnician than of an Egyptian form," while the mixture of Assyrian with Egyptian types, which is characteristic of the entire number, is not unnatural if they were the products of a country over which Egypt and Assyria exercised about equal influence. Assuming then the more ornamental of these works to be Phœnician, we may note, first, that the bronze is of excellent quality, containing exactly those proportions of tin and copper which were decided by the Greeks and which are still regarded by modern artists as the best, viz., one part of the former to nine of the latter metal; secondly, that the ornamental work is effected by two different processes, partly by punching the bronze with a blunt instrument from the back or outside, and partly by a careful but sparing use of the

PATERA FROM CURIUM.

graving tool on the inside after the embossing was completed ; and thirdly, that the designs, while not of any high artistic merit, are curious and interesting, showing in the patterns a lively and elegant fancy, and in the figures, which are both human and animal, a great vigour, boldness, and force. The animal forms include lions, bulls, antelopes, horses, wild goats, leopards, bears, deer, hares, greyhounds, serpents, sphinxes, and vultures ; they are, in every instance, unmistakably characterized, and, in some, leave little to be desired. The human forms are inferior, and mostly verge on the grotesque ; but they show considerable power of drawing.

In some instances, small bosses of silver or gold have been inlaid into the bronze. In others, the dishes have a rim, or border, made in a separate piece, running round about one-third of the dish, and fastened to it by nails or bosses. To this rim is attached the handle, which is of horse-shoe shape, and works freely through two rings, the intention apparently being that the dish should be hung up by it.

Sir A. Layard conjectures,[1] that the set of dishes may have been carried away from Tyre, or from some other Phœnician city, when it was captured by the Assyrians, and may have been used by the captors for sacrificial purposes, at royal banquets, or when the king performed certain religious ceremonies ; or that they may have been selected from the spoil of some city, to be laid up in one of the temples of Nimrud, as

---

[1] "Nineveh and Babylon," pp. 192, 193. Similar dishes and bowls have been found in Cyprus on Phœnician sites, which tend strongly to confirm the Phœnician origin of the Nimrud bronzes.

the holy utensils of the Jews, after the destruction of the Temple, were kept in the treasury of the great sanctuary of Bel-Merodach at Babylon. Either alternative is possible ; but neither can be regarded as having distinct claim to acceptance ; and severe critics may perhaps question whether the evidence on which is based our view that the dishes are really Phœnician is altogether satisfactory.

Perhaps it must be said that the only objects in metal that can be positively assigned to Phœnicia Proper are its coins. Even these are not numerous ;

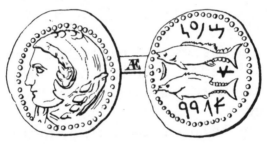

COIN OF GADES.

and they have few marked peculiarities. The earlier have the irregular shape and clumsy thickness of all coins of ancient workmanship ; the later are thinner, and more nearly approach to the circular form. The favourite emblem in the more primitive times is a trireme, beaked in front, and with a lofty stern, ending sometimes in a fish's tail. On the coins of Sidon is sometimes found the figure of Ashtoreth accompanied by a star, sometimes the front of a temple resting on four columns. Coins of the later period have mostly Greek emblems—Neptune with his trident ; Bacchus with the cista, diota, and thyrsus ; Europa riding upon the bull ; Cadmus killing the serpent ; Hercules with his club and lion's skin ; and the like. Bilingual legends, Greek and Phœnician, are common ; but the subject matter of the two legends is generally different. Under the Seleucidæ, the royal name and title are in Greek, while the name of the locality, for which the coin is struck, is in Phœnician. Coins of Phœnician colonies have, for the most part, a single legend, which is in the native character. One of Tarsus shows Baal seated on a throne, with a sceptre in his right hand, and the legend *l'Baal Tarz*, "To Baal of Tarsus." Another of Gades has two tunny fish, with the inscription *m'baali Agadir*, "from the citizens of Gades."

The chief arts practised by the Phœnicians were, besides architecture, sculpture, navigation, mining, working in ivory, gem-engraving, and ornamental metallurgy.

It is from the ornamentation of the tombs that we obtain our main knowledge (such as it is) of the characteristics of Phœnician sculpture. Complete statues, which can be positively assigned to Phœnician artists, scarcely exist ; but on the walls of tombs, and still more, on the richly-ornamented sarcophagi contained in them, are not infrequently found reliefs, which must in reason be ascribed to the same people as the tombs themselves. Unfortunately, none have been discovered of any very great antiquity. Even the earliest belong to a time when Greek influence had begun to be felt, and when the sculptor, consciously or unconsciously, imitated Greek models. In one, at Amathus in Cyprus, a purely Phœnician

city, we see a funeral procession, consisting of two
men on horseback, four *bigæ*, or chariots drawn by
two horses, with either two or three persons in
each chariot, and three footmen behind the *bigæ*,
walking fast, to keep up with the horses. There
is some, though not much, variety in the postures of
the horses, which are of a strong compact make, like
those seen in Greek friezes. They wear top-knots,
like the Assyrian and Lycian horses, but larger and
more in the shape of an open fan. The human figures
are, in every case, draped, wearing the chitôn and
chlamys, or at any rate the latter, except the horsemen, who seem to have on a tight-fitting dress of
leather. A few of the figures are bare-headed, but the
generality wear a turban or a close-fitting cap. One
carries a parasol, but whether to shade himself or his
companion, is uncertain. The proportions of the
figures and of the horses are good, the workmanship
not very refined, but fairly good ; and, if the composition must be said, on the whole, to lack life and
spirit, we must remember that the solemnity of the
subject would make lively action—prancings and cur-
vettings of horses or gesticulations of men—inappro-
priate.

Two other reliefs occupy the two ends of the sarcophagus. In these the Greek ideal has been discarded,
and Oriental art shows itself without a possibility of
mistake. It is needless to say that the result is a
lamentable falling off. One end is occupied by four
figures of Astarte, or Ashtoreth, perfectly similar,
which stand side by side, like Caryatides, except that
their heads do not *quite* touch the entablature above

BAS-RELIEF ON SIDE OF SARCOPHAGUS FROM AMATHUS.

BAS-RELIEF ON SIDE OF SARCOPHAGUS FROM AMATHUS.

them.   The figures are nude, except that each is adorned with a double necklace of beads, and have the two hands so placed as to support the two breasts. They are ill-proportioned, the heads being too small, and the bodies considerably too short, not to mention that they are almost without necks.   At the other end the bas-relief is injured, a large hole having been there knocked in the sarcophagus ; but enough remains to indicate that here too were four nearly similar figures, but male instead of female, and intentionally grotesque and hideous.   They have been called figures of Melkarth, but more probably represent four of the eight Cabiri, or else Eshmun four times repeated.   They are fat pigmy figures, with unduly large heads, fearfully ugly faces, and mis-shapen legs, recalling the description which Herodotus gives of the Patæci, wherewith the Phœnicians ornamented the prows of their warships.   The lid of the sarcophagus was ornamented with figures *in the round.*   These represented sphinxes or harpies, having a woman's head, a lion's body, and the wings of a bird.   They were carefully carved, and quite equal to the ordinary sculptures of the Egyptians.

The sculptures in the sepulchral chambers discovered in the present year (1887) near Sidon, and already briefly described,[1] appear to be even more remarkable.   An eye - witness gives the following account of them :—

" Impossible is it to describe the splendour, the perfection of the tombs of this locality ; so perfect an art is not to be described but admired.   The variety of forms, of styles, of workmanship, is no less astonishing;

[1] See p. 268.

SARCOPHAGUS FROM AMATHUS.
(First Short side.)

SARCOPHAGUS FROM AMATHUS.
(Second Short side.)

it still laughs to scorn all the conjectures that can be made as to the origin of the sepulchres. The chamber situated towards the east contained two large sarcophagi in white marble, placed on the same level, and separated the one from the other by an interval of rather more than half a yard. Their dimensions are alike—a length of eight feet, a breadth of four, and a height of only a few inches less, without counting in the lid, which measures above one and a half feet. One of the two, that which the visitor has on his left upon entering, is entirely without sculpture or ornamentation of any kind ; but the other is, on the contrary, covered with sculptures, and immediately attracts attention.

" Around the entire chamber there runs a colonnade which rests on fluted pillars of the Ionian order, diversified by Doric pilasters in the corners. In each of the eighteen niches there is the figure of a mourner in high relief, dressed according to the Grecian fashion. All are in different attitudes ; and each of them has a sorrowful expression peculiar to itself, which is at once perfectly natural, and full of dignity.

" The lid of the sarcophagus resembles a pointed roof, sloping two ways, and formed of flat stones overlapping one another, like the flat Marseilles tiles which are employed for roofing houses at Beyrout. There extends along its whole length an attic, a foot and a half high, about level with the top of the roof, and adorned with sculptures representing a funeral procession. At the head of the procession marches a man dressed like a Greek ; next come two horses, led by grooms ; then a triumphal car, a man carrying fillets, and a *biga*, or two-horse chariot, laden with the sarcophagus of the departed. Behind this chariot is an attendant, and last of all a horse, walking alone. Along the edge of the base there runs a bas-relief of great delicacy, representing the chase of the stag, the wild boar, the lion, and the leopard.

" The chamber towards the south contained also two sarcophagi. Though the entrance to it was on the same level with the other chambers, its floor, on which the sarcophagi rested, was six feet below the floor of the others. One sarcophagus was of black marble, called improperly Egyptian basalt, and was not distinguished by any sculpture. At its side the visitor saw another of white marble, placed towards the left, clearly made to provoke his admiration by the singularity of its form and the richness of its ornamentation. The lid, ogive in shape, had a height of four and a half feet; the sarcophagus which it covered, a length of seven and a half feet, a width of four feet, and a height equal to that of the lid.

" It is a tomb which may be called Lycian. Previous to its discovery, only seven tombs of the kind were known, and all these had been discovered in the tract called Lycia; of these, six are now at Constantinople and one at Vienna. The back of the vault forming the lid is smooth and without ornament. On the two upright ends are sculptured, in the one case, two magnificent Greek sphinxes, winged, with the breasts of a woman, and with human heads that are exceedingly fine and graceful ; in the other, two gryphons with the heads of birds, and the bodies of mammals, the one male and the other female.

" Upon the sarcophagus one sees two *quadrigæ*, or four-horse chariots, driven by Amazons.   The horses have the archaïc and conventional form of those sculptured on the Parthenon by Phidias.   The mane is straight, like the dorsal fin of a fish ; in the mouth is a bit ending in two flat squares, which tightly compress the lips of the animal.   But the thing which is most worthy of admiration is the expression of the horses' heads, which live, speak, have a finish that is absolute perfection.   The muscles, the veins, the quiverings of the nostrils, the folds of the skin are rendered with unequalled precision.   ' I would give,' said the discoverer, ' one of the other sarcophagi, all complete, for the head of one of these horses.'

" The opposite side of the sarcophagus represents a boar hunt.   A horseman in Greek costume, with arm outstretched and two of his fingers—the first and second—extended, seems to be giving an order.   ' He looks like one of our bishops giving us his blessing,' say the Greek women of the modern Sidon (Saïda). On one of the smaller sides or ends, two centaurs, standing up on their hind legs, hold a doe between their forelegs, and dispute possession of it ; their figures are full of expression and extremely beautiful. On the other end are also two centaurs, each of whom empties a jug of water over the other.   The intention of this sculpture is hard to conjecture.   There can be no doubt that it is the great height of this sarcophagus which induced the original excavator to lower the floor of the chamber.

" The chamber on the west, which was of little depth, contained only one sarcophagus—a sarcophagus in white marble, shaped like a mummy case. It will be described later on. This excavation served as the vestibule of a sepulchral chamber of greater size and more elaborate than the others, which opened from its southern wall. Here were drains against the wall, prepared to receive such moisture as might exude from them, and in the upper part of the walls were holes, corresponding each to each, made to receive the ends of the beams, by aid of which the lids of the sarcophagi were put in place, while a red line was traced upon the wall horizontally, to serve as a mark for the workmen who had to emplace the lids. There were four tombs in this chamber. The largest, which was also the most richly ornamented and the finest of all the sarcophagi discovered in the entire burial-place, occupied the south-west corner. It is a little more than ten feet long, five feet four inches broad, and, without the lid, four feet five inches high. The height of the lid is two feet seven inches. It is *a masterpiece of sculpture, architecture, and colouring, the discovery of which will form an epoch in the history of art.* All the museums of Europe will need to have casts of it. It is a work of Greek type, whereof the forms hold a middle place between the archaïc conventionalism of the earlier times and the realism of the latter period of ancient art. By its truth to nature, its nobility, and its grace, it seems to be comparable to the most beautiful of all the works of art previously known.

" The whole is painted in natural colours, among which are predominant the various shades of the purple dye, from deep crimson, through intense violet, to blue. It is well-known that Sidon possessed large manufactories of the purple dye. One can see even now, on the slopes of the hill whereon stands the ancient citadel, known as that of St. Louis, great heaps of *murex* shells, all of them opened on the same side, with the object of extracting from them the molluscs inside, which furnished the Tyrian purple. The other colours used appear to have been ochres, such as are common in the neighbouring Lebanon. All the tints are admirably harmonized, in spite of their brilliancy. No detail is forgotten. There is nothing which is not painted in the hue appropriate to it, down to the eyes of the men, horses, and lions ; and this, although the sculptor has not marked by any incision in the marble the outline of either the iris or the pupil.

"All the sculptures are in high relief ; and, when the limbs of the figures are detached from the background, they are not even given supports.

"Two subjects occupy the four sides of the sarcophagus. One large and one small side are occupied with a battle-scene, while the remaining two sides are filled with hunting subjects. The same persons are figured in both cases, in the one as enemies, in the other as friends. The fight is between Greeks and Persians. The Greeks, easily recognized by their physiognomy, are naked ; they wear nothing but a helmet on their heads, and the large round buckler with broad border, which is peculiar to them, on their left arm. The Persians are completely clothed. They are to be recognized by the peculiar head-dress called *mitra*, which envelops the whole head from the forehead to the nape of the neck, and covers the cheeks and the chin, the same that is worn by the companions of Darius in the great mosaïc of Pompeii. They are also distinguishable by their long trousers (*braccæ laxæ*), a garment peculiar to the people of Asia and of the north. The Greeks never wore trousers ; and the Romans only adopted them late under the Empire. All the arms of the combatants were of gold, and had been removed very carefully by those who first broke into the tombs.

" In the centre of the battle is a frightful confusion of horsemen, foot soldiers, corpses, men in the act of dying ; an amputated hand lies on the ground, disregarded and trampled under foot. The Persians are animated by a fury which is in strong contrast with the calm intrepidity and martial serenity of the Greeks. We can see which side will gain the victory ; almost everywhere the Greek combatant plunges his sword into the breast of the barbarian, before the latter can strike him with the mace, or battle-axe, or spear, which he brandishes in the air. There are figures, there are attitudes, of every kind of beauty. The animation of the combatants, the pain and alarm of the dying, even the fright of the horses—each and all are admirable.

" As was the Greek usage, the two principal personages appear at the two ends of the picture. They are horsemen clothed in purple. One of them, conspicuous by his attitude, his martial air, and the richness of his apparel, may well be the prince who was entombed in the sarcophagus. The other, whose head is Greek and of the finest type, and who wears on it the skin of a lion, may, perhaps, be Alexander the Great, who is represented on several coins with this Herculean adornment.

" In the other relief a lion has leapt upon a horseman, and begun to tear with his claws the breast of
the horse on which he rides.   Bloody masses of flesh
hang from the wound.   The rider has pierced the
lion with his spear, and endeavours to master his
steed ; but the lion still keeps hold of his prey, despite
the efforts of a huge dog, who has rushed upon him
determinedly, and bites him with the utmost fury.
Two huntsmen are running up with their hunting-
knives in their hands, and in the distance an archer is
about to discharge an arrow from his bow.   The men
and the animals are alike magnificent for their spirit,
their courage, and their strength.   At no great distance, a poor stag, trapped by a couple of hunters
from whom it is not possible that he can escape, excites
the spectator's compassion and forms a contrast with
the rest of the *tableau.*

" The lid of the sarcophagus is not inferior in
beauty.   It is shaped like a gabled roof, covered with
tiles resembling the scales of a fish.   All around, both
on the border and on the line of the roof, there stand
up heads of genii, which are of a ravishing grace, and
are surrounded by glories or haloes.   The heads on
the roof have two faces, and are somewhat larger than
those along the border.   Rams' heads, projecting from
the cornice like gurgoyles, alternate here with the
heads of the genii.   At the four corners are couched
four lions, which seemed to us incomparable masterpieces.   One might say that they were lamenting over
the dead man, and endeavouring to catch a sight of
him by bending their heads down over the edge of
the roof.

" The other three sarcophagi of white marble found in the chamber were exactly similar the one to the others. They measure eight feet in length, and have a height altogether of a little more than six feet. Their form is that of a Greek temple of the most harmonious proportions. The wal s are smooth ; but the cornice is very delicately sculptured, and below it runs an astragal, on which the foliage of a vine is depicted in yellow on a ground of purple. On the base and on the pediments, the sculptured ornamentation is equally pleasing. On the whole it must be said of this entire series of tombs, that they are real masterpièces of good taste, harmony, and elegance. In this class of work nothing has ever been seen of such a noble, such a royal simplicity.

" The chamber towards the north presented at first sight no more than two sarcophagi, one of which belonged to the class of Egyptian coffins which represent roughly the human form in the manner of the cases of mummies, and have been called ' anthropoid sarcophagi.' Like that in the vestibule of the western chamber, it is of white marble. The head is roughly traced upon the lid, and the arms melt into the bust ; but from the point where the hips begin, everything is more carefully marked. The projections of the knees, the calves of the legs, and the ankle-bones, are indicated with sufficient clearness. In this respect the present specimen differs from the ' anthropoid sarcophagi ' found at Sidon which may be seen in the museum of the Louvre, where the head is very well made out, while the lower portion is a simple case turned up at the foot.

" A plank of sycomore, the wood used in Egypt for the cases of mummies, covers the bottom of the sarcophagus. Small holes are bored all round it towards the edge, through which no doubt strings were passed to retain the body in its place upon the plank. To judge by what remains of the bandages and bones, the body must have been very imperfectly mummified.

" During the process of removing the rubbish which covered the floor of the chamber, the existence of two other chambers became apparent, situated respectively to the east and to the west, and at a lower level. Of these the eastern one contained nothing but a small tomb of no interest, but the other held four sarcophagi in white marble. Only one of them—that which stood furthest from the entrance, had any sculptures. One of its smaller sides exhibited a prince, crowned with the Assyrian tiara, extended on his funeral-bed. Food was being offered to him, and drink out of a large horn. Two servants standing behind his pillow appeared to act as guards ; his wife, seated beside his feet, was bewailing her spouse. The scene appears to represent the making of an offering to the dead.

" All the tombs of which we have spoken hitherto had been violated at some considerable distance of time by persons greedy of gain, who had carried off everything of intrinsic value. Consequently nothing was found in the way of trinkets, except fifty-four gold buttons, of the diameter of a half franc, ball-shaped, and without any chasing. These were buried in the earth deposited at the bottom of the tomb of the Assyrian personage. The violators had in every case broken into the sarcophagi by fracturing one of the corners of the lid, without damaging any other part.

"The excavator, had, however, the good fortune to open one sarcophagus which had not been violated. He discovered it in an under-chamber, exactly beneath the tomb of the eighteen mourners. It was a sarcophagus in black stone, of a semi-anthropoid form sufficiently singular, flat and about a yard broad. It contained a mass of long hair, the bones of a woman with the remains of bandages, a royal diadem in gold, smooth and of the width of three fingers, a gold wedding-ring, quite plain, like the ring of a curtain, and, at the bottom, a plank of sycomore wood, like the one already described.

"The 'diggings' furnished, besides, some earthenware lamps, rudely modelled, in the shape of a round plate, the edge of which has been pinched and turned up, to form a spout for the wick ; and also several alabastrums, or vases in alabaster intended to hold perfumes. These are all of Egyptian alabaster, pear-shaped, and about ten inches in height, without any other marking beyond the raised circles left by the lathe of the potter : the neck is narrow, and the vase fragile, since it is little more than one-third of an inch thick. Alabastrums of a similar character were brought from Cyprus by M. di Cesnola.

"The character of the art exhibited by the sculptured tombs is decidedly Greek. The blocks of marble must have been imported from the islands of the Archipelago, since no marble is furnished by the Asiatic coast between Egypt and the neighbourhood

of Smyrna.　They must, however, have been sculptured at Sidon, since it would have been impossible to
bring from Greece objects at once so heavy and so
delicate.　The body of the largest sarcophagus weighs
above ten tons and its lid above four tons.　It is to be
presumed that the mode employed for lowering them
into the pit was the same as that which was in use in
Egypt, viz., the following :—the pit was filled with
sand and the sarcophagus emplaced upon this artificial ground; the sand was then by degrees extracted,
and the sarcophagus sank as the amount of sand in
the pit diminished.

"At the extreme end of the northern chamber
above described, the excavator remarked a hole which
appeared to lead to other excavations.　Guided by
this indication, he discovered, at the distance of six
yards and a half from the pit in which his researches
had hitherto been made, a second similar pit, thirteen
feet broad in one direction and nine feet nine inches
in the other.　When this pit or shaft had been cleared
out to the depth of about twenty-three feet, there was
seen to be an opening in its northern face.　The
chamber to which this opening gave access was sixteen feet three inches long by eleven feet in width.
The rock was covered with a thick layer of rough-cast
and stucco, which in places had fallen to the ground.
In one corner were found on the floor two large bronze
candelabra.　They are simple and beautiful :—a
tripod forms the base ; the stem, which is of the
thickness of a man's arm, terminates in two blossoms,
placed upside down, one over the other, and having
above them a long basket, designed to hold the torch.

Both are modelled on the same type, but they are of unequal size : one is four feet ten and a half inches in height ; the other is an inch or two less. A very similar candelabrum was found in Cyprus, at Curium, and is now in the Museum of New York. The floor of the chamber was formed of a bed of huge stones, about two feet thick, and fitting closely ; below this was a second bed, still thicker ; and then a third ; finally, there was an enormous monolith, measuring ten cubic mètres, which covered a grave, cut in the natural rock, wherein lay concealed a magnificent anthropoid sarcophagus of black stone. It recalls very strikingly the sarcophagus of Esmunazar, king of Sidon, which was also discovered in the gardens about Saïda, but more to the south, and which is in the Museum of the Louvre. It has a length of eight feet, and a medium width of two feet seven inches. The head is magnificently sculptured ; both head-dress and beard are in the Egyptian style ; the chest, and the upright sides of the coffin are covered with hiero- glyphics ; on the raised part, which is in the form of a foot-stool, and which covers the feet, is a Phœnician incription of eight lines. The whole was perfectly intact.

"On the removal of the lid, the mummy appeared to be in a good state of preservation ; but there almost immediately took place a partial decomposition of the body, accompanied by the emission of a fetid smell, which did injury to the middle part of the corpse. The hands and the bottom of the feet dis- appeared ; the rest of the body was covered by the sand, with which the sarcophagus appears to have been originally filled, and which had sunk in consequence of the body having dried up. The hands and the feet, remaining uncovered, were destroyed by the moist atmosphere. The body reposed on a concave plank of sycomore-wood, to which were attached on either side six silver rings, made to receive the cords with which the body was kept in place. In the coffin was found a golden diadem without ornament.

"On the same level with this royal sepulchre, an opening in the southern wall of the shaft gave admission to a sepulchral chamber divided into two compartments. That on the west contained a tomb which had not been violated ; and in it were found a great number of women's trinkets, a golden collar, two bracelets in gold of fine workmanship, another bracelet ornamented with coloured stones, and having in the centre the kind of opal which is called ' cat's-eye.' There were also recovered a number of rings which seem to have been anklets, sixteen finger rings, a bronze mirror, several ' symbolic eyes '—an Egyptian ornament which is shaped like an elongated eye, with a tear falling from the inner corner. Some of these ornaments were in gold, the others in carnelian. The compartment on the west, and another chamber which opens into it and is in the same direction, contained nothing but tombs which had been violated and were of no interest."[1]

The extent of Phœnician navigation has been already considered in the account which has been given of the Phœnician colonies, and in the section on the

---

[1] From the " Journal le Bachir," of the 8th of June, 1887 (published at Beyrout).

circumnavigation of Africa. It is certain that the Phœnicians affronted the perils of the open ocean, and probable that they succeeded in rounding the Cape of Good Hope, and making their way from Suez by the Red Sea, the Indian Ocean, and the Atlantic to the Mediterranean. But their art of navigation was, no doubt, rude and primitive. For the most part their traders hugged the shore, or at any rate shrank from venturing out of sight of land; and when direct voyages were undertaken from shore to shore, or from island to island, it was only when the direction was well ascertained and the interval moderate. Still, some of the more elementary portions of the art must have been known to them, since it is certain that they occasionally ventured into the open ocean, and also that they made voyages by night, and steered their course by the Polar star. They undoubtedly from an ancient date made themselves charts of the seas which they frequented, calculated distances, and laid down the relative position of place to place. Strabo says that the Sidonians especially cultivated the arts of astronomy and arithmetic, as being necessary for reckoning a ship's course, and particularly needed in sailing by night. They must have had some mode of estimating the rate of a ship's progress, or night voyages would have been too dangerous to have become common, as they seem to have been. In the Mediterranean it was not requisite to devote any attention to tides; but in the Atlantic, Red Sea, and Indian Ocean a knowledge of them was important, and the Phœnicians are found to have paid attention to the subject. They noted the occurrence of spring and neap tides, and were aware of their connection with the position of the sun and moon relatively to the earth ; but they made the mistake of supposing that the spring-tides were highest at the summer solstice, whereas they are really highest in December, since the sun at that time approaches the earth more nearly than at any other season. " Observations," in the nautical sense of the word, were of course impossible before the invention of optical instruments ; but meteorology was carefully studied, and the captains of the Phœnician ships made, we may be sure, excellent " weather forecasts."

The little which we know of Phœnician mining is derived from Posidonius. Posidonius was a Tyrian Greek of the first and second centuries B.C. He travelled extensively, and, among other countries, visited Spain, Liguria, Gaul, and Italy. In Spain he carefully examined the mines which had been first opened by the Phœnicians, then enlarged by the Carthaginians, and finally worked extensively by the Romans. He did not distinguish, probably he had no means of distinguishing, between the methods originally pursued and those which he found in actual operation. But there is no reason to suppose that they were very different. The Carthaginians inherited the system of the Phœnicians, and the Romans that of the Carthaginians. No doubt improvements were from time to time introduced ; but, after the first surface scratching, the main features of mining must always have been the same ; and the Book of Job is a witness that they were all in use at the time when it was written, which few will now place later than B.C.

5oo, long before Carthaginian superseded Phœnician influence in Spain.

The Spanish mines were the result of prolonged and thoroughly scientific labour. Perpendicular shafts were bored down to a great depth in the solid rock, and from the bottom of them horizontal adits were driven through the hardest strata, while from these adits branched out to right and left numerous galleries. Air-shafts were at intervals opened from the workings to the surface. To keep the mines free from water, tunnels had been constructed wherever it was possible, down which the water flowed to a lower level. In the time of Posidonius some of the water was pumped up by means of Archimedes screws; but it is probable that this was a Roman improvement. When the ore had been extracted, it was first subjected to a certain degree of heat, then crushed by water power and pounded into a paste, after which, by repeated washings and siftings, the pure metal was separated from the stony matrix which had contained it. To obtain the necessary water-power, reservoirs were made at a great height among the mountains, and channels formed from them to conduct the fluid to the crushing mills, and the sifting-works. Altogether, it may be said that the method employed was very much that which is still in use, except that the steam-engine has superseded the Archimedes screw for pumping purposes, and that no attempt was made to separate one metal from another where two were intermixed, whence it resulted that the gold obtained was often much alloyed with silver, and the silver with lead.

It has been conjectured that the author of the Book

of Job had the mines of Spain in his view when he wrote the subjoined passage—

> " Surely there is a mine for silver,
> And a place for the gold which they refine.
> Iron is taken out of the earth,
> And brass is molten out of the stone.
> Man setteth an end to darkness,
> And searcheth out to the furthest bound
> The stones of darkness and of the shadow of death.
> He breaketh open a shaft away from where men sojourn ;
> They are forgotten of the foot that passeth by;
> They hang afar from men ; they swing to and fro.
> As for the earth, out of it cometh bread,
> But underneath it is turned up as it were by fire.
> The stones thereof are the place of sapphires,
> And it hath dust of gold.
> That path no bird of prey knoweth,
> Neither hath the falcon's eye seen it :
> The proud beasts have not trodden it,
> Nor hath the fierce lion passed thereby.
> He putteth forth his hand upon the flinty rock ;
> He overturneth the mountains by the roots,
> He cutteth out channels among the rocks ;
> And his eye seeth every precious thing.
> He bindeth the streams, that they trickle not,
> And the thing that is hid bringeth he forth to light "
>
> (Job xxviii. 1–11).

We are justified in regarding the Phœnicians as workers in ivory by the statement of Athenæus that they were the first to use that material in the construction of musical instruments, and perhaps by the fact that Solomon's throne was made chiefly of ivory, since it is difficult to regard Solomon as employing for his artistic works any artificers who were not Phœnicians. Ahab's " ivory house," moreover, may reasonably be connected with the close relations which he established with Sidon. Tyre certainly imported ivory to a considerable extent (Ezek. xxvii. 15), and most probably exported it in an ornamental and artistic form. If any extant specimens in our museums are to be regarded as Phœnician, they would seem to be those which present that mixture of Assyrian with Egyptian features which we have noted in the set of bronze dishes found at Nimrud. Objects in ivory of this kind exist ; and the same reasons, which incline us to admit the Phœnician workmanship of the Assyro-Egyptian dishes, would be valid if applied to the Assyro-Egyptian ivories.

Gem engraving was certainly a Phœnician art. Seals exist of Babylonian or Perso-Babylonian type with Phœnician legends, which have evidently been engraved for, and probably by, Phœnicians. The writer of Chronicles declares that Hiram of Tyre was " skilful to grave *any manner* of graving " (2 Chron. ii. 14). The precious stones which adorned the vest-ments of the Tyrian monarchs in Ezekiel's time—the " sardius, topaz, diamond, beryl, onyx, jasper, sapphire, emerald, and carbuncle" (Ezek. xxviii. 13)—were undoubtedly cut, and may in some cases have been further ornamented by engravings. Specimens of Phœnician cut gems were not till lately very numerous ; but the discoveries made in Cyprus seem to furnish a means of distinguishing Phœnician gems from others, and reveal to the careful student certain interesting peculiarities. In the first place, it appears that the Phœnicians had two instructors in gem-engraving, Babylonia and Egypt, and derived from each certain features of their own practice. From

Egypt they adopted the scarab, instead of the cylinder, as the ordinary form on which to impress their
devices, not perhaps so much from any mystic value
which they attached to the form as a symbol, as from
its greater compactness and convenience. From
Babylonia they derived a preference for the harder
kinds of stones, for sards, carnelians, agates, chalce-
donies, onyxes, and rock crystals, instead of the soft
steaschist, and the other still softer substances, on
which alone the Egyptian lapidaries appear to have
been able to make impression. In the next place, it
is found that the skill and proficiency of the Phœnicians is vastly superior to that of their instructors in
the art, and especially to that of the Egyptians. They
draw their figures with greater spirit and correctness
than either of their rivals, and execute the work
" with a precision that proves the mechanical part of
the engraver's art to have been carried by them
to a degree of perfection never afterwards surpassed.
Animals, for the most part imaginary, gryphons and
sphinxes, but often accurately copied from nature, form
the great staple of Phœnician art. The human figure,
in a mere mortal sense, their gem-engravers never attempted. It is evident that all their gems served the
double purpose of signets and of talismans, all embodying religious ideas ; and that even the real
animals so often represented only received this honour
as being the attributes and by ready transition the
emblems of the deities whose good graces the wearer
hoped in this material way to secure to himself." [1]
The subjects of their designs show, however, little

[1] C. W. King in Di Cesnola's " Cyprus," p. 357.

originality, being in almost every case adopted, either
from Egypt or from Babylonia. The hawk of Ra, the
Egyptian Sun-God; the cynocephalous ape, sacred
to Thoth; the Baris, or sacred boat of the Nile,
carrying the terrestrial globe between two asps;
sphinxes, gryphons, serpents, winged disks, recall
unmistakably the symbolism of the land of Mizraim;
while "Sacred Trees," men contending with lions,
and lions contending against each other, are well-
known Babylonian types. Drawing of an original
character is shown only in a very few instances, as in a
scarab from Curium, where a warrior
in a conical helmet and with a plain
round shield, strikes his spear into the
breast of another, whose head is
covered with a kind of hood, while
his shield has a large boss or *umbo.*
Here the forms are spirited and un-
conventional, the proportion is good,
and the attitude lifelike and natural.

SCARABÆOID.

Phœnician ornamental metallurgy has been already
touched upon in the present section, and also in the
section on the "Rise of Tyre to the first rank among
the Phœnician Cities;" but a few more remarks may
be added in this place based upon the evidence
derived from recent discoveries in Cyprus. At
Curium, one of the towns most certainly Phœnician,
there were opened in the year 1875, a set of treasure
chambers, concealed beneath the pavement of a temple,
which contained objects in metal of various kinds,
pronounced by the best archæologists to be Phœnician
in their general character, and to belong to a time

GOLD BRACELET.

BRACELET.

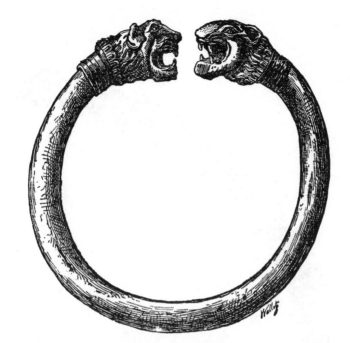

GOLD BRACELET.

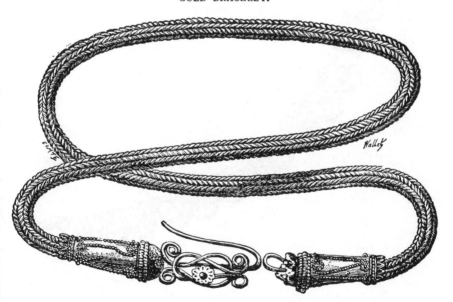

GOLD NECKLACE.

JEWELRY FOUND AT CURIUM.

anterior to the fifth century before our era. The most
remarkable are gold necklaces. Of these, "one is
composed of seventy finely wrought gold beads and
some twenty large gold acorns as pendants, with a head
of Medusa (?) as a centre-piece. Another is formed
of beads, having pomegranates and segments of
fruits as pendants, and a gold bottle as centre-piece.
A third consists of a quantity of alternate lotus flowers
and lotus buds in gold, with an Egyptian head as
centre-piece. A fourth has a number of small carnelian
and onyx bugles, alternating with very fine granulated
gold beads, and a number of gold amulets as pendants.
A fifth is composed of alternate carnelian and gold
beads, with a carnelian cone in the centre. A sixth
is made of gold and rock-crystal beads, with a beautiful little vase of crystal as pendant ; nearly the whole
of this necklace was found strung on a gold wire in
its original order. But the finest necklace of all is
one made of a thick solid gold cord, having at both
extremities lions' heads of very fine granulated work,
and with a curiously made gold knot forming the
clasp at the end." Next in interest are a number of
gold armlets and bracelets. Two of the former, very
heavy and massive, weighing about two pounds each,
are plain twists of the precious metal, engraved along
the inner side with an inscription in the Cypriote
character, which shows them to have belonged to an
" Eteandros, King of Paphos." The inscription dates
the armlets, and helps to date the entire collection ;
for as there was a Paphian monarch of this name
contemporary with Esarhaddon and his son Asshurbanipal, who lived in the seventh century before

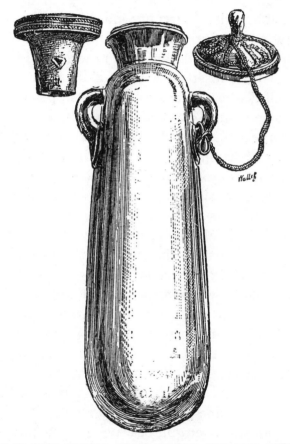

VASE IN ROCK CRYSTAL, WITH FUNNEL AND GOLD COVER.

22

Christ, and as no other Paphian king of the name is known to history, it is reasonable to conclude that the ornaments in question were made for this personage.   Among the bracelets the most remarkable are one which consists of a plain ring of solid gold, wrought at either extremity into lions' heads of great beauty and spirit ; another, or rather two others, which are flat bands an inch in width, adorned externally with rosettes, flowers, and other designs in high relief, whereon are still visible in places remains of a blue enamel ; and a fourth, composed of fifty-four large ribbed gold heads, soldered together by threes, and having a gold medallion in the centre, with a large onyx set in it, and four gold pendants. Bracelets of a similiar character are seen worn by kings on the bas-reliefs from Nineveh and Calah, now in the British Museum ; but none appears to have equalled in beauty this unique specimen.   Other objects found in the same collection at Curium are : (1) a gold bowl, ornamented internally with extremely elegant *repoussé* work, consisting of a rosette at the bottom, and then two rows of palm-trees, among which disport themselves stags and antelopes and aquatic birds ; (2) a vase in rock-crystal, with a gold funnel, through which to fill it, and a lid in gold fastened by a fine gold chain to one of its handles ; (3) a patera, silver gilt, bearing designs that closely resemble those on the bowls brought by Sir A. Layard from Nimrud, but are perhaps even more markedly Assyrian ; (4) numerous gold and silver finger-rings and ear-rings, some set with stones, others ornamented with pendants, all delicately wrought, and some

FINGER-RING.

EAR-RING IN GOLD.

SIGNET-RING.

RING FOUND IN SARDINIA.

RING FOR FASTENING THE HAIR.

in exquisite taste, with chasings of a most refined
character.   One pair of ear-rings seems to deserve
special description.   To the shaft which passes
through the ear is attached a gold medallion, chased
with concentric circles, partly ribbed, partly plain,
gathered round a central rosette, from which hang
three pendants, two of them pear-shaped, and the
third, which is in the middle, consisting of a female
head above a covered inverted cone.   The cone and
cover are alike ornamented with fine chasings ; and
the three pendants are attached to the medallion by
gold cords.   The finger-rings are mostly, but not
always, signet-rings.   Some are of solid gold, with
gold bezels, on which a design is engraved in intaglio.
Others have, in the place of a bezel, a scarab or
scaraboid attached by a swivel.   These scarabs and
scaraboids are of agate, onyx, carnelian, jasper, sard,
chalcedony, and other stones ; they are engraved with
designs, and have commonly been used as signets.
Some rings are in the form of coiled snakes, but are
so small that they could not possibly have been worn
on a finger ; these have at one end the head of a
lion, goat, gryphon, or chimæra, while the other
extremity finishes in a point, probably intended to
represent a serpent's tail.   It has been thought by
some that they may have been women's ear ornaments, but perhaps it is as likely that they were
fastenings for the hair or for dresses.

Altogether, the metallurgy of the Phœnicians, like
their sculpture, though certainly remarkable, and exhibiting abundant manual dexterity, is deficient in
the higher qualities of mimetic art, genius and origin-

alitv. In the metallurgy, the "motives" are invariably either Egyptian or Assyrian; in the sculpture, they are ordinarily Greek. There are some who think that Greece must have supplied, not only the artistic forms followed by those who carved the sarcophagi of Sidon and Amathus, but the very artists themselves, since they cannot imagine that Asiatics of the true Oriental type can have risen to the æsthetic level reached by those sculptures. For ourselves, we question this conclusion; but, whether it ultimately prevails or not, we see no room to doubt that Phœnicia herself produced the school of workers in metal, whose masterly productions have been found at Nimrud, Dali (Idalium), Golgoi, Amathus, Curium, and Tharros in Sardinia. With the exception of Nimrud, the places that have furnished embossed metal bowls, dishes, and pateræ of the character which we have described, are, all of them, well-known Phœnician sites; and the works themselves, which clearly belong to one nation and one school, have in some cases Phœnician legends. But, if it be allowed that Phœnician artists have embossed and engraved the bowls and pateræ, while other members of the nation have chased the gold ornaments and cut the gems, it will be impossible to deny to the Phœnicians a considerable amount of artistic talent, although we may admit they were wanting in originality and inventive genius.

If we had the greatest masterpieces of the Phœnician metallurgists before us, the verdict might be even more favourable. Jachin and Boaz, the lavers of Solomon and his "molten sea," if they still existed in our day, would not improbably have placed the

Phœnicians in the front rank of metal-workers. Their animal and vegetable forms were in excellent taste. If they showed the talent indicated by their gems and pateræ on the large scale required by the works which they executed for the Temple of Jerusalem, they must have deserved a high, if not the very highest, place among the artists of antiquity. But the barbarism of the Babylonians under Nebuchadnezzar [1]—unequalled perhaps, except by that of the Romans under Mummius—has left us without any means of forming an *exact* judgment on the subject. We can only say that the people, who could show such taste and skill in their smaller productions as our eyes witness, carried their art probably to a still higher pitch, when they constructed for the wealthiest king of the time ornamental bronzes on a colossal scale.

---

[1] The Babylonians broke up the works in question for the sake of their material (Jer. lii. 17).

XIX.

PHŒNICIAN LANGUAGE, WRITING, AND LITERATURE.

IT is now generally allowed that the Phœnicians spoke a Semitic tongue, very closely allied to the Hebrew. Among the ancients, Jerome, Augustine, and Priscian, state the fact in the clearest terms. The inscriptions which exist confirm it. A few of them are bilingual, either Phœnician and Greek, or Phœnician and Assyrian. They are mostly rather paraphases than translations; but they fix the sense of some dozen words, which are all of them identical, or nearly identical, with Hebrew ones of the same meaning. The other inscriptions are, for the most part, readily explicable, if Hebrew be assumed as the key to them, but not otherwise. The same may be said of the long Punic passage in Plautus. A good Hebrew scholar has no difficulty in understanding any legible Phœnician inscription, as soon as he knows the letters.

The letters themselves are identical with those which the Hebrews used anciently, as is evident from the series of Maccabee coins, and from the inscription recently discovered in the channel which conveys the water from the "Virgin's Pool" through the rocky spur of Ophel to the " Pool of Siloam." A uniform alphabetic system, with slight modifications, appears to have been employed by the Phœnicians, the Jews, the Samaritans, and the Moabites, and to have prevailed from the mountain barrier of Casius upon the north to beyond the further end of the Dead Sea upon the south. This alphabet is that which has commonly been called Phœnician, because the Greeks ascribed its invention to that people. It is, like the Hebrew, an alphabet of twenty-two letters. These consist of four gutturals, *aleph, he, heth,* and *ain,* corresponding to the Hebrew א, ה, ח, and ע—four labials, *beth, vau, mem,* and *pe,* corresponding to ב, ו, מ, and פ—four palatals, *gimel, caph; koph,* and *yod,* or ג, כ, ק, and י— three dentals, *daleth, teth,* and *tau,* or ד, ט, and ת—three linguals, *lamed, nun,* and *resh, or* ל, נ, and ר—and four sibilants, *zain, samech, tsade,* and *shin,* or ז, ס, צ, ש. The gutturals and sibilants seem unnecessarily numerous ; and the distinction between *caph* and *koph, teth* and *tau* is infinitesimally small ; so that four or five letters appear to be redundant, while, on the other, the sounds of *j* and *w* are un-represented, and there is no distinct form for *f.*

It has generally been supposed that some very extraordinary credit attaches to the Phœnicians in respect of their invention of this alphabet, and no doubt it was much simpler than the other alphabets which prevailed among the neighbouring nations at the time when it was first brought into use. But it is to be remembered that Egypt had possessed an alphabetic system for above a thousand years before the date of the first known use of Phœnician characters, and the Babylonians, Elamites, and Assyrians had modes of writing not very much less ancient. Phœnicia is rather to be praised for curtailing the excessive redundance of the primitive methods of expressing speech in a written form than for any actual invention or discovery. The Egyptians had two or more quite different forms for almost every letter of their alphabet; and, besides this, employed also an enormous syllabarium and a vast number of determinatives, so that to read Egyptian we have to be familiar with more than a thousand symbols. The Mesopotamians did not go quite to this length; but Sir H. Rawlinson gives a list of two hundred and forty-six cuneiform characters in use among the Babylonians and Assyrians, while at the same time he notes that "the list does not pretend to be complete"; and M. Oppert represents the signs most in use ("les signes les plus usités") as exceeding three hundred. The characters had also frequently, both in Assyrian and in Assyro-Babylonian, several values, and values often wholly unconnected one with another. Thus to read either Egyptian or Assyrian with facility requires a life-long study, while Phœnician may be read and pronounced with almost as much facility as Greek or Hebrew.

Whether the Phœnicians were the actual inventors of the signs which they employed is uncertain, since the same characters were certainly in use from a very early date among the neighbouring nations; but, on the whole, the tradition that the invention was theirs may be accepted as, at any rate, highly probable. Commercial transactions, on a larger scale, are almost impossible without " book-keeping," and book-keeping necessitates the use, both of figures and letters. Whence they took their signs is a curious subject for inquiry. There are a certain number which more or less resemble the hieroglyphics of Egypt, and it has been argued that the entire alphabet is really derived from this source ; but the real resemblances do not attach to more than three or four letters, and in only one instance are they unmistakable. Moreover, the names of the letters, in Hebrew at any rate, designate objects ; while the objects are in no case identical with those represented by the corresponding hierogly-phic. *Aleph* in Hebrew is " an ox " ; but the Egyptian sign for *a* is an eagle, or the leaf of a water-plant, or else a hand and arm to the elbow. *Beth* means " a house " ; but in Egyptian *b* is expressed by the leg and foot of a man, or by a bird with a tuft growing from the breast. *Gimel* means " a camel " ; but the camel is not used as a hieroglyph, or otherwise represented, in Egypt. *Lamed* is " a goad " ; but the hieroglyph for *l* in Egyptian is a lion. We must assume from the names of the Phœnician letters that each character was originally the picture of an object ; but the objects were never, so far as appears, the same that represent the corresponding sounds in the alphabet of the Egyptians.

It was among the merits of the Phœnicians that they chose simple objects to depict, and then depicted them in the simplest possible way. Thus their characters were, from the first, simple. Instead of attempting to depict an entire ox, they were content to take the animal's head, which they represented by three lines, sufficiently marking the animal's face, his two ears, and his two horns. *Beth*, " a house," they represented by a tent, the house of early times, but, a diacritic mark being needed to distinguish this form from their forms for *d* and *r*, they added a horizontal line under the tent, representing the ground in which it stood. To depict the camel it was enough to give his long neck and head, which are traceable alike in the Hebrew *Gimel* and in the Grecian *Gamma*. *Daleth*, " a door," could only, in consistency with the sign for *beth*, be a tent door, which in the primitive tent was triangular, like the tent itself; hence *daleth* took the form familiar to us in the Greek *Delta*. *Vau*, " a nail," was a single vertical line, with a small mark, which might be angular or semicircular, for the head. And the other letters were, for the most part, equally simple.

Some have argued that it was the simplicity of the Phœnician alphabet which caused its general adoption by the nations of the West, the Greeks, Etruscans, Romans, and others. But this is to suppose that the Western nations had a choice, and deliberately preferred the Phœnician to other systems ; whereas, in fact, it does not appear that they had any choice at all. The Phœnicians were, for many ages, the only people who navigated the Mediterranean, and thus they alone had the power of introducing into the West the civilization and arts of the East. Naturally, they introduced their own alphabetic signs, since they were familiar with no others ; and the tribes with which they traded naturally adopted them, not because, on a comparison, they found them preferable to the other signs in use at the time, but because they recognized their utility, and knew of no other set of signs with which to compare them.

Like most other Semitic races, the Phœnicians wrote from right to left ; and their letters were for the most part sloped in the opposite direction from ours. This slope, however, is not universal. The *k*, the *l*, the *m*, the *n*, and the *p*, have often a decided slope in the same direction as our own ; and the other letters seem to be sloped more or less, according to the fancy of the engraver. In no case did the Phœnicians write *boustro-phedon*, as the early Greeks did, *i.e.*, alternately from right to left and from left to right, much less did they, as the Egyptians, adopt either direction indifferently.

A representation of the ordinary Phœnician alphabet, and a specimen of Phœnician writing, are appended by way of illustration.

The extant Phœnician literature is entirely epigraphic. It consists of two fairly long, and several short, inscriptions on tombs, and of a number of curt legends on votive offerings, coins, gems, vases, pateræ, and the like. The inscription of Marseilles, and the passage in the Pœnulus of Plautus, commonly called Phœnician, belong rather to the literature of Carthage. The longest and most important of the tomb inscriptions of Phœnicia is that on the sepulchre of Esmunazar, which extends to twenty-two lines. It has been translated by M. Jules Oppert, as follows :—

" In the month of Bul (October), in the fourteenth year of the reign of King Esmunazar, King of the Two Sidons, son of King Tabnit, King of the Two Sidons, King Esmunazar, King of the Two Sidons,

Greek Name	Phoenician	Early Greek	Early & Later Hebrew	Hebrew Name
Alpha				Aleph
Beta				Beth
Gamma				Gimel
Delta				Daleth
Epsilon				He
Upsilon				Vau
Zēta				Zain
Eta				Heth
Thēta				Teth
Iōta				Yod
Kappa				Caph
Lambda				Lamed
Mu				Mem
Nu				Nun
Xi				Samech
Omicron				Ain
Pi				Pe
				Tsadde
Koppa				Koph
Rho				Resch
San or Sigma				Shin
Tau				Tau

THE PHOENICIAN ALPHABET

said as follows :—' I am carried away ; the time of my non-existence has come ; my spirit has disappeared, like the day from whence I am silent, since which I became mute ; and I am lying in this coffin, and in this tomb, in the place which I have built. O thou [who readest] remember this :—May no royal race, nor any other man open my funeral chamber—may they not seek after treasures, for no one has hidden treasures here ; nor move the coffin out of my funeral chamber, nor molest me in this funeral bed, by putting another tomb over it. Whatever a man may tell thee, do not listen to him, for the punishment [of the violation] shall be :—Every royal race and every man, who shall open the covering of this tomb, or who shall carry away the coffin wherein I repose, or who shall molest me in this chamber, they shall have no funeral chamber with the departed, nor shall be buried in graves, nor shall there be any son or off-spring to succeed to them, and the holy gods shall inflict extirpation on them. Thou, whosoever thou art, who shalt be king [hereafter], inspire those over whom thou wilt reign, that they may exterminate the members of that royal race which shall open the covering of this chamber, or shall take away this coffin, and exterminate also the offspring of that royal race, or of the common men [who shall do so]. They shall have no root below, nor fruit above, nor living form under the sun.

" For, by the grace of the gods, I am carried away ; the time of my non-existence is come ; my spirit has disappeared, like the day from whence I am silent, since which I became mute.

" For it is I, Esmunazar, King of the Two Sidons, son of King Tabnit, King of the Two Sidons, and grandson of King Esmunazar, King of the Two Sidons, and my mother, Amastarte, the priestess of Astarté, our mistress, the Queen, the daughter of King Esmunazar, King of the Two Sidons—it is we who have built the Temple of the gods, and the Temple of the Ashteroth at Sidon, which is by the seaside, and have placed there the images of the Ashteroth, since we are sanctifiers [of the gods]. It is we who have built the Temple of Esmun, and the sanctuary of the murex-shell river in the mountain, and have placed there his [Esmun's] image, since we are sanctifiers [of the gods]. And it is we who have built the Temples of the gods of the two Sidons, in the maritime Sidon, the Temple of Baal-Sidon, and the Temple of Ashteroth, who bears the name of Baal.

" May in the future the Lords of the Kings give us Dora and Japhia (Joppa), and the fertile cornlands, which are in the plain of Sharon, and may they annex it to the boundaries of the land, that it may belong to the two Sidons for ever.

" O thou [who readest], remember this :—May no royal race, and no man, open my sarcophagus, nor deface the inscriptions of my sarcophagus, nor molest me in this funeral chamber, nor carry away the coffin wherein I repose. Otherwise the Holy gods shall inflict extirpation on them, and exterminate the royal race, or the common man, that shall so do, with their offspring for ever." [1]

---

[1] " Records of the Past," vol. ix. pp. 111-114.

The shorter inscription of Tabnit, probably Es-munazar's father, has been already given.[1] In both of them the main idea is to prevent the disturbance of the tombs, partly by imprecations and partly by the assurance that there is no treasure buried with the corpses. It seems to have escaped the observation of those who set them up, that they could not be read until the disturbance of the tombs had, at any rate, proceeded to a certain length.

Literary merit was scarcely to be expected in compositions which were intended to be concealed from sight, and, if ever uncovered, to serve simply a practical purpose. Even less was it to be looked for in the still briefer legends upon votive offerings, gems, coins, and pateræ. The utmost that can be said of these is that they are neat and to the point, without superfluous words or far-fetched ideas. On a candelabrum from Malta, a votive offering to Mel-karth, we read, "To our lord, Melkarth, lord of Tyre. The man that vowed it is thy servant, Abd-Osiris, with his brother, Osiri-Shamar, both [of us] sons of Osiri-Shamar, son of Abd-Osiris. When he hears their voice, may he bless them !" On a stone from the same place, "Melchi-Baal, a man of Jamblicha (?), offered this stone to Baal-Ammon, when he had heard my prayer." On a cippus, also from Malta, "The cippus of Melchi-Osiris, a man of * * *, [offered] to Baal. The stone was vowed by my father."

Of the more ambitious efforts of the later Phœnicians, who, discarding their own language, wrote their works in the language of the Greeks, we may obtain some

[1] Supra, p. 269.

general idea from the fragments, which have come down to us, of the (so-called) " Phœnician History " of Philo Byblius. The first fragment runs as follows :—

" The beginning of all things was a dark and stormy air, or dark air and a turbid chaos resembling Erebus ; and these were at the first unbounded, and for a long series of ages had no limit. But after a time this wind became enamoured of its own first principles, and an intimate union took place between them, a connection which was called Desire (Pothos) ; and this was the beginning of the creation of all things. But it (the Desire) had no consciousness of its own creation ; however, from its embrace with the wind was generated Môt, which some call slime, and others putrescence of watery secretion. And from this sprang all the seed of creation, and the generation of the universe.

" And there were certain animals without sensation, from which intelligent animals were produced, and these were called ' Zôpha-Sêmin,' *i.e.*, ' beholders of the heavens ' ; and they were made in the shape of an egg, and from Môt shone forth the sun, and the moon, and the lesser and the greater stars. And when the air began to send forth light, by the conflagration of land and sea, winds were produced, and clouds, and very great downpours, and effusions of the heavenly waters. And when these were thus separated, and carried, through the heat of the sun, out of their proper places, and all met again in the air, and came into collision, there ensued thunderings and lightnings ; and through the rattle of the thunder, the intelligent animals above mentioned were woke up, and startled by the noise began to move about both in the sea and on the land, alike such as were male and such as were female. All these things were found written in the Cosmogony of Taaut, and in his commentaries, and were drawn from his conjectures, and from the proofs which his intellect perceived and discovered, and which he made clear to us."

The most important of the other fragments are the following :—

Fragment 2.—" These men first consecrated the fruits of the earth, and accounted them gods, and worshipped those very things on which they themselves lived, and their posterity after them, and their ancestors before them ; and to these things they poured libations and offered sacrifices. The ideas which underlay the worship corresponded to their own weakness and timidity of soul."

Fragment 3.—" From the wind, Colpia, and his wife Baau, which is by interpretation ' Night,' were born Æon and Protogonus, mortal men so named ; of whom one, viz., Æon, discovered that life might be sustained by the fruits of trees. Their immediate descendants were called Genos and Genea ; who lived in Phœnicia, and in time of drought stretched forth their hands to heaven towards the Sun ; for him they regarded as the sole lord of heaven, and called him Baal-samin, which means ' Lord of Heaven ' in the Phœnician tongue, and is equivalent to Zeus in Greek. . . . Moreover, from Genos, son of Æon and Protogonus, were begotten mortal children, called Phôs, and Pyr, and Phlox (*i.e.*, Light, and Fire, and Flame). These persons invented the method of producing fire by rubbing two pieces of wood together, and taught men to employ it. They begat sons of surpassing size and stature, whose names were given to the mountains whereof they had obtained possession, viz., Casius, Libanus, Anti-Libanus, and Brathy. From them were produced Memrumus and Hypsuranius, who took their names from their mothers, women in those days yielding themselves without shame to any man whom they happened to meet. Hypsuranius lived at Tyre, and invented the art of building huts with reeds and rushes and the papyrus plant. He quarrelled with his brother Usôus, who was the first to make clothing for the body out of the skins of the wild beasts which he slew. On one occasion when there was a great storm of rain and wind, the trees in the neighbourhood of Tyre so rubbed against each other that they took fire and the whole forest was burnt; whereupon Usôus took a tree, and, having cleared it of its boughs, was the first to venture on the sea in a boat. He also consecrated two pillars to Fire and Wind, and worshipped them, and poured upon them the blood of the animals which he took by hunting. And when the two brothers were dead, those who remained alive consecrated rods to their memory and continued to worship the pillars, and to hold a festival in their honour year by year.

"At a time long subsequent to this, there were born of the race of Hypsuranius Agreus (Hunter) and Halieus (Fisherman), the inventors of hunting and fishing, from whom hunters and fishermen took their names. From them again were born two other brothers, who discovered iron and the method of working it. One of them named Chrysor, who is the same as Hephæstus, applied himself to the study of words, and invented charms and oracles; he was moreover, the discoverer of the hook, and the bait, and the fishing-line, and the raft, and the first man to navigate ships. On this account he was after his death worshipped as a god, and called Molech, or Zeus Meilichios. According to some, his brothers (brother?) invented the art of building party-walls of brick.

" Later on, there were born of the same family two youths, called respectively Technites (Artificer) and Geïnos Autochthôn (Earth-born). They discovered the art of mixing straw with the clay of bricks, and of drying bricks in the sun; and further they invented roofs. From these came two others, one called Agrus, and the other Agruêrus or Agrotes. Of the latter there is a wooden image greatly venerated in Phœnicia, and a shrine which is carried about by a pair of oxen; he is called by the people of Byblus, by way of pre-eminence, 'the greatest of the gods.' These persons invented courts to houses, and walls of enclosure, and cellars. From them are descended those who till the soil, and those who hunt with dogs. They are also called Aletæ (nomads) and Titans (giants). From them descended Amynus and Magus, who taught men to live in villages and to tend flocks; and from Amynus and Magus descended Misor and Sydyk, or 'the Redeemed' and 'the Just.' By them was discovered the use of salt. From Misor came Taaut, who invented written characters: the Egyptians call him Thoth, and the Greeks Hermes. From Sydyk came the Dioscuri, or Cabeiri, or Korybantes or Samothracians, who were the first to invent a ship. From them descended others, who discovered medicinal herbs, and found out how to cure the bites of venomous creatures, and how to compose charms. In their time was born a man called Eliun, or 'the Highest,' and a woman called Beruth ; and they dwelt near Byblus. Of these two was born Epigeius or Autochthôn, who was afterwards called Uranus (Heaven) ; and it was from him that the element which is above us, by reason of its superlative beauty, received the same name. He had a sister born of the same parents, who was named Gê (Earth), and from her the earth, on account of its beauty, was so called. Hypsistus, their father, having died in a conflict with wild beasts, was consecrated by his sons, and worshipped with libations and sacrifices.

" Now Uranus, having received the kingdom of his father, contracted a marriage with his sister, Gê, and had by her four sons, El, who is also called Kronus, and Bætulus, and Dagon (or Siton), and Atlas. Uranus had also by other wives a numerous issue ; on which account Gê, being vexed and jealous of her husband, reproached him, so that they parted the one from the other. Uranus, however, though he had quitted her, returned whenever he pleased, and had commerce with her, and again departed ; he likewise attempted to destroy the children which he had had by her ; and Gê had often to protect herself from him by calling in the aid of auxiliaries. And Cronus, when he arrived at man's estate, with the advice and assistance of Hermes Trismegistus, who was his secretary, opposed himself to his father Uranus, that he might avenge his mother.

" And to Cronus were born two children, Persephone and Athene, of whom the former died a virgin. And Cronus, at the suggestion of Athene and Hermes, constructed of iron a falchion and a spear ; after which Hermes having addressed the assistants of Cronus with enchanted words, wrought in them a keen desire to make war on Uranus in behalf of Gê. And it was thus that Cronus, having engaged in battle with Uranus, drove him from his kingdom, and succeeded him in the government. In this battle was taken the favourite concubine of Uranus, who was with child ; and Kronus gave her in marriage to his brother Dagon. And after the marriage she gave birth to the child whom she had conceived of Uranus, and called his name Demarous. After these events, Kronus built a wall about his dwelling-place, and founded the first of the Phœnician cities, viz., Byblus. And later on, Kronus, having conceived a suspicion of his own brother, Atlas, by the advice of Hermes, threw him into a deep pit and piled earth upon him. About the same time, the descendants of the Dióscuri, having built rafts and ships, put to sea, and, being cast away over against Mount Casius, built and dedicated a temple there.

" Now the allies of El, who is the same as Kronus, were called Eloeim, as one might call them Kronians, after Kronus. And Kronus, having a son called Sadid, whom he had come to suspect, despatched him with his own sword, thus with his own hand depriving his child of life. And in like manner he cut off the head of his own daughter, so that all the gods were struck with astonishment at the disposition of Kronus. But after the lapse of some time, Uranus, who was under sentence of banishment, sent secretly his virgin daughter, Astarte, with two of her sisters, Rhea and Dione, to cut off Kronus by treachery; but Kronus took them, and made them his legitimate wives, notwithstanding that they were his sisters. Now, when Uranus heard of it, he sent Eimarmene and Hora with other auxiliaries to make war on Kronus; but the latter contrived to win their affections also, and kept them with him in his house. Moreover, the god Uranus devised Bætylia, which were stones possessed of life.

"By Astarte Cronus had seven daughters—the Titanides, or Artemides; and by Rhea he had seven sons, of whom the youngest was consecrated from his birth; by Dione he had daughters, and by Astarte two sons, Pothos and Erôs (Desire and Love). Now Dagon, after he had discovered bread-corn and invented the plough, was called Zeus Arotrius (the patron of ploughing). And to Sydyk (or 'the Just') one of the Titanides bore Asclepius. Kronus, moreover, had three sons born to him in Peræa, one called Kronus after his father, another called Zeus Belus, and a third known as Apollo.

"Contemporary with these were Pontus, and Typhon, and Nereus, the father of Pontus; from Pontus descended Sidon, whose sweetness of voice caused her to be the first to invent a metrical hymn, and also Poseidon. And Demarous had a son called Melkarth, who is the same as Hercules. Uranus then again made war upon Pontus; but afterwards, relinquishing his attack, he attached himself to Demarous; then

Demarous proceeded against Pontus, but Pontus repulsed him, and Demarous offered a sacrifice for his escape.

"In the thirty-second year of his power and sovereignty, El (or Kronus), having laid an ambuscade for his father Uranus, and got him into his hands, emasculated him near some fountains and rivers. There was Uranus consecrated, and his spirit was separated (*i.e.*, quitted his body) ; and the blood of his parts dripped into the fountains and the waters of the rivers; and the place where this happened is shown even to this day."

Fragment 4.—"Now Astarte, who is called the Great Goddess, and Zeus Demarous, and Adad, the king of the gods, reigned over the country, with the consent of Kronus. And Astarte put upon her own head, as a mark of sovereignty, the head of a bull ; and, as she travelled about the habitable world, she found a star falling through the air, which she caught and consecrated in the holy isle of Tyre ; and the Phœnicians say that Astarte is the same as Aphrodite. Moreover, Kronus, as he went round the world, gave the sovereignty of Attica to his daughter Athene ; and on the occurrence of a plague, accompanied by a great mortality, he offered up his only-begotten son as a burnt-offering to his father Uranus, and circumcised himself, and compelled his followers to do the same. And, not long afterwards, he consecrated another of the sons whom he had by Rhea, Muth by name, after his decease. This Muth, the Phœnicians say, is the same with Death and Pluto. And after this, Kronus gave the city of Byblus to Baaltis, who is the same as

Dione, and the city of Berytus to Poseidon, and to the Cabeiri, who were husbandmen and fishermen; and the Cabeiri consecrated at Berytus the remains of Pontus. But before this, the god Taaut, having portrayed the countenances of the heavenly deities, such as Kronus, Dagon, and the rest, gave form to the sacred characters of the elements (?). And he invented for Kronus, as emblems of his royal power, four eyes in front and four behind, [two open, and] two shut as if in sleep, and on his shoulders four wings, two of them in the act of flying, and two closed and at rest. And the symbolic meaning was [in the case of the eyes] that Kronus could see when he was asleep and rest his eyes even when he was awake; and in the case of the wings it was the same, that while he rested he flew, and while he flew he was resting. To the other gods he gave two wings only upon their shoulders, to intimate that they flew with the aid of Kronus; and to Kronus he gave two wings also upon the head, one for the directing intellect, and one for perception. And Kronus, when he reached the country of the south, bestowed the whole of Egypt on the god Taaut, that it might be his kingdom. These things did the seven sons of Sydyk, the Cabeiri, and Asclepius their brother, the eighth son, first of all write down in the records, as the god Taaut had enjoined upon them."

Fragment 5.—" It was the custom among the ancients, in times of great calamity and danger, for the rulers of the city or nation to avert the ruin of all by sacrificing to the avenging deities the best beloved of their children as the price of redemption; and such

as were thus devoted were offered with mystic ceremonies. Kronus, therefore, who was called El by the
Phœnicians and who after his death was deified and
attached to the planet which bears his name, having
an only son by a nymph of the country, who was
called Anobret, took this son, who was named Jeoud,
which means 'only son' in Phœnician, and when a
great danger from war impended over the land, adorned
him with the ensigns of royalty, and, having prepared
an altar for the purpose, voluntarily sacrificed him."

It must be freely granted that the lucubrations of
Philo Byblius scarcely deserve, any more than the
epigraphs on Phœnician tombs, the name of literature.
They are curious; they are to some extent instructive;
they embody Phœnician ideas and traditions which
we should be sorry to have lost; but their merit, as
compositions, is a negative quantity. The probability
however is, that they are a fair sample of what the
nation could produce in the way of literary achieve-
ment—neither better nor worse than the other productions of Phœnician intellect after it had been
brought into contact with Greek thought, and become
saturated with Greek ideas. The notion of a cosmogony is not indeed specially Greek, since it is found
also among the Babylonians and among the Hebrews;
but the form which Philo's cosmogony takes allies it
far more closely with the Theogonies of Hesiod and
Apollodorus than with the accounts of creation given
by Berosus and Moses. It may have also owed much
to Euemerus, whose reduction of the whole of the
Grecian Mythology to history in disguise is so well-

known and so generally condemned as mistaken and foolish. Philo evidently belonged to the Euemeristic School, and based his explanations of the Phœnician religion upon Euemeristic principles. The system reaches the climax of absurdity when Phôs and Pyr and Phlox (φῶς and πῦρ and φλόξ) become men who discovered the means of lighting a fire by rubbing two pieces of stick together, and Casius, Libanus, and Anti-Libanus represent also *men of superior stature*, whose names were given to those lofty mountain chains.

It is, as Bunsen says, a " real difficulty " how a man of such learning and discretion as Philo Byblius could have been brought to advocate so shallow and silly a system. His explanation is that Philo did not believe it, but " thought anything better than the allegorical interpretations " which were in vogue in his day. The account he regards as " the result of a philosophical re-action in the sense of Voltaire." It is scarcely per-missible in this place to enter upon so abstruse an inquiry. We are concerned with the literary, not with the philosophical, merit of Philo's work, and our ver-dict must be, that whatever is to be thought of his " historical erudition," or of his " talent," and his rank among " serious thinkers," he is, as a writer, to be placed in a very humble, if not quite in the humblest, position.

This conclusion harmonizes with the general result of our investigations into the idiosyncrasy of the Phœnician nation. The race was formed to excel, not in the field of speculation, or of thought, or of literary composition, or even of artistic perfection, but in the sphere of action and of practical ingenuity. As shipbuilders, as navigators, as merchants, as miners, as metallurgists, as dyers, as engravers of hard stones, as engineers, they surpassed all who preceded them, and were scarcely surpassed in later times by many. They were the great pioneers of civilization, and by their boldness, their intrepidity, and their manual dexterity, prepared the way for the triumphs of later but more advanced nations. They adventured themselves, in many cases, where none had ever gone before them, entrusted themselves to fragile boats, dared the many perils of unknown seas, penetrated deep into untrodden continents, mixed with savages, affronted the dangers of extreme heat and extreme cold, risked their lives continually night after night and day after day, not so much stimulated by the expectation of large profits, as by the pure love of adventure ; they explored all the shores of the Mediterranean, the Propontis, and the Euxine, passed the Pillars of Hercules, and launched their fleets bravely into the Atlantic, circumnavigated Africa in one direction, and reached the shores of Britain, perhaps of Norway, in another ; at the same time they were, in their own homes, skilled artizans and manufacturers, weavers of delicate fabrics, inventors of dyes of unrivalled beauty, excellent metallurgists, good gem-engravers, no contemptible sculptors ; while, abroad, they were the boldest navigators and the most successful traders that the Old World ever saw, worthy rivals of the Cabots and Columbuses and Di Gamas and Drakes and Raleighs of later times. Active, energetic, persevering, ingenious, inventive, dexterous, not much troubled with scruples, they had all the qualities which ensure a nation, in the long run, commercial prosperity and the wealth which flows from it ; while, by their natural vigour and adventurousness, their rough lives and hardy habits, they were well qualified to resist for long ages the corrupting influence of that luxury which is almost certain to follow upon the accumulation of riches. Phœnicia maintained her greatness, and took rank among the chief of the secondary powers of the earth, for nearly nine hundred years, from the beginning of the twelfth century before our era to near the end of the fourth, and retained some traces of her early glories for about six centuries longer. Her decline, when it came, was caused, not by internal weakness or corruption, but by the necessity of yielding to external force. Assyria, Babylon, Persia, had each in turn compelled her to submit, but had respected her character and position so far as to allow her a sort of qualified independence. But with the conquest by Alexander, this was changed. What the great conqueror would himself have done we cannot say ; but it was the policy of his " Successors " to destroy every nationality that was not strong enough to resist them. Phœnicia almost ceased to be Phœnicia, partly won over, partly compelled to Hellenism, under the rule of the Syro-Macedonians. She was finally trampled to death by the Romans. Under the iron heel of that relentless power, " the Scourge of God," far more truly than any Goth, or Hun, or Vandal, the unhappy country ceased to be in any sense a political entity, and passed into a " geographical expression."

FINIS.

INDEX.

A.

Abd-Ashtoreth, king of Tyre, 107
Abdemon and King Solomon, 104
Abdera, 68
Abdi-Milkut, king of Sidon, defeated and beheaded by Esarhaddon, 140, 141
Acre, formerly Aké or Akko, 10, 53, 54, 144, 237 ; mercilessly treated by the Assyrians, 148
Adonis, the myth of, 35, 36
Africa, circumnavigation of, by the Phœnicians, 175–180
Agesilaus, 206
"Aggry beads," 283
Agrippa, Herod, 242, 243
Ahab, 108, 109, 117
Alexander the Great, 172-174 ; invades Asia, 212, 213 ; destroys the army of Darius, 214 ; obtains the submission of Phœnician cities, 214–216 ; Tyre stands out for terms, which are refused, 116–118 ; he connects the island city with the mainland, 219–229 ; storms the city, 229-236, 350
Algesiras, the bay of, 68, 69
Alphabet, the Phœnician, 87, 327–332
Amasis, king of Egypt, 184
Amathus, bas-reliefs at, 290-294
Amrit, monuments at, 260-267
Andalusia, the fertile plains of, 66
Antalcidas, peace of, 205
Antaradus, or Carnus, 51, 52

Antigonous, 237
Antiochus the Great, 237, 239, 240
Apollonius, a philosopher of Tyre, 245, 249
Apries, king of Egypt, invades Syria, 181, 183
Architectural remains, Phœnician, 250-274
Arvad, or Aradus, 51, 52, 55 ; pays tribute to the Assyrians, 133, 134, 144 ; surrenders to Alexander, 215 ; the great wall of, 257–260
Aserymus, 107
Ashtoreth (Astarté), worship of, 32, 37, 109–112
Asshurbanipal conquers Egypt and Phœnicia, 143–147
Asshur-nazir-pal, 129, 131, 132
Assyria, contest of, with Phœnicia, 129 ; military strength of, 131–133 ; severity to rebellious provinces, 141, 148 ; tribute exacted, 146–148 ; decline of, 149, 165
Athaliah, daughter of Jezebel, 110, 117
Athanasius, condemned at Tyre, 244
Attalus, 212
Azemilchus, king of Tyre, 216, 222, 235
Azibaal, 144

B.

Baal, made king of Tyre by

Esarhaddon, whom he afterwards defied, 142; compelled by Asshurbanipal to submit, 143, 144

Baal-uzur, son of Hiram, 107

Baal-worship, 29, 37, 111–114

Babylon, rise of, 165, 166

Bætica, 66

Bargylus, and its beautiful valleys, 16

Bas-reliefs, Phœnician, 290–308

Berytus (Beyrout), extensive gardens of, 12; anciently a place of little note, 48; school of Roman law, 248; the great sepulchre near, 265, 266

Bostrenus, the river, 12

Buccinum lapillus, 5, 276–279

Bunsen on Philo Byblius, 348

Buonarotti, Michael Angelo, 97

Byblus, an early Phœnician settlement, 48; one of the chief scenes of the licentious orgies to Adonis, 49, 50; submits to Assyria, 133, 134; surrenders to Alexander, 215

C.

Cadiz, formerly Gadeira or Gades, 67, 68

Cambyses, prepares to invade Egypt, 188; treats with Phœnicia for assistance by sea, 188–192

Canaanites, the, 20

Caravans, Phœnician, 155–164

Carteïa, 68, 69

Carmel, the promontory of, 10

Carthage, a Tyrian colony, 64, 65; "dumb commerce," 85; mythical story of origin, 118–128

Casius, geological formation of, 15

Cesnola's, M. di, explorations in Cyprus, 255, 305, 314

Cicilia, Phœnician connection with, 57, 58

Cimon, son of Miltiades, defeats the Persian fleet, 204

Cleopatra, Palestine made over to, 242

Commercial honesty, 85–87

Constantine, 244, 245

Cornwall and its natives, visited by the Phœnicians, 70, 164

Craterus, 228

Crete, Phœnician influence in, 59, 60

Curium, Phœnician jewelry found at, 315–322

Currency, a general metallic, established by Persia, 193

Cyaxares, founder of the Median monarchy, 149

Cyprus, colonized by Phœnicians, 58, 136; occupied by Amasis, 187; assists Cambyses against Egypt, 189–190

Cyrus becomes master of Babylon, 186, 187

D.

Dagon, the god of Ashdod, 34, 35

Damer, Mrs., cited, 76

Darius Codomannus, defeated by Alexander, 214, 221

Darius Hystaspis, his uniform system of finance and government, 192, 193; contemplates the conquest of Greece, 197

David, King, and Hiram, king of Tyre, 92–94

Demetrius, son of Antigonous, 237

Democedes, sent by Darius to survey the Grecian shores, 197

Deutsch, E., cited, 39

Dollinger, Dr., cited, 76

E.

Egypt, Phœnician traffic with, 56, 57; conquered by Asshurbanipal, 143; rises with the decline of Assyria, 165, 168; ravaged by Nebuchadnezzar, 183, 184; reduced to subjection by Cambyses, 188–190; throws off the Persian yoke, 205, 207

Elissa and Pygmalion, 118–128

Epiphanes visits Sidon, 238;
sends Lysias against Judea, 240
Esarhaddon ravages Phœnicia,
140, 141; hastens forward to
Egypt, 142
Esmunazar, "King of the Two
Sidons," 209, 210; inscription
on his sepulchre, 332-347
Eth-baal (Ithobalus), high-priest
of Ashtoreth, and king of Tyre,
108
Eth-baal II., 168, 182
Eumæus, the tale of, 82-84
Evagoras, a Cypriot Greek, becomes master of Cyprus, 205,
266
Ezekiel, cited, 37, 46, 55, 150,
169, 170, 313; description of
the prosperity of Tyre, 151-
153

G.

Gama, Vasco di, 179
Gebal, *see* Byblus
Gerostratus, 215
Glass manufacture, Sidonian, 282-
284
Greek colonization, 60, 61, 71;
Greek maidens, 80, 81; begin-
ning of the Greek struggle with
Persia, 197-199; battle of
Ladé, 199, 200; of Salamis,
203; Phœnician influence, 204,
205

H.

Hecatomnus, prince of Caria, 206
Helix ianthina, 279
Hermippus, disciple of Philo
Byblius, 246, 249
Herodotus, an authority second to
no other, 21; cited, 56, 57, 60,
63, 79, 176, 190, 200
Hiram, king of Tyre, 42; the
improvement of his capital, his
first care, 91, 253; magnificent
services to David and Solomon,
92-100; commercial alliance
with the latter, 101-103; a
friendly contest of wits, 103,
104

Hiram's Tomb, 104
Hiram the Tyrian, master-worker
at Solomon's Temple, 97

I.

Illyrians of the Adriatic, 88
Io, rape of, 79-81
Isaiah, cited, 131, 132, 135

J.

Jachin and Boaz, the two pillars,
97, 100, 285, 325
Jehoiakim, tributary king of
Judah, 166; deposed, 168,
169
Jeremiah, cited, 183
Jezebel, daughter of Eth-baal,
introduces obscene abominations
into Samaria, 108-110
Job, extract from the Book of,
312
Josiah, king of Judah, 165, 166
"Journal le Bacher," cited, 183
Julius Cæsar, 242
Justin, on the Phœnician migra-
tion, 21, 22; cited, 108

K.

Kenrick, cited, 225
King, C. W., cited, 314

L.

Ladé, battle of, 199, 200
Læstrygonians of Sicily, 88
Laodicea, formerly Ramantha, 52
Layard's, Sir A., series of bronze
dishes from Nimrod, 286-289;
ornamented bowls, 322
Lebanon, the glory of Syria, 16-
19
Litany, or Leontes, the river, 11
Luliya, or Elulæus, king of Tyre,
repels the Assyrians, 136-138;
retreats before the attack of
Sennacherib, 139
Lycus, the river, 14
Lycians, the, 59

M.

Maccabæus, Judas, defeats the army of Nicanor, 240

Malaga, 68

Maranthus, 50, 215

Marinus, the first scientific geographer, 246, 249

Maximin, persecutes the Christians, 245

Maximus of Tyre, 247-249

Mediterranean, storms of the, 75-78

Memphis, the Phœnicians at, 56; surrenders to Cambyses, 190

Menand, cited, 138

Menelaus, Jewish high-priest, 239

Mentor, the Rhodian general, sent to assist Sidon, 207, 208; the best strategist of the Persians, 212, 213

Merbal, king of Tyre, 182, 185

Metallurgy, Phœnician, 285, 290, 310, 311, 324-326

Methodius, bishop of Tyre, 248

Metiochus, son of Miltiades, 201

Melkarth, another form of Baal, 34, 114

Miltiades, 201

Moloch, worship of, 34, 112-114

Murex trunculus, 5, 276-279

N.

Nabonidus, king of Babylon, 185

Nabopolassar, 166

Nebuchadnezzar, invades Syria, 166; is recalled to Babylon, 167; lays siege to Tyre, Sidon, and Jerusalem, 168-174; ravages Egypt, 183, 184

Nectanebo II., 207

Neco, king of Egypt, invades Palestine and Syria, 165, 166; defeated by Nebuchadnezzar, 166; engages a Phœnician crew to circumnavigate Africa, 175, 176

O.

Ochus, Artaxerxes, avenges himself on Sidon, 207-209; revives the Persian authority, 210

Onca, the goddess, 36

Ophir, the gold of, 102

Oppert, M. Jules, 329; cited, 332-336

Origen, at Tyre, 247

P.

Paphos, temple of, 255-257

Parmenio, 202

Paul, St., at Tyre, 243

Paulus of Tyre, 247, 249

Philo Byblius, 28; his Phœnician history, 246, 249, 347, 348; cited, 337-347

Phœnicia, "the land of palaces," 1; its small size, but important position and advantages, 2-9; boundaries of, 15; the chief cities on friendly terms with one another, 54, 55

Phœnicians, migration of the, from the Persian Gulf to the Mediterranean, 20-22; much in their career common with that of the English, 25; their language and physical appearance, 24, 25; moral characteristics, 25-28; polytheism, 29-37; religious prostitution, and human sacrifices, 37; unscrupulousness, enterprise, and practical industry, 38, 39; early traffic with Egypt and Cilicia, 56-58; they colonize Cyprus, 58; effect settlements in Rhodes, 59; also in Crete and the Grecian islands, 59, 60; early intercourse with Greece, 60-63; settlements on the African coast, Utica, Carthage, 63-65; they cross over to Sicily, Malta, &c., 65, 66; pass through the Straits of Gibraltar, and plant colonies in Spain, 66-69; also in the Scilly Isles, for the sake of tin and lead, 69, 70; their earliest ships little more than open boats, 72-74; danger from storms and pirates, 75–78 ; fair trade, sometimes ending in man- and woman-stealing, 79–84 ; Homeric and Biblical testimony to the excellence of their work, 86, 87 ; their remarkable civili- zing influences, 87, 88, 348, 349 ; their skilled artizans extensively employed by David and Solo- mon, 93–100 ; Solomon's temple essentially a Phœnician build- ing, 98–101, 325, 326 ; com- mercial league with King Solomon ; extensive traffic with the East, 101–103 (*see* Hiram) ; fearful corruptions of Phœnician religion, 107–117 ; they become tributary to Assyria, 130–135 ; partial repulse of the invaders, 136-139 ; no permanent confede- racy among the cities, 145 ; they recover independence at the decline of Assyria, 149, 150 ; Tyre gains ascendency ; testi- mony of Ezekiel to her exceed- ing prosperity, 150–153 ; vast extent of her commercial rela- tions, 153–164 ; circumnavigation of Africa, 175–180 ; the Phœni- cians assist Cambyses with their fleet against Egypt, but refuse to join in an attack upon Carthage, 190–192 ; practical in- dependence under the Persian rule, 194, 195 ; excellent equip- ment of Phœnician ships, 195, 196, 202 ; they assist Darius against Greece, 197–201 ; superior military engineering, 201, 202 ; defeated at Salamis, 203 ; also at the mouth of the Eurymedon, 204 ; influence in the internal quarrels of Greece, 204, 205 ; waver in their allegiance to Persia, 205, 206 ; join with Egypt in revolt, 207 ; destruction of Sidon, 208, 209 ; an interval of peace and repose, 210, 211 ; the cities generally surrender to Alexander, and then aid him in the destruction

of Tyre, 214–235 ; Phœnicia becomes the battle-field of the two great monarchies of Syria and Egypt, 237 ; the popula- tion becomes more and more Grecized, 238, 241 ; privilege of " free cities " under the Romans, 242 ; architectural remains, 250–274 ; manufactures and works of art, 275–290, 312– 326 ; navigation, 308–310 ; mining, 310–311 ; alphabet, and meagre literature, 327–348 ; the great pioneers of civiliza- tion, 348–350

Pnytagoras, 228, 230
Porphyry, the neo-Platonist, 247– 249
Psamatik I., king of Egypt, 165
Ptolemy Lagi, 236
Ptolemy of Pelusium, 246
Pygmalion, son of Matgen, 118– 128

R.

Rawlinson, Sir H., on the Assyrian alphabet, 329
Renan, cited, 22, 253, 255, 257– 260, 270–274
Rhodes, Phœnician settlements in, 59, 60

S.

Salamis, 38 ; battle of, 203
Sanduarri, 140, 141
Sarepta, the plain of, 11
Sargon invades Syria and Pales- tine, 139
Sataspes, 179, 180
Satraps, the war of the, 206, 207
Schliemann's, Dr., researches on the site of Argos, 80
Scilly Islands, the, visited by the Phœnicians, 69, 70, 164
Sennacherib invades Phœnicia, 139
Shalmaneser IV., 134 ; invades Phœnicia, 137, 138
Ships, Phœnician, little more than open boats, **72–75**

Sicily, the Phœnicians at, 65

Sidon, 46 ; excellence of her workmanship, 86, 87, 282–285 ; decline of, 89, 90; submits to Assyria, 133, 134 : devastated by Esarhaddon, 140 ; taken by assault by Nebuchadnezzar, 169 ; again rises to importance, 181 ; desperately burnt by her own citizens, 209 ; becomes once more a flourishing city, 209, 210 ; surrenders to Alexander, 215, 216 ; varying fate between Egypt and Syria, 237 ; privileges granted, 238

Simyra, 50, 136

Solomon's temple, built by Phœnicians, 95–101, 253–255, 325, 326 ; commercial league between Solomon and Hiram, king of Tyre, 101–103

Spain, Phœnician colonies in, 66–69

Stanley, cited, 109, 111

Strato surrenders Marathus to Alexander, 215

T.

Tachos, king of Egypt, 207

Tarshish, 69

Tennes, king of Sidon, foully betrays his city to the Persian vengeance, 208, 209

Terah, migration of, 20

Thasos, gold mines in, 60

Thebes, 62

Theodore of Samos, 97

Theseus and the Minotaur, 114

Thirlwall, cited, 62

Tiglath-pileser I., 129, 136

Tigranes, 242

Timber-rafts of Norway and Switzerland, 96

Tirhakah, king of Egypt, 142, 143

Tissaphernes, 204

Tripolis, now Tarabolus, 50

Tubaal, or Tubal, 140

Tyre, the plain of, 10, 11 ; the city and its harbours, 40–46 ; ascendency over Phœnicia, 89–92, 156 ; submits to Assyria, 133, 134 ; repels Shalmaneser's attack, 136–138 ; her wonderful prosperity, 150–164 ; heroic defence against Nebuchadnezzar, 167–174; constitutional changes, 181, 182, 184, 185 ; assists Evagoras against Persia, 206 ; desperate but futile resistance to Alexander, 216–236 ; again becomes a flourishing community, 236, 242 ; connection with Christianity, 243–249

Tyrian dye, 5, 6, 275–282

U.

Utica, the earliest Mid-African settlement, 63, 64

W.

William of Tyre, 248

Winckelmann on Phœnician art, 284

X.

Xenophon's testimony to the excellent appointment of Phœnician shipping, 195, 196

Xerxes prepares to attack Greece, 201, 202 ; at Salamis, 203

Y.

Yakinlu, king of Arvad, shakes off the Assyrian yoke ; but compelled to submit, 144

Z.

Zedekiah, 169

Zerubbabel returns to Jerusalem, 186